Postmodern Representations

Postmodern Representations

TRUTH, POWER, AND MIMESIS IN THE
HUMAN SCIENCES AND PUBLIC CULTURE

Edited by **Richard Harvey Brown**

University of Illinois Press Urbana and Chicago

This book is printed on acid-free paper.

Library of Congress Cataloging-in-Publication Data

Postmodern representations : truth, power, and mimesis in the human
    sciences and public culture / edited by Richard Harvey Brown.
        p.   cm.
    Includes index.
    ISBN 0-252-02176-2 (cloth : acid-free paper).—
ISBN 0-252-06465-8 (paper : acid-free paper)
    1. Postmodernism—Social aspects.   I. Brown, Richard Harvey.
HM73.P644   1995
303.4—dc20   94-24083
                                                                   CIP

Contents

Preface

Richard Harvey Brown

During the past decade scholars from a number of disciplines have challenged objectivist credos and reconceived their activities in rhetorical or postmodern terms. This has intensified critical attention to the language and logic of the human sciences and of public culture. As part of this broad intellectual movement, the essays in this volume focus on the *how* of representation more than on the what and why. That is, we look at modes of mimesis from a rhetorical or postmodern perspective and try to show how truth is represented (misrepresented) poetically and politically.

The concept of postmodern representation derives from such challenges to objectivist notions of representation. New forms of textwork, new methodologies, and retheorizations indicate the possibilities of a rhetorical social theory of representation that accepts the complexities of language and the limitations of human knowledge. The essays in this volume define and extend this general project, drawing from, even as they reconceptualize, the disciplines of sociology, anthropology and ethnography, literary criticism, Soviet studies, film and media studies, and social theory. Postmodern representations emerge from a rhetorical conceptualization of social texts, genealogical analyses of power/knowledge, the reflexive practice of disciplinary work, the critique of sex, gender, and desire, and the effort to create an authentic form of democratic participation.

In the opening essay, "Postmodern Representation, Postmodern Affirmation," I describe how a renewed practice of rhetoric might move postmodern critique toward civic affirmation. With the relative decline of the United States in recent decades, Americans have become more open to critical and even pessimistic discourses imported from Europe and have invented a few of their own. Positivism, foundationalism, and essentialism are increasingly being subverted or replaced by rhetorical, feminist, and deconstructive approaches—all, perhaps, signs of the postmodern. But what exactly is the postmodern, what are its challenges, and how might these be met?

I engage these questions and suggest that postmodern discourses need not remain merely deconstructive and suspicious but might also enable more affirmative academic and civic interventions. Such a shift would require us to exploit, rather than reject, the contradictions between relativism and foundationalism—that is, to cultivate the tensions between them as a field of ironic affirmation. Such irony, however, would not be the endless negative regress for which Hegel criticized Schlegel, but rather a mastered irony in the manner of Kierkegaard, one that accepts the contradiction of affirming modernist values such as truth, freedom, and justice, but doing so with the provisionality, open-endedness, and playful gravity characteristic of postmodern representations.

Ricca Edmondson treats relations between "Rhetoric and Truthfulness" in the social sciences and shows how textual truth is linguistically constructed. There are two focal questions in Edmondson's rhetorical approach to understanding how true claims are produced: first, *what can be said* (that is, the communicative consequences of who is speaking to whom, in what circumstances), and second, *in what time.* Such an approach radically opposes both objectivist and pragmatist methodologies, which suppress many of the social processes of the inquiries they seek to explain. By contrast, a rhetorical analysis of the production and assessment of sociological claims shows that their meaning or objectivity and, indeed, their very intelligibility are dependent on social and temporal contexts. This means that the expressed content in such accounts is not intrinsically static but may appropriately vary according to circumstances. Thus, for Edmondson the truthfulness of accounts in social science does not reside exclusively in their denotative terms but is produced by the arguer *in conjunction with* the audience. This implies that limiting criteria for constructing and evaluating sociological claims urgently need reformulation. Such criteria should be enlarged to deal with the implications of the moral, communicative, and political aspects of social science in its historical and social contexts.

Norman K. Denzin further explores these themes as a "Poststructural Crisis in the Social Sciences" and finds a path out of the crisis in the works of James Joyce. Denzin notes a double crisis in the human sciences—of representation and of legitimation. The representational crisis is engendered by the rhetorical, poststructural turn in social theory that has made problematic the traditional assumption that lived experience can be captured in a text. Poststructural discourse also has prompted deep doubts about the traditional criteria for evaluation of interpretive theory and research. This is the legitimation crisis. Denzin locates these two crises within the history of twentieth-century social theory and qualitative research in the United States. After suggesting new criteria of validity and legitimacy of representation, he turns to history and literature, specifically to James Joyce's four major works—*Dubliners, A Portrait of the Artist as a Young Man, Ulysses,* and *Finnegans Wake.* These texts are used to illustrate how the representation and legitimation crises have been resolved in earlier historical moments. Drawing on Joyce's texts, Denzin concludes with a brief discussion of possible new directions for critical interpretive research and theory.

In the same spirit, John Van Maanen reveals the "Trade Secrets" by which ethnographers disguise their methods of rhetorical construction in order to produce unreflective but objective texts. In the past, Van Maanen notes, doing ethnography entailed living with members of a group, observing their conduct, taking notes, and later writing it up. Today, ethnography is being criticized epistemologically, morally, and politically, and the field is now in deep reflection and repentance. A central concern in these critiques has been how ethnographers inscribe social reality—the specific textual practices through which truth in ethnography is constructed. Van Maanen's concern here is with ethnography as textual mimesis—how ethnographers persuade readers to accept what is being said. Because these techniques of persuasion generally are not acknowledged to the reader, or even to the writer, we may call them "trade secrets." Most prominent among these are the techniques of conveying that ethnography is fact, that it is real, methodically done, and technical in nature. By maintaining these postures ethnographers persuade others that their words should be heard and their texts believed.

A still more focused treatment of this theme is presented by Jon W. Anderson, who unearths the methods by which Bronislaw Malinowski objectified his subjects while suppressing from his text a recognition of those methods of objectification. Malinowski advanced ethnography as a conceptual-analytical method and research practice for the social sciences. He argued for including a subjective understanding of native customs and beliefs in ethnographies and launched what is now commonly known as the "fieldwork revolution" in anthropology. His study of the Trobrianders, *Argonauts of the Western Pacific* (1922), now serves as an anthropological point of departure and an exemplar of the much-cited Malinowskian instruction to "get the native's point of view." A subjective understanding of customs and

beliefs consists of "concrete, statistical documentation," "imponderabilia of everyday life," and "corpus inscriptionum." The latter refers
to native discourse in both formal compositions and informal telling
phrases. Yet in Malinowski's *Argonauts,* these modern ethnographic
formulas are absent in the layered construction of the text. Instead,
"getting the native's point of view" becomes the construction of a
point of view on this native's point of view. In the *Argonauts* and in
subsequent anthropological practice, native views remain objects
until the conclusion of the study, when they become subjects for
edification. The objectivity of Malinowski's reconstruction of the
subjectivity of natives is achieved by disguising its own rhetorical
construction.

Thomas Cushman undertakes a parallel inquiry by analyzing discourses on the dead (obituaries) to deconstruct the ideological construction of the Soviet other. Our knowledge of the Soviet Union (and
of post-Soviet Russia and the Commonwealth of Independent States)
is a system of socially constructed representations. But how precisely are such mimeses accomplished? Drawing on the writings of
Pierre Bourdieu, Cushman answers this question by construing Soviet
studies as an intellectual field comprised of social actors who construct representations about the Soviet other. Although these representations are presented as factual truths, they also can be seen as
forms of symbolic capital with which status among Sovietologists is
gained. Both representational practices and the representations that
are the outcomes of such practices have value. They may satisfy
political and economic imperatives of the larger social system in
which this intellectual field exists or they may foster the status
mobility of academics within this intellectual field through promotion,
tenure, and material capital.

These systemic and professional imperatives are not, however,
always entirely consistent. For example, many academics within the
field of Soviet studies have maintained close, public ties to the
political and economic sectors of American society. These ties have
decisively affected both the autonomy of knowledge producers and
the character of the knowledge they produce. Nonetheless, not all
Soviet scholars have such ties, and representations produced within
this intellectual field are not solely determined by external influences.
Rather, there is a complex, dialectical interplay of representations
among the academic, political, economic, and media sectors of American society. The role of representation in satisfying material and symbolic objectives implies a symbiotic relationship between the political
and economic sectors and the intellectual field of Soviet studies.

I explore power/knowledge relations in my chapter on "Realism and Power in Aesthetic Representation." I show how the representation of realism in art is achieved through effective deployment of poetic and political resources of specific genres, as in the techniques of the modern novel or the use of perspective in painting. I identify methods by which people represent aesthetically what is taken as normal and real, to be accepted without question and even without awareness. Realistic representations are not just accurate copies of pregiven objects; rather, these representations are codified practices of making and seeing. Thus, there is a radical entanglement between the artistic and the political—between the paradigms of aesthetic discourse, the privileges of their practitioners, the requirements of patrons and publics, and the reigning ontology. By untangling these relationships, we can gain insights into the ways in which the real not only has been fashioned through conscious acts but also how it has been imposed historically, institutionally, and discursively.

I begin by showing how "realism" is constructed within aesthetic paradigms and genres. I then argue that realism itself is an historically relative construction. We can see this in the creation of a modern public culture through the French Academy, in the "scientific" aesthetics of realism and the professionalism of producers of art, and in the changing definitions of realism in Western literary art. Modern modes of aesthetic representation project visual and fictional realities that reinforce through homologies the modern factual realities of psychological individualism, economic capitalism, and political statism. But in the postmodern culture of late capitalism, realism, like reality, becomes uncertain. Postmodern aesthetic representations invite us to ask not "Is it beautiful?" but rather "What is art? What are the modes of its construction?"

Linda S. Kauffman's essay, "Dangerous Liaisons," reveals how Woman is reproduced in the texts of Roland Barthes and Jacques Derrida. Barthes's *Lover's Discourse* and Derrida's *Post Card* are anatomies of the kinds of death that attend love, yet each is a wake, simultaneously commemorating and contributing to the multiple deaths of the author, of literature, and of the unitary subject. Each text is a "desedimentation" of the semantic and semiotic mythologies surrounding love and literature in the modern world. The aim is to stretch language to its limits and "beyond"—beyond the pleasure principle, the narratable, the boundaries of genre and gender. The lines of relay and dissemination connecting Barthes's and Derrida's projects overlap at numerous "switch points" (*coup d'aiguillage*),

especially on their respective representations of Woman. Each text is
a sustained attempt to write from the place of Woman. How do they
construct the Woman as other and what are their motives? Where do
their textual constructions of subjectivity overlap and diverge with
feminism? What is at stake in their appropriation of a quintessentially
female mode, the epistle? What do their interventions signify about
current politics of both deconstruction and feminism? What moves
are still needed for feminism and deconstruction to have a joint
impact in transforming society? Kauffman develops these questions
in relation to the amatory discourses of Barthes and Derrida.

In his chapter on "Postmodernity and Modern Film," Paul Shapiro
extends the rhetorical, deconstructive mode of analysis to popular
culture by focusing on the transformation of moral and political
images and meanings over several decades of American films. Traditional Hollywood films were characterized by obligatory happy endings that could be interpreted by audiences as affirming life and by
critics as affirming culture. Within the last twenty years, however, a
new film ending has emerged. The protagonist can be killed or
frustrated, or the film can have no conclusive ending or resolution.
Evil can be smashingly and leeringly triumphant. The universe in this
representation becomes morally decentered. There is ambivalence as
to whether such endings have a Brechtian alienation effect, lead
beyond that to a totally amoral disenchantment, or somehow ironically reaffirm the established order. Such endings lie within three
postmodern parameters: "the death of the subject" (in Shapiro's
examples, literal demise), the transformation of reality into image,
and the fragmentation of time into a series of perpetual presents.
Glimmers of such denouements are seen in film noir and horror films
of the 1940s and in some recent popular theater releases and made-
for-TV films. The tendencies toward postmodern spectacle, decentration
of the subject, and post-Christian anhedonia have become even more
pronounced in popular films of the eighties and early nineties. Shapiro
concludes that such endings more likely and ironically provide their
own thrust for cultural affirmation and reside comfortably within the
culture industry.

In the final essay, "Rhetoric, Ethics, and Telespectacles in the
Post-everything Age," Bruce E. Gronbeck analyzes limits and contributions within the rhetorical approach and suggests how a reformulated,
critical rhetoric could better illuminate media politics and telespectacles
in a postmodern era. The political world of advanced capitalist
democracies, especially the United States, has changed radically in
the last two decades. Political messages have become more complex

composites of discourses created across verbal, visual, and acoustic languages. Paradoxically, even as information increases, political messages have become shorter and more focused. Controversial or adversarial propositions (debate) have given way to emotion-laden, narrative depictions of political acts (storytelling). Political constituencies are fractured and then added together (but not integrated) in spectacle. Further, political parties play reduced roles when political elites can build their constituencies electronically via television and computerized mail sorted by nine-digit zip codes.

How are we to assess political morality in such a world? Three positions currently hold center stage: (1) the "immorality of electric rhetoric" position, which offers judgmental criteria, applies them to teledemocracy, and calls for renewal, (2) the "disappearance of modernist politics" position, which asserts the disappearance of politics in the age of spectacle and the ensuing irrelevance of ethics, and (3) the "construction of public moral judgment" position, which recognizes that people's sense of community and public morality is always crafted in public discourses through which the world is construed and assessed. In this final chapter, Gronbeck develops this third position and urges us to think of moral and political judgment not simply as a relativist exercise or even one wherein the personal is public and the public is personal. Instead, he argues that in an age of cultural fragmentation and electronic extravagance—which, after all, is merely a remade, symbolically constructed political arena—critics still must engage in moral assessment via public argument. The emerging political ethics suitable for today's telespectacles understands that the visual is every bit as discursive as the verbal, that political meaning in the age of telespectacles is derived from relationships among the visual, the acoustic, and the verbal, and that, for any collectivity, standards of inclusiveness and exclusiveness always provide guidelines for public morality and character in the polity.

Together these essays describe and illustrate postmodern representations. They all take a critical rhetorical approach to reveal interchanges of truth, power, and mimesis in the human sciences and public culture.

Postmodern Representations

1 Postmodern Representation, Postmodern Affirmation

Richard Harvey Brown

The modern academic disciplines were largely formed as disciplines, professionalized and institutionalized, during the proud days of nineteenth-century industrial expansion, state formation, and imperialism. The optimism of that era began to falter as the twentieth century brought global wars, Nazism and Stalinism, the end of empires, and the threat of ecological collapse. This relative decline of the West has been reflected within the academic disciplines, earlier in Europe, later in the United States. The very success of academic knowledge contributed to this. Comparative history, religion, and sociology relativized claims to positive knowledge and showed how truths are constrained and shaped by their historical, social, and linguistic contexts. In the United States, however, military victory, economic success, and global hegemony discouraged such critical self-reflection in the two postwar decades. Instead, this was the heyday of academic and popular discussion of the affluent society, the end of ideology, and the postindustrial society. But around 1970 the United States began to experience declines in economic growth ("stagflation"), political empire ("Vietnam"), and cultural legitimacy ("the sixties"). Although this loss of stature and self-confidence elicited jingoism and reactionism, it also created space within American academia for critical and self-reflective discourses such as Marxism, critical theory, phenomenology, ethnomethodology, existentialism, feminism, poststructuralism, and, most recently, postmodernism.

These tendencies in academic knowledge have matured within the past decade to become an important intellectual movement. The unifying perspective of this movement has variously been called social constructionism, the rhetorical turn, society as text, deconstructionism, and postmodernism. Many analysts have attempted to define postmodernism in order to eliminate the confusion surrounding this term. Others argue that ambiguity is the preeminent characteristic of postmodernism, not only because it eschews the linearity, order, and rationality of modernity, but also because postmodernism has abandoned the modern but has not yet defined itself. Indeed, this ambiguous temporal and terminological status is implied in postmodernism's very name, as after but still tied to the modernism from which it departs. Nonetheless, more and more people recognize that late capitalism, postindustrial society, and postmodern culture are qualitatively different from what had come before. Whether such changes are conceptualized in terms of a late, consumer, global capitalism bearing a hypermodern culture or of a postindustrial information society embodying a postmodern sensibility, it appears that things are no longer as once they seemed.

This accounts in part for the often hostile reception of postmodern thought, because postmodernism suggests that the limits of modernist optimism have been reached, at least in the West. Indeed, for many thinkers the pursuit of unshakable foundations for analytic truth seems pointless (Kellner 1988; Featherstone 1988), the promise of modernity to emancipate humanity from poverty and prejudice is no longer believable (Lyotard 1988, 302), and the liberating potential of revolution, knowledge, and subjective experiences are less than once was thought. Some modernist intellectuals also have been hostile to postmodernism because it undermines their position as guardians of the universal metanarratives of progress or emancipation.

Postmodernists hold that the consumption of information has replaced the production of things. The media, which used to report (or distort) reality, have *become* reality. Former President Ronald Reagan could not distinguish his old movie roles from his real life actions; both children and adults confuse real incest with fantasy projections or guided retrospections; youths spend more time in front of televisions than in the classroom; the exchange of commodities has become an exchange of signs; meanings, like eating, are reduced to a narrow range of standardized flavors designed for easy vending to the masses—"57 Channels (and Nothing On)," as Bruce Springsteen's song goes. Books also are part of this world: they are either commoditized signs of status or information for consumption. Reflexivity, irony, and deconstruction then become ways of negating these functions and creating a critical distance from what is taken as real. This allows words to do their critical work as they mark their difference from the world they attempt to capture.

In much of the debate on postmodernism, it is said that either postmodernism is continuous with modernism, in which case the whole "debate" is specious, or that there is a radical rupture, a break with modernism, which is then evaluated in either positive or negative terms. The principal discussants fall into four major groups. The first camp views postmodernism as a rupture with modernism and, like Georges Bataille, Michel Foucault, or Jacques Derrida, characterizes it in terms of "a decentered subjectivity, emancipated from the imperatives of work and usefulness" (Habermas 1987, 14). Some of these thinkers see postmodernism as positive and welcome it as a triumph of heterogeneity over consensus. They envision artists and writers "working without rules in order to formulate the rules for what *will have been done*" after the event has happened and who are thereby able to resist capture by any form of ideology (Lyotard 1988, 81; 1992).

A second group decries postmodernism because it reinforces the logic of consumer capitalism (Jameson 1987; 1992), it parodies the formal resolution of art and social life while remorselessly emptying it of its political content (Eagleton 1987), or it is merely a cultural reflection of the "transition from Fordism to flexible accumulation" (Harvey 1989). A third interpretation of postmodernism is exemplified by Jürgen Habermas (1987), who eschews literary Marxism even as he criticizes postmodernists for overlooking political economy and thereby drifting unwittingly into the neoconservative camp. Instead, he champions a renewed liberalism guided by a rational ethics of discourse.

Finally, some scholars are radically reconsidering Marxism in light of an "avalanche of historical mutations" and a "whole series of positive new phenomena" (Laclau and Mouffe 1985; 1987). These scholars might be called post-Marxist (Smart 1992, 184) or perhaps postmodern Marxists. Many of them view Nietzsche not only as the great critic of Enlightenment pretentions but also as the harbinger of a new order whose values would be self-consciously invented "myths." Thus, they seek a concept of the normative that avoids both absolutism and its nihilistic counterparts; instead of rejecting the political, they wish to redefine it (e.g., Aronowitz 1988; Huyssen 1986; Agger 1990). For example, Ben Agger (1990, 17-19) asserts that "postmodernity is a myth"—not a new historical epoch where "class, race, gender and geographic inequalities" have been overcome—but, on the contrary, merely a way of "casting doubt on the standard left-wing attempts to specify definitive values" and to undermine the Marxist historical project. Nonetheless, Agger takes postmodernism with great seriousness. He wants to appropriate it for his own Marxist and feminist project.

Thus, postmodern social theory implies a larger set of questions: How can we create a politically constructive moment for an intellectually deconstructive critique? Accepting that some forms of rationality bring advantages for certain groups over others (e.g., colonial anthropology, feminism, expertise), how might we form a discourse that would include more of society or humanity as its implicit public? How are we to develop a more liberating textwork in relation to the institutionalized interests and ideologies of scholars, the contexts of public presentation (press, museums, policy councils), and the larger political economy? Many textual leftists responded to an era of conservative politics by retreating into deconstructive hermeneutics and eschewing civic engagement. But what basis for political actions, rather than retreatism, could be established within the consciousness engendered by deconstructive criticism? How can textual reflectiveness within disciplines yield greater empowerment of citizens? If all forms of truth are ultimately fictions or myths, what myths might be more adequate for our polity and how might textwork contribute to their creation (see Brown 1989b)?

Despite the lure of such questions, the practical scope of postmodern ideas seems limited to a politics of resistance, since the grounds, goals, or even stable meaning of any positive social historical project are radically relativized by postmodern thought. As Jean-François Lyotard (1988, 302) suggests, "The real political task today, at least insofar as it is also concerned with the cultural . . . is to carry forward the resistance that writing offers to established thought, to what has already been done, to what everyone thinks, to what is well known, to what is widely recognized, to what is 'readable,' to everything which can change its form and make itself acceptable to opinion in general. . . . The name most often given to this is postmodernism."

The notion of postmodernism as resistance to any form of reified meaning is central for those who believe in its radical potential. But is this enough? Is it sufficient to stress the marginal against any sense of collectivity? For example, the feminist critique of patriarchy and the postmodernist critique of representation intersect most fruitfully when they go beyond criticism of hegemonic discourses. Alternately, if we agree that *everything* is representation, that there is nothing outside the text, then postmodernism becomes a metaphysics so broad that it tells us little about anything in particular. Indeed, the debate over pros and cons of representation as such has impeded a postmodern politics in which "the power of representation is something sought, indeed passionately struggled for, by groups that consider themselves dominated by alien and alienating representations" (Arac 1986).

In the case of studies of alcohol use, for example, a deconstructive rhetorical analysis can show us how an historic shift was effected in America since 1950 in the definition of the research object from "habitual drunkard" to "alcoholic." In this movement from a moral vocabulary of sin and redemption to a scientific vocabulary of sickness and cure, a number of other changes occurred. The sociology of social problems became a new version of the theology of evil, personal identities were transformed accordingly, and power shifted from church and community to medical institutions and the state (Gusfield 1992). Such postmodern analyses are no longer "merely theoretical." Instead, they make something happen. By revealing the power of naming to shape reality, they empower people and enable action.

How then can postmodern scholarship and culture encourage a responsible public order and discourse? In the postmodernism view, order is not associated automatically with reason. Instead, reason and society are both subject to definition. Scientific rationality is one among many language games and, "because languages are finite, no game can legitimately dominate others. In fact, according to postmodernists, repression results from the belief that selected games are infinite, and thus can rob others of their integrity" (Murphy 1989, 73). Thus, for postmodernists, order is not abandoned, but only "reality sui generis," which is usually used to legitimize existing social arrangements. In this sense, postmodernists radicalize contract theory because their perspective invites us to negotiate the entire framework within which discussions about norms are conducted (Murphy 1989, 67). Hence, postmodernism is neither apolitical, nor conservative, nor nihilistic. Instead, it is radically democratic in its focus on discourse, its disavowal of any permanent ends, systems, or essences of social order, and its affirmation that the world is made here and now through communicative interaction.

Given such a perspective, what would constitute a socially responsible institution and what would be the culture and politics through which such institutions would be formed? In the postmodern view, politics is a competition between language games, none of which has any ultimate priority over any other. Instead, the polity is where shared realities are formed. Accordingly, socially responsible institutions are those that provide the maximum space for public discourse and citizen self-direction and, reciprocally, such discourse is precisely the means for engendering those socially responsible institutions.

This is postmodernism as dialogical and dialectical practice. Against positivist rationality and reified bureaucracies, it affirms the centrality of human authorship of the world. Workplace democratization is an example of such a dialogic process, as is community justice and community-based mental health care. With the latter, for instance, "anti-psychiatry has a postmodern orientation because madness is understood to occur within language. With madness lodged within language, the usual 'monologue of Reason about madness' is no longer sufficient to sustain a diagnosis. [Instead] anti-psychiatrists contend that madness is indicative of communicative inadequacy. Accordingly, the purpose of treatment is reestablishing a dialogue between patients and residents in their communities" (Murphy 1989, 85–87).

Thus, for postmodernists, the philosophical and political meanings of representation are closely linked. Classical and modernist theories of representation hold that meanings or truths precede and determine the representations that communicated them. By contrast, for postmodernists, representatons are causes as well as effects; they can create the substance they supposedly reflect. Postmodernists also argue that the modernist theory of representation reinforces social norms by grounding them in a determinate reality or social order. Thus, the critique of representation comes to have a political edge. The postmodern argument that representation constitutes the world is also an argument against earlier ideologies that legitimated social institutions by grounding them in truths about a reality that was viewed as outside representation altogether (Ryan 1989, 82). Thus, postmodernism can be seen negatively, as the theoretical emblem of an information society and a technoculture of entirely simulated realities that support capitalist ideology by mystifying the realm of production and exploitation. But postmodernism also can be seen as a progressive critique because it undermines conceptions of a supposedly immovable material universe that is external to and determines culture (Ryan 1989, 83). Instead, for postmodernists the real is subsumed within the realm of human intentionality and collective creativity.

Having dispatched the philosophic problems of moral essences, universals, and foundations, postmodern analysis need not rest in smugness or unease. The interesting question is not *whether* there is truth, reality, or virtue independent of all possible accounts of it, but *how* such accounts are made adequate to their respective purposes and publics through poetic and political practices: "The problem is not finding with Michel Foucault that power/knowledge is a unity, and hoping that unmasking this connection is a liberation from power and passion. Rather, the human sciences should be seeking ways of managing the inevitable integration of power/knowledge within discourses that give life direction. This is what it must mean to treat knowledge claims rhetorically, if rhetoric is not to slide into sophistry, on the one hand, or become a new mode of academic self-perpetuation on the other" (McGee and Lyne 1987, 400).

Perhaps then, textual reflection has been treading in the wrong direction. Rather than focusing on the impossibility of objectivity or total truth, it would be more fruitful to understand the conditions in which statements or actions are nonetheless accepted as objective, valid, or legitimate. That everything is a sign for some other sign can have practical import if we move from Saussure's question, "What stands for what?," toward Lenin's question, "Who stands for whom?," and from there to the question, "What discursive and cultural practices would support each person standing for themselves and for each other?"

I believe that, if practiced in a dialectical, ironic mode, a postmodern rhetoric engages such questions not to resolve them but to exploit their tensions. Such an ironic discourse is one of both resistance and affirmation. After all, there are affirmative forms of resistance and resisting forms of affirmation. The space of fruitful tensions between a hermeneutic of suspicion and a hermeneutic of affirmation is always shifting. But this need not and should not keep us from making moral judgments. Thus, an affirmative postmodern discourse can occur neither on an absolute foundation nor in the dissolving imperium of language but rather in the space between the two. Indeed, both scientific realists and language relativists seem to be aware of this. Although each tends to be imperialistic about their assumptions, they rarely advocate strong, comprehensive programs. Instead, the play between realists and relativists is usually about where to draw the (bottom) line—what shall be considered actual and what symbolic. For most realists, that line defines certain ontological and ethical absolutes—beliefs in things or values, the abandonment or even the questioning of which seems too awful to contemplate. For realists, "stones," "nature," or "this table" are factual realities that common sense tells us are unshakable; human suffering, the Holocaust, and death are also moral truths. But even relativists often seek a fortress of facticity to defend what they see as the corrosive effects of their own otherwise relativistic thinking. One example is the usually relativistic ethnographer of science, Harry Collins (1990, 41, 50), who includes animals and rocks as part of the natural world in contrast to human beings who exist through culture: "A rock instructs everyone equally, without needing to be recognized. As we stumble against a rock, our actions are directly caused by the rock rather than our interpretations of what the rock is." Similarly, James Hikins and Kenneth Zagacki (1988, 208) draw a moral line between realism and relativism at genocide: "There are numerous truths in which we can reasonably place our confidence, such as 'The Mi Lai Massacre is morally abhorrent,' and 'Adolph Hitler was a wicked man.'"

A number of remarks can be made about such line drawings that, building on Derek Edwards, Malcolm Ashmore, and Jonathan Potter (1992), I will call the unwitting concession, the misguided attack, the epistemic/judgmental conflation, the gesture child morality, and the joyless unwisdom. First, those who take a realist stance on some ultimate category like stones or suffering are making large, though usually unwitting, concessions to the relativist position. That is, in resorting to such cases, "realists appear to be setting aside, even conceding, a huge amount of more contentious stuff of relativism—language, madness, the social order, cognition, even science" (Edwards et al. 1992, 3). In building a wall around certain core verities, realists confine themselves to the castle keep. Instead of continuing an attack on this apparent stronghold, relativists might do well to simply cavort in their command of everything else.

Second, when realists insist on some absolute truths or essences of the real, they believe they are striking a blow against relativists. They are not. They argue: "But what about this table, rock, etc.? [Thump, kick] You're not going to tell me that *that's* not real?!" But if this is an argument, it is against a caricatured *inversion of realism*, not of relativism. The relativist does not assert the nonreality of things or values but only challenges their self-evidentness. He or she always asks, "How do you know?" "How is it made evident or true, by whom, to whom, where, and for what practical purposes?" This is not a denial of the reality of anything but only an inquiry into methods by which such assertions are socially, historically, and rhetorically manifested. For example, Larry Laudan (1990, 74) distorts the relativist's position that *nature* does not choose theories into her saying that *evidence* does not shape them. Thus, the relativist position that matter-doesn't-reason is inverted into reason-doesn't-matter, and the relativist is presented as a self-refuting irrationalist (Fuller 1993, 329).

In the same spirit, Harry Collins (1990) asserts that rocks instruct without needing to be recognized. But how could one stumble on

Collins's rock without recognizing it? How could a rock be the "cause" of "actions"? How does his "rock" become a rock for the stumbler and not a Gibraltar for the British or coal for the miner? Why does the realist invoke stones or suffering at that moment, in that discussion, for that audience? And to what effect, and why? These are the interesting questions for relativists, and they are not necessarily inconsistent with, nor should they be overcome or silenced by, commonsensical or morally cherished truths.

Rhetorical criticism, then, relativizes Truth by showing different versions of it as alternative constructions, none of which corresponds absolutely and universally to an external reality that is knowable without symbolic mediation. Rhetoric is not only the technique that realists use in producing cognitive or moral effects; as used by relativists, rhetoric is also a means of keeping the production of such effects transparent and thus more open to challenge or refinement. Absolutists retort that such rhetorical accounts cannot themselves be credited because they are subject to the same deconstruction that was applied to the initial assertion. But this is not an attack of the *relativist's* position.

Put somewhat differently, antirelativists argue that relativists refute themselves by asserting universally the principle that there are no universal principles of truth. But this attack also is misguided, for two reasons. First, its presupposition is false because relativists claim only local, situated truthfulness for their assertions; second, local truth is not equivalent to falsity. Again, what is attacked are absolutist positions, not relativist ones. Indeed, relativists can elaborate Hans-Georg Gadamer's (1975) and Alasdair MacIntyre's (1981) thinking to argue that absolute relativism, like complete universalism (or any other absolutism), is impossible because complete independence of a tradition of argumentation is impossible, even for radical relativists.

Thus, such attacks make sense only if one assumes that relativists are inverted clones of realists and that rhetoricians are attempting to provide a universally true account of Science, Ethics, or Reality. If this is not the rhetoricians' purpose, however, the attack is without consequence. And, as Kenneth Gergen (1990, 297) states:

> Why should truth be the point of rhetorical analysis? The concept truth, as commonly employed during the present century (e.g., correspondence with fact), is already saturated with empiricist foundationalism. Thus, the point of such analysis is not to be truthful (or untruthful), because this concept presupposes the very

structure that is under attack. Rather, the point is to invite the reader into linguistic space that, once understood, enables one to transcend the ontology into which he or she was previously locked.

It also seems useful to distinguish between epistemic relativism and judgmental relativism, which are usually conflated by antirelativists and sometimes by relativists themselves (Bhasker 1979; Rorty 1988; 1989). Epistemic relativism asserts that all knowledge emerges from and is shaped by particular historical and social circumstances and that, therefore, there is no realm of "pure data" describable either extralinguistically or in a nonindexical language (Barnes and Law 1976; Collins 1983, 102). By contrast, judgmental relativism makes the further claim that because all forms of knowledge are epistemically relative they are all equally valid (or invalid). That is, because different forms of knowledge all are embedded in local historical, social, and linguistic practices, we cannot compare and discriminate among them. But these latter assertions of *judgmental* relativism are not in the least entailed by the position of *epistemological* relativism. Indeed, in some ways the two are opposite. First, judgmental relativists assume that standards must be absolute or universal to be valid, whereas epistemological relativists identify alternative forms of valid knowledge. Second, epistemological relativism is a stance one may assume when *talking about* forms of knowledge. But it usually is quite inappropriate when *actually using* one of them. Thus, for example, the fact that any explanatory category can be analyzed rhetorically does not count, by itself, as a criticism of the usability of that category (Collins 1983, 101). Nor could we very well analyze the category rhetorically and simultaneously deploy it as an explanation within its specific domain. Concepts can be treated as *topics of* research or *resources for* research. The epistemological relativism implied in the former does not warrant a judgmental relativism about the latter.

Accordingly, epistemological relativism appears to be a precondition for the need and possibility of making determinations about the validity of knowledge systems. This is far from the disavowal by judgmental relativists of such determinations. As Karin Knorr-Cetina and Michael Mulkay (1983, 6) note:

> The belief that scientific knowledge does not merely replicate nature *in no way* commits the epistemic relativist to the view that therefore all forms of knowledge will be equally successful in solving a practical problem, equally adequate in explaining a puzzling phenomenon or, in general, equally acceptable to all partici-

pants. Nor does it follow that we cannot discriminate between different forms of knowledge with a view to their relevance or adequacy in regard to a specific goal.

Of course I have distinguished epistemological relativism from an absolutist type of judgmental relativism. But, as we have seen, such absolutism is a caricature of relativist thinking. Moreover, precisely expressed, a nonabsolutist form of judgmental relativism is perfectly consistent with epistemological relativism. For example, we might take copies of both *Moby Dick* and *Celestial Navigation* on our sailboat, both of which we may judge useful for the larger purpose of our voyage, respecting the validity of each for their specific purposes.

This leads to a fourth observation—the gesture child morality of absolutist assertions. The gesture child, remember, is that thwarted and abused creature who will be satisfied by the mere appearance of caring without anything of substance being delivered. Realists who invoke torture, for example, as a stop on relativizing analyses seem to think they are engaged in moral conduct simply by censuring others for inquiring into the argumentative devices inherent in their (or any other) moral position. But moral truths, like facts of nature, do not come already labeled and categorized in language. They must be articulated in order to become public moral facts—the way that slavery-is-evil became a moral fact for Western humanity only in the past century or so. To forbid inquiry into this process does not contribute to its advancement. Indeed, such censure prohibits the very discursive practices of which democratic communities are made. And, by itself, it does nothing whatever to help the enslaved or tortured. Instead, it treats them as gesture children.

Some realists argue that the promise of a realist ontology "lies in encouraging social scientists to engage in critical social theory" (Wendt and Shapiro 1993, 3; see also Harvey 1989; Nussbaum 1992; 1993). But even on its own terms, the assertion of essential values, social forces, or human needs on realist grounds is a weak rhetorical move because realist language could readily be invoked (and often is) to justify immoral conditions. The disasters of nationalist *realpolitik* or biologies of racism of the past and present centuries should teach us that. Fewer atrocities in the history of the world have been the result of excessive tolerance than the result of absolutism. Which is worse, the possibility that evil will be tolerated in the name of cultural relativism or the promise that future atrocities will be justi-fied by some group's assurance that they are absolutely right? Whereas tyranny is or depends on absolutism, in a democratic polity we are and must be relativists in practice because we exercise judgment as citizens in shaping or finding ethical truth. Democratic practice requires prudent judgment, and such judgment presupposes critical, even deconstructive, reflection on political experience that is inherently contingent. Hence, our best defense, relativists would argue, is always to insist on knowing the reasons and methods of persuasion in such matters and how they may be justified.

There also is a certain joyless unwisdom in the framing of the choice as one between realistic descriptions and relativistic constructions. The unwisdom for the realist is in the elimination of the imagination, the refusal to consider how facts are manufactured, the reluctance to stretch the mind beyond what can be "concretely" known. The joylessness is in refusing the creative delight of intellectual and aesthetic play. Conversely, if relativists dogmatically ignore "recalcitrance in experience," as Kenneth Burke (1984) called it, they diminish the heroic and tragic dimensions of life that deepen our joy and wisdom. By contrast, a serious playfulness is available to those who exploit the tension between opposing dogmatisms and extremes. In the spirit of Søren Kierkegaard's (1965) mastered irony, this could be the relativist libertine donning the garb of the realist monk, or the realist playing the relativist, each to make a moral or intellectual point. Why, after all, should we let the opposing players have all the good parts? For example, in this essay I have relativized realism and essentialized a kind of postmodernism for the purpose of framing the essays in this volume. Thus, relativists are not so much antirealist as they are against heavy spirited absolutists.

The point, then, is not simply to blast realists for their dogmatic foundationalism, but to explore the various rhetorics of foundationalism. In a time when such foundationalisms proliferate in deadly competition, rhetoricians need to assess the practices that flow from them (Nelson 1990, 259). Indeed, relativists can *become* realists for particular occasions of persuasion, and they can affirm with many realists that humane values must be supported by just social conditions and defended with good reasons. Relativists also want critique to lead somewhere worth going. But they want as well always to keep the discussions of ends open through critique of discourse, for they know that our strategies of discourse shape what we will find when we get there.

Thus, an affirmative postmodern discursive practice is open-ended, dialectical, and ironic (Brown 1989a, 172–220; 1987, 172–92; Woolgar 1983, 259–60). It acknowledges the contradictions between the reflection of reality *in* language and the constitution of reality *by* language.

It recognizes that the very debate over whether language makes or fakes reality is itself foundationalist (Fish 1989, 482). It accepts that the literal and the metaphoric are reciprocally defining and mutually transforming. Indeed, the very effectiveness of such a practice *as* ironic depends on its constituting at least part of the world as literally true in order to unmask false versions. Such an irony also builds solidarity between speaker and audience since the audience is presumed, unlike naive outsiders, to be capable of *noting* the irony. Such irony also fosters agency and enlightenment because it never states absolutely which of the terms of opposition is intended to be the truer or better one. This must be decided by the auditors. Unlike Lyotard, the ironicist plays two language games at once, making opposites seem perhaps commensurable. But unlike Habermas, the ironicist does *not* want to be universally understood (Capel 1965, 32). In deploying the dialectics of irony, in *seeing* the irony or in *being* ironic, we take more seriously the deep ambiguities of all representations, all quests, all truths.

I think these observations illuminate important aspects of the essays in this volume. All of us gathered here are relativists in that we explore postmodern *representations*—of objectivity, of the Soviet other, of Woman, and so on. For this purpose, we need not take a stance on what the essential reality of method or Russians or gender might be. Instead, the essential reality is bracketed, perhaps indefinitely.

Further, although I believe these essays are deeply informed by moral intentions, they are not moralistic in propounding any specific doctrine, except perhaps the "doctrine" of reflexivity itself. But this kind of relativity must be endorsed by all persons who call themselves scholars. Further, the mode of discourse of these essays arguably is itself an ethical practice. Alasdair MacIntyre insisted "that the contemporary period is one of fundamental moral disorder. In this situation, it is not possible to do ethics by argument, because the relevant parties do not share commensurate argumentative fields (to use Toulmin's vocabulary) or intellectual traditions (to use MacIntyre's) in which persuasive discourse can be framed. MacIntyre suggests the neo-Aristotelian concept of historically continuous traditions as the locus of both meaning and ethics which will stave off the specter of chaotic relativism" (Pearce and Chen 1989, 129). In a similar move, postmodernists gravitate toward rhetoric because they want to create an ethical *community*, not just produce a list of moral precepts or a philosophic defense of pluralism. The *practices* of decoding and re-encoding, of translation and interlocution, and of rhetorical deconstruction are acts of social and moral creation, closer to an initiation ritual than a philosophic treatise. By engaging in these practices we can produce a community in which the felicity conditions for enacting them are met.

Finally, I believe these essays invite deconstruction of their judgments by the very rhetorical, relativizing methods and criteria that they direct to their topics. Edwards, Ashmore, and Potter (1992, 30-31) summarize these criteria of reflexive judgment: (1) "*Provisionality*. That is the principle that for common sense, science, and textual analysis alike, any version or presentation of the world is to be understood as provisional, as susceptible to deconstruction or doubt, disproof or cancellation." (2) "*Shorthand*. This is the principle that any version or demonstration of reality is held to be a kind of shorthand for all the processes of construction that produce it, or would have to be produced to warrant it if challenged." (3) "*Irony*. This is the notion that, since reality claims and demonstrations are rhetorical devices, they are at the disposal of everyone" and are potentially contestable and even invertible.

The practice of such an open discourse encourages us to put our own cherished views at risk and recognize the rationality and humanity of people whose ideas and values may be radically different from our own. We also are encouraged to recognize the paradoxical nature of our own pursuit—that the truth (or justice, etc.) that we seek is shaped in our own quest to discover it. This realization of truth in discourse seems to require that we posit Truth outside of discourse itself. To figuratively manifest truth we take it to be literally existent. Why should this be so? Why have people so *wanted* the notion of a certain Truth? Why has it been a central and continuing desire of philosophers, theologians, and scientists, not to speak of lay believers, for millennia, at least in the West? I believe this is largely because the creation of truths locally, historically, and provisionally responds to particular needs that the concept of one universal Truth seeks to unify in the interest of cognitive and social order. Thus, the creation of local, relative truths and the belief in a universal, absolute, or essential Truth are both complementary and incompatible. Each contradicts but is logically dependent on the other.

The same tensions exist between the various justifications of any universal concept of Truth itself (or Good or Beauty, etc.). Here we find that each such justification expresses a different particular function that a unified concept of Truth is expected to perform. As Amelia Rorty (1987, 70-72) notes, particular theories of Truth excise some of the diversity of the concept in the name of cogency or elegance, but then the theory usually loses more in richness than it gains in closure. Because most of the various functions of Truth, Reality, or Good are *unifying* functions, we continue to posit *the* method of knowledge, *the* definition of the real, *the* subject of experience. Such theories serve better *as* unifying concepts if a unified source and authority of Truth or Reality can be attributed to them.

Of course this is logically confused. We cannot with consistency assert a transcendental unity of the concept of truth that unifies the *variety* of distinct, independently unifying functions that each concept plays in its inevitably local domain of application. To be sure, we could legislate one central notion of truth and fend off strong contending candidates for definition. Such legislation might express, and even *be*, a moral or an ideological victory. It would not, however, on that account alone, insightfully illuminate the nature of the True, the Good, or other essence (Rorty 1987, 70-72). In contrast, it *would* obfuscate the poetic and political operations of such concepts.

Put somewhat differently, the relativist could allow "that reality is, after all, a common factor or even foundation in all the vastly different cognitive responses that humans or even scientists have produced to explain it (Barnes and Bloor 1982, 34). Being a common factor, however, Reality is not a very promising candidate as an explanation for this variation. Realists have argued that science does provide a privileged access to reality, but the *justification* of this claim, relativists argue, is not provided by "reality itself," whatever that may be, but only reality as (rhetorically) construed by scientists and their companion philosophers.

We might conclude that there is no such thing as *the* concept of Truth or Reality and that there are only highly regionalized, unsystematically connected functions that seem, erroneously, to be subsumable in a structured concept. Or we might conclude that although the various functions of the concept are sometimes at odds, the concept of Truth still provides decision procedures for resolving conflicts among competing claims for cognitive (and political) rights and obligations even though it partially embeds and expresses just those conflicts.

Or we may conclude, as I do for the moment, that we need not take a definitive position on such issues. Instead, we can hold that literal grounds are necessary for metaphoric flights and that the solidarity and cohesion fostered by universal Truth presuppose the openness and innovation fostered by many local truths. The interesting space for civic-minded scholars is the aporia between such conflicting necessities. Indeed, if we are modernist in our ethical commitments (to truth, freedom, or justice) and postmodern in our criticality, that aporia will be our precise location. Let us have the courage to accept and cultivate that garden and to harvest, if we can, its thorny wisdom.

References Cited

Agger, Ben. 1990. *The Decline of Discourse: Reading, Writing, and Resistance in Postmodern Capitalism.* New York: Falmer.

Arac, Jonathan. 1986. *Postmodernism and Politics.* Minneapolis: University of Minnesota Press.

Aronowitz, Stanley. 1988. "Postmodernism and Politics." Pp. 46–62 in *Universal Abandon? The Politics of Postmodernism,* ed. Andrew Ross. Minneapolis: University of Minnesota Press.

Barnes, Barry, and David Bloor. 1982. "Relativism, Rationalism, and the Sociology of Knowledge." In *Rationality and Relativism,* ed. Martin Hollis and Steven Lukes. Cambridge, Mass.: MIT Press.

Barnes, S. B., and John Law. 1976. "Whatever Should Be Done with Indexical Expressions?" *Theory and Society* 3:223–37.

Barthes, Roland. 1975. *The Pleasures of the Text.* New York: Hill and Wang.

Bataille, Georges. 1988a. *A Curse to Share.* New York: Zone.

———. 1988b. *Inner Experience.* Albany: State University of New York Press.

Bhaskar, Roy. 1979. *The Possibility of Naturalism: A Critique of the Contemporary Human Sciences.* Brighton, U.K.: Harvester.

Brown, Richard Harvey. 1987. *Society as Text: Essays on Rhetoric, Reason, and Reality.* Chicago: University of Chicago Press.

———. [1977] 1989a. *A Poetic for Sociology: Toward a Logic of Discovery for the Human Sciences.* Chicago: University of Chicago Press.

———. 1989b. *Social Science as Civic Discourse: Essays on the Invention, Legitimation, and Uses of Social Theory.* Chicago: University of Chicago Press.

———. 1994. "Reconstructing Social Theory after the Postmodern Critique." Pp. 12–37 in *After Postmodernism,* ed. Herbert Simons and Michael Billig. London: Sage.

Burke, Kenneth. 1964. *Perspectives by Incongruity.* Bloomington: Indiana University Press.

———. 1984. *Permanence and Change: An Anatomy of Purpose.* Berkeley: University of California Press.

Capel, Leo M. 1965. "Historical Introduction." Pp. 7–41 (introduction) in *The Concept of Irony,* by Søren Kirkegaard. Translated by Leo M. Capel. Bloomington: University of Indiana Press.

Collins, Harry M. 1990. *Artificial Experts: Social Knowledge and Intelligent Machines.* Cambridge, Mass.: MIT Press.

Collins, Michael. 1983. "An Empirical Relativist Programme in Sociology of Scientific Knowledge." Pp. 85-113 in *Science Observed: Perspectives on the Social Study of Science,* ed. Karin D. Knorr-Cetina and Michael Mulkay. Beverly Hills, Calif.: Sage.

Derrida, Jacques. 1974. *Of Grammatology.* Baltimore, Md.: Johns Hopkins University Press.

Eagleton, Terry. 1987. "Awakening from Modernity." *Times Literary Supplement,* Feb. 20.

Edwards, Derek, Malcolm Ashmore, and Jonathan Potter. 1992. "Death and Furniture: The Rhetoric, Politics, and Theology of Bottom Line Arguments Against Relativism." Discourse and Rhetoric Group, Loughborough University, United Kingdom.

Featherstone, Mike. 1988. *Consumer Culture and Postmodernism.* London: Sage.

Fish, Stanley. 1989. *Doing What Comes Naturally: Change, Rhetoric, and the Practice of Theory in Literary and Legal Studies.* Durham, N.C.: Duke University Press.

Foucault, Michel. 1970. *The Order of Things: An Archeology of the Human Sciences.* New York: Pantheon.

———. 1972. *The Archaeology of Knowledge.* Translated by A. M. Sheridan. New York: Harper Colophon.

———. 1980. *Power/Knowledge: Selected Interviews and Other Writings, 1972-1977.* Edited by Colin Gordon. New York: Pantheon.

Fuller, Steve. 1993. *Philosophy, Rhetoric, and the End of Knowledge: The Coming of Science and Technology Studies.* Madison: University of Wisconsin Press.

Gadamer, Hans-Georg. 1975. *Truth and Method.* New York: Seabury Press.

Gergen, Kenneth J. 1990. "The Checkmate of Rhetoric (But Can Our Reasons Become Causes?)." Pp. 293-307 in *The Rhetorical Turn: Invention and Persuasion in the Conduct of Inquiry,* ed. Herbert W. Simons. Chicago: University of Chicago Press.

Gusfield, Joseph R. 1992. "Listening to the Silences: The Rhetorics of the Research Field." Pp. 117-34 in *Writing the Social Text: Poetics and Politics in Social Science Discourse,* ed. Richard Harvey Brown. New York and Berlin: Aldine De Gruyter.

Habermas, Jurgen. 1987. *The Philosophic Discourse of Modernity: Twelve Lectures.* Cambridge, Mass.: MIT Press.

Harvey, David. 1989. *The Condition of Postmodernity.* Oxford: Basil Blackwell.

Hikins, James W., and Kenneth S. Zagacki. 1988. "Rhetoric, Philosophy, and Objectivism: An Attenuation of the Claims of the Rhetoric of Inquiry." *Quarterly Journal of Speech* 74:201-28.

Huyssen, Andreas. 1984. "Mapping the Postmodern." *New German Critique* 33 (Fall): 5-52.

————. 1986. *After the Great Divide: Modernism, Mass Culture, Post-Modernism.* Bloomington: Indiana University Press.

Jameson, Fredric. 1984. "Postmodernism and the Cultural Logic of Late Capitalism." *New Left Review* 146:53-92.

————. 1992. *Postmodernism, or, The Cultural Logic of Late Capitalism.* Durham: University of North Carolina Press.

Kellner, Douglas. 1988. "Postmodernism as Social Theory: Some Challenges and Problems." *Theory, Culture, and Society* 5, nos. 2-3: 329-70.

Kierkegaard, Søren. 1965. *The Concept of Irony.* Translated by Leo M. Capel. New York: Harper and Row.

Knorr-Cetina, Karin D., and Michael Mulkay, eds. *Science Observed: Perspectives on the Social Study of Science.* Beverly Hills, Calif.: Sage.

Laclau, Ernest, and Chantal Mouffe. 1985. *Hegemony and Socialist Strategy: Towards a Radical Democratic Politics.* London: Verso.

Laudan, Larry. 1990. *Science and Relativism.* Chicago: University of Chicago Press.

Lyotard, Jean-François. 1988. *The Postmodern Condition: A Report on Knowledge.* Minneapolis: University of Minnesota Press.

————. 1992. *Postmodernism Explained.* Minneapolis: University of Minnesota Press.

MacIntyre, Alasdair. 1981. *After Virtue: A Study in Moral Theory.* Notre Dame, Ind.: Notre Dame University Press.

McGee, Michael Calvin, and John R. Lyne. 1987. "What Are Nice Folks Like You Doing in a Place Like This? Some Entailments of Treating Knowledge Claims Rhetorically." Pp. 381-406 in *The Rhetoric of the Human Sciences: Language and Argumentation in Scholarship and Public Affairs,* ed. John S. Nelson, Allan Negill, and Donald N. McCloskey. Madison: University of Wisconsin Press.

Murphy, John W. 1989. *Postmodern Social Analysis and Criticism.* New York: Greenwood Press.

Nelson, John. 1990. "Political Foundations for the Rhetoric of Inquiry." Pp. 258-91 in *The Rhetorical Turn: Invention and Persuasion in the Conduct of Inquiry,* ed. Herbert W. Simons. Chicago: University of Chicago Press.

Nussbaum, Martha. 1992. "Human Functioning and Social Justice: In Defense of Aristotelian Essentialism." *Political Theory* 20:202-46.

————. 1993. "Non-Relative Virtues: An Aristotelian Approach." In *The Quality of Life,* ed. Martha Nussbaum and Amarta Sen. Oxford: Clarendon Press.

Pearce, W. Barnett, and Victoria Chen. 1989. "Ethnography as Sermonics: The Rhetorics of Clifford Geertz and James Clifford." Pp. 109-32 in *Rhetoric in the Human Sciences,* ed. Herbert W. Simons. Newbury Park, Calif.: Sage.

Rorty, Amelie Oskenberg. 1987. "Persons as Rhetorical Categories." *Social Research* 54, no. 1:55-72.

Rorty, Richard. 1988. "The Propriety of Democracy to Philosophy." In *The Virginia Statute for Religious Freedom: Its Evolution and Consequences in American History*, ed. M. D. Peterson and R. C. Vaughn. Cambridge: Cambridge University Press.

———. 1989. *Contingency, Irony, and Solidarity*. Cambridge: Cambridge University Press.

Ryan, Michael. 1989. *Politics and Culture: Working Hypotheses for a Post-Revolutionary Society*. Baltimore: Johns Hopkins University Press.

Smart, Barry. 1992. *Postmodern Conditions, Postmodern Controversies*. London and New York: Routledge.

Wendt, Alexander, and Ian Shapiro. 1993. "The Misunderstood Promise of 'Realist Social Theory.'" Paper presented to the meetings of the American Political Science Association, Washington, D.C.

Woolgar, Steve. 1983. "Irony in the Social Study of Science." Pp. 239-66 in *Science Observed: Perspectives on the Social Study of Science*, ed. Karin D. Knorr-Cetina and Michael Mulkay. Beverly Hills, Calif.: Sage.

2 Rhetoric and Truthfulness: Reporting in the Social Sciences

Ricca Edmondson

Doing sociology, trying to come to terms with what goes on in society, is an enterprise that involves considerable concern about the reliability and validity of the statements made. Understandable as this concern is, it is also partly misdirected: by being preoccupied with claims, proofs, and propositions, this concern ignores the communicative contexts in which these are made. Despite their sociological avocations, methodological scholars ignore the processes by which readers construct various forms of sense from what they read. Despite their supposed acquaintance with social components of sense-making in the interpersonal world, methodologists write as though social processes go into abeyance during the time it takes to read a sociological text. This concentration on static aspects of statements and states of affairs amounts to an evasion of the processes involved in communicating, and to ignore what readers make of sociological claims is in effect to *decrease* the truthfulness of sociological accounts.

It is an ironic fact that even in the most hermeneutically oriented of the human sciences, elaborate attention may be paid to interpreting a piece of interaction but almost none is given to how the interpretation is communicated. Methodological texts in sociology concentrate on how to arrive at opinions; how they are communicated to readers is not considered a problem. Apparently, once a view has been formed in the interpreter's mind, it can simply be transferred to readers with no further ado. To replace this concentration, this essay offers a *rhetorical* conception of truth, which contends that, since the meaning of what is said on any occasion results from a *combination* of what is contributed by both speaker and hearer, or reader and writer, within the context of the situation in which they find themselves, the notion of truthfulness is properly applied to the fruits of this combination. This implies that if writers are to achieve the effects they believe to be valid, they cannot concentrate their attention solely on what they are analyzing but must also respond to how readers are likely to react. Not only *should* they do this, but sharp differentiations in academic style between different times and places show that they already do. Far from directing their work toward the consistent demands of a universal audience, academic writers knowingly or unknowingly frame their discussions in terms they hope or believe that putative audiences will understand. The use of rhetorical instruments to show how this happens, however, can transform the status of this framing. Rather than a regrettable divergence, it can be revealed as a justifiable part of the process of trying to communicate truthfully. Adapting traditional conceptual tools used in rhetoric can thus help to shift the quest for trustworthy accounts away from an exclusive preoccupation with the *objects* of discussion. Truthfulness needs to be promoted by attending also to the sociopolitical and interpersonal conditions of what can, in any particular circumstances, be said.

It is highly reasonable that in sociology, as in any study of human concerns, practitioners should feel a passion to find and be faithful to the truth. It may also be understandable that they should wish to protect the intuition that this truth lies somehow outside the contingent realm of human communication. After all, a rhetorical analysis of language, which for our purpose means an analysis that takes into account how communication between people actually works, at first seems to pose problems for understanding what finding and telling the truth really mean. Certainly, a rhetorical analysis built on Aristotle's concepts is able to examine the functioning of social and personal aspects of language itself and to chart the interactions and developments through time that all communication involves.[1] The effect of this, though, is to increase the complexity of the elements known to be involved in talking or writing about social developments. For those anxious to discover hard-and-fast criteria for valid claims about society, the subtleties inherent in communication may seem to imply that there is no hope of making any statement correspond to any state of affairs in the world—no hope of telling anything identifiable as the truth. This cause may appear especially hopeless given the special features of sociology's subject matter: it can rearrange itself at a moment's notice, deliberately contradicting prediction and willfully concocting novel motivations. Under these circumstances, attempting to devise processual and communicative accounts of truthful claiming can seem more than daunting.

Nonetheless, the cause of accuracy is served better by trying to come to terms with the realities of communication than by pretending to a simplicity that cannot be achieved. Clean-cut versions of "description" and "analysis" used to be assumed, on a scientistic model of communication, to be attainable by distinguishing between empirical and evaluative claims and then sifting away the latter in order to be left with a straightforward account of what occurred on some given occasion. On this model, "bias," "opinion," and "feeling" count as deviations from the norm; what we need to do by way of communication is to find the words that best fit what is happening in the world and set them down in print. This is a model that has been rejected in theory; it is harder to relinquish in practice, and a replacement set of conceptual instruments is needed in order to discern what *telling* the truth is about.

This essay discusses some of what a rhetorical account of language in sociology can reveal, in order to begin to examine the notion of truth-telling. This project will be divided into three parts. The first discusses the aspect of communication that concerns the adaptation of arguments to hearers' feelings and predispositions, an aspect traditionally referred to under the Aristotelian term "pathos." In particular, it is important to consider what difference pathos makes to communication when we take into account the passage of time. Second, the least overtly personal part of an argument, its inferential structure, is termed "logos." On examination, this too will be seen as subject to social influences as well as those of chronology and time. Third, "ethos," the role in arguing played by the hearer's relationship with the speaker, forms a further complex of attitudes that can evolve over time and from which grounds for an argument's acceptability may be derived.

All these features of argumentation contribute to the version of truth-telling offered here as a model for elucidating the "telling" aspect of the operation. This aspect refers to the developing, interpersonal activities of comunication itself. These features recall that sociological reporting occurs within evolving social structures. These structures themselves can conduce more or less effectively to the ability to communicate truthfully to other people, and they are therefore in just as urgent need of critical appreciation as are the relatively static, technical practices with which sociologists are more often concerned.

Pathos and the Passage of Time: The Instability of Accounts

This discussion, I should emphasize, is not concerned so directly with sociologists' reports on the social world as with *what can be said* about it. Like other kinds of activity, *saying* is done in a particular place, for a particular reason, at a particular time, and to a particular audience. Thus, there cannot be any such thing as talking about the social world in a vacuum, with no hearer or reader involved (most of what is said here will apply to either). Nor has anyone ever shown that any language can be established to mean exactly the same thing to everyone, irrespective of time, place, reason for speaking, or participants; universal languages, like universal audiences, appear to inhabit the realm of myth. The contention that there is no "theory-neutral" language has been discussed at length in the philosophy of the natural and social sciences, so this discussion need not be rehearsed here in its usual form; it need only be recalled that there is no *context*-neutral language either. Instead, an account of what is offered by rhetorical instruments is presented here in order to examine some of the *differences* that a lack of neutrality can make.

The point of Aristotle's category of pathos is that it permits a conceptualization of what is *changed* by the fact that *what* is said is said *to* someone, to some person with habits of thought derived from his or her cognitive or emotional disposition. Again, the phenomenon of changing styles in sociology shows us that what the audience is assumed already to think and feel forms part of the process shaping what is written. The background to statements about the capacities and values of human beings that was accepted in the 1920s or 1930s, for example, could not be taken for granted now, and what is written now presupposes notions of human behavior that would have seemed distinctly odd then.

Pathos: Legitimate, Inevitable, but Generally Covert

According to the classical notion of pathos, the emotional dispositions that writing evokes are more than just extraneous emotional or political attitudes that may be counteracted by public admission of such deviations from a neutral account. It is almost banal to admit that people's emotional backgrounds may influence their judgments in relation to abortion, for example, or the legalization of hanging, and that arguments may be composed to take advantage of this fact; but that is not exactly what I meant. There is no need to deny that emotions may provide *motivations* for one standpoint or another and perhaps it is even possible to discern these motivations and remove oneself from undue influence by them. But the phenomena to which the concept of pathos points are somewhat different. They form a state of affairs so ubiquitous that it is seldom noticed and even less frequently acknowledged: namely, that *any* argument about human activities requires components that are social, emotional, and political if it is even to be *intelligible*. Since these components confer intelligibility, they of course cannot be removed.

Consider, for example, the argument of whether schoolchildren's educational attainments can be influenced significantly by the headteacher's personality and the school atmosphere he or she promotes. (This example is suitable because it is a relatively ordinary instance of a sociological argument and, though important enough, it is not exceptionally emotion-laden.) Suppose someone wishes to argue that children *can* be influenced. It would be a routine procedure in terms of this sort of argument to seek instances of school types and headteachers' influence on those schools, defined in terms of some identifiable style or other, to identify the sorts of interaction characteristic of the schools concerned, and to define and discover their educational "results" and check for influences on these of factors external to schooling. In this context it would be appropriate to give instances of types of interaction common or crucial in particular types of schools. If arguing with people who did *not* believe styles of interaction to be significant in pupils' educational lives, one might naturally and sensibly give instances of such interactions into which readers could *enter*, so that they could *appreciate* what sort of difference it might make to be in, for example, a school in which critical inquiry is encouraged or a school where discipline is the highest value. If readers were unable to appreciate such differences on the grounds of the text, they would merely resort to their own preconceived notions of what impact school interaction has on pupils—they could not ignore the question altogether.

Appreciation is a partially socioemotional faculty, and arguments using pathos in this sense all attempt to put the reader in a socioemotional position to *take in* the emphases and inferences involved. This is not a question of bludgeoning readers into agreement as much as of providing socioemotional *enabling devices* so that the argument can be understood. If readers cannot imagine how it would feel to belong to one type of school rather than another, they can neither form nor judge hypotheses arising from such matters. This is a further reason for which there can in reality be no neutral, invariant "scientific attitude" to replace adaptation to a particular audience: certain dispositions on the reader's part are actually necessary to make comprehensible and credible statements about human behavior (and statements made without reliance on such dispositions tend *not* to be credible). It is this connection with intelligibility in communication that makes rhetorical aspects such as pathos a *methodological* question in sociology and not merely a pragmatic one concerning the way in which a text happens advantageously to be arranged.

It is worth noting that one of the features of academic style that changes over time concerns the extent to which professional writers are prepared to recognize the actual existence of operations using features such as pathos—that is, operations whose function is to sensitize the reader to the import of what is being said. These are in essence always present, but certain climates of opinion about academic writing may dictate that they should be heavily disguised, for example, as matters relating exclusively to evidence or method. "Background material" and "case studies" may in practice have much less to do with "evidence" in a technical sense than with putting readers in a position to *appreciate* arguments, in the sense that "pathos" describes. Texts written earlier this century may appear long-winded or old-fashioned; this is not an amorphous question of "style" but relates to the fact that it used to be more acceptable to acknowledge that writing is performed by people addressing other people. Possibly this fashion will alter again in the future. Although this is an interesting topic in itself, fluctuation in academic style is not my focus here. More relevant are the effects of the passing of time on the *internal* structures of sociological communication.

Communication as a Performance in Space and Time

If we accept that communicating about human beings and their affairs involves aspects that are not exclusively cognitive, if communication is an *action*, then like other actions it is carried out in circumstances that change and are affected by change.[2] It is not simply the passage of time in an abstract sense with which we are concerned here. In sociology, what is said or written does not exist statically in a personless vacuum; it occurs in some specific context. In this regard, what is said must be determined not only by the speaker's view about what happened but also *by the other person*. If writers think that their audiences underestimate the effects of daily microinteractions on pupils' states of mind, that is what will need to be stressed, whereas if these matters have recently been discussed widely and ad nauseam, authors are free to take another tack. This is not, nor should it be, a matter of manipulation; it is rather a matter of making comprehensible contact. Nonetheless, it complicates the question of what should be written down about any given state of affairs. It is not just the state of affairs and a sociologist's perceptions and judgments in relation to it that form the touchstone of what he or she writes. A work dealing with the social world is formed also by what the other person, the reader, has been estimated most to need—in order to take in what is necessary if the argument is to be understood. When these needs change, the content of that same work effectively also changes.

Acknowledging such features of communication about society is difficult because it demands a reconceptualization of sociological inquiry—one that can account for its three-dimensional character. It requires an acknowledgment of what has previously been recognized only covertly: that the audience or imputed audience can actually *alter* what a sociologist is obliged to write about a given situation. Many professional sociologists attempt to circumnavigate this issue by regarding each other as the only members of a potential audience, but this in itself is a political rather than a neutral decision, and it by no means lacks social consequences. Thus, anyone wishing to be intelligible to another person must consider what will take effect given that person's state of mind. This is complicated further in view of the fact that, in sociology, both speaker and hearer are members of their own subject matter. If the sociologist has to address two audiences with very different attitudes and preconceptions, what he or she says will need to take two different forms; different accounts of the same "thing" may be influenced by factors other than the immediate characteristics of the "thing" itself. Hence the search for conditions of sociological integrity and truthfulness must be recast to respond to, rather than repress, considerations of interpersonal intelligibility as these develop over time.

Taking other people into account requires, then, injecting life into the static elements of the conventional view of what sociological reporting achieves. This is necessary to respond to the fact that other people and their perceptions change and develop—not least because of what they have read. The concept of pathos supplies an organizing framework to deal with the fact that, in reading about social theories, readers bring emotional, sociopolitical dispositions that are, rightly, not abandoned lightly. But anything interesting enough to report in sociology is, by definition, not what everyone knew already. Insofar as it fails to match exactly the dispositions already held by its audience, it cannot help confronting and challenging them. This innocent aspect of the nature of communication would by itself be enough to compromise the strict impartiality of reporting about society. But it also suggests that we need stronger criteria than an effectively bogus "neutrality" to keep sociologists in order. It also implies that *what can effectively be said* about society is not just nonneutral in import. It *fluctuates in content,* according to both the interventions of the audience and the passage of time.

This may be seen most clearly in cases with obvious political implications, though it is by no means restricted to these. What is written today about feminism or environmentalism, for instance, differs from what could be said a decade or two earlier. Communication often deliberately addresses itself to the baseline socioemotional attitudes of its audience. The works of Betty Friedan or Germaine Greer are only the most visible instances in which authors have sought to respond to the changed positions of their audiences. In a different arena, one may cite William Butler Yeats's interventions into Irish cultural life at the beginning of this century. Addressing an audience accustomed to confronting textual images of national incompetence and stage Irishry, Yeats (among others) offered an awe-inspiring richness of Irish language and tradition that had hitherto been forcibly neglected. After decades, Yeats's accounts could be seen as taken-for-granted, even naive, not only by a later audience, but even—as poems such as "The Fisherman" and "The Circus Animals' Desertion" show—*by the author himself.* In the latter work, one of Yeats's "Last Poems" of the late 1930s, the author repudiates the reality of the struggles that had formerly engrossed him: "Players and painted stage took all my love, / And not those things that they were emblems of." His earlier efforts had seemed, to him and others, real enough at the time but a different cultural context made them look, in retrospect, exclusively theatrical.

Sociology, as communication by and to people, is equally subject to the requirement that the same tale be told again and again, depending on who is listening, what they already feel and know, and whether, in what circumstances, and how long ago they had heard the tale before. The facts of pathos mean that the audience-dependency of accounts, developing and changing over time, renders the success of any piece of communication a generally unstable matter—a process rather than a state of affairs.

Logos and What Really Happens in Social Time

There is a certain antithesis to this thesis in the reminder that things do after all occur, even if it is never possible to rest secure in having said or written the last word about them. Moreover, the impact of communication varies in degree. This impact increases, no doubt, the more intentionality is concerned, and it correspondingly decreases—to a certain point—the less intentionality is concerned. Its *apparent* impact decreases, too, the more participants in a discourse agree about the general framework within which they are talking; enormous communicative effects can simply be pushed beyond the horizons of notice. (Most such agreements about general frameworks are unconscious and emanate from the surrounding culture—thus they can give participants the subjective illusion of complete naturalness and even objectivity.)

Even so, within some (sub)cultures in particular, great attempts are made to strive for loyalty to whatever did occur. The definition of "what occurred" is itself culturally dependent; rather than stressing loyalty to external aspects of events, other cultures locate the significance of what transpired in terms of relationships or ultimate aims. In highly rural cultures, for example, people may often hold that the harmony of future interaction is more important than loyalty to what somebody identifies as the bare facts. But cultures that emphasize the importance of external, nonsocial reality have evolved batteries of techniques that constrain discourse to a tight relationship with what can be thought actually to have happened; techniques associated with reliability and validity in sociology are intended to achieve this relation. For this reason, rhetorical conceptions may seem difficult to accept; they reintroduce process-immanent elements to a type of discourse that has tried to rid itself of them.

Acknowledging the legitimate and indispensable place of pathos in arguing is not intended altogether to undermine the relation between discourse and its content, however; it is not intended to imply that *anything* goes if somebody feels that it does. On the one hand, there is force in the reproach that the more texts rely upon "facts" about society, the less meaning they are able to supply. Nonetheless, though the knowledge that 25 percent of a defined population ticked a box marked "yes" on a certain day may not yield knowledge of very much, it certainly imposes *limits* on what can be said about people resembling that population. Such a "finding" is not by itself, without the addition of heavily theoreticized interpretations, highly significant; even naked percentages cannot be calculated without such interpretations. Nonetheless, the interpreted finding still imposes barriers on what can reasonably be said that cannot be transcended without establishing a very good excuse. The impact of sayability and understandability on communication is immensely far-reaching, but nothing said here is intended to indicate that this impact is manipulable at will.

Rhetorical analysis does not imply that the impact of communication on what can be communicated is manipulable at whim but neither is it as regulable and stable as more positivistic models would imply. Processes between people, acting in space and time, inevitably add content to whatever they say—but not just *any* content. As Pierre Bourdieu indicates, even the most apparently innocent and technical of activities, such as that of drawing a distinction, conveys social messages that alter the lines of communication between author and reader, or speaker and hearer. The very fact that statisticians are able to draw fine lines between different categories of unemployment puts them in a position of power vis-à-vis the people who actually are unemployed. Moreover, the public use of such distinctions inevitably occurs in some social context. Holding conferences on unemployment without involving any unemployed people, for example, as sometimes occurs at prestigious universities, entails a social standpoint that necessarily prejudices the outcome. Yet for Harvard University, for example, to invite people with firsthand experience of unemployment would equally make a social impact experienced as alarming by certain observers. In all these cases, however, the differences made to communication by the people and the distinctions involved can be traced, explicated, and linked intelligibly to their settings: they do not strike randomly across the social world.

The question of evidence and communication, in short, cannot be adjudicated in blanket fashion between positivistic and postmodernist positions. Instead, rhetorical analysis can be used to trace in detail what processes occur when communication takes place. Social assumptions about what it is worth distinguishing between, for example, inevitably contain elements that confer pathos in that setting at that time, and these can be traced. We can demonstrate how investigating a given area augments the social importance attached to it, whereas failing to investigate it declares it relatively unworthy of attention. This explains, for instance, why it is not just a poetical or religious fancy to declare that applying names to things is a high-risk activity. Naming or counting alleged phenomena confers on them social viability and launches them into new careers in other people's consciousnesses. At the least this cannot but select and shape some—previously vague or imperceptible—items at the expense of others. And allowing them to take up space in people's minds also shapes and blocks out what is *not* attended to (as the rhetorical concept of "presence" is used to indicate). None of this means that social construction occurs in some free-floating communicative sphere where people can just choose, like Humpty Dumpty, what everything should mean. It does show that we have instruments with which to trace and analyze the influences of communicative processes.

In attempting to describe this work of tracing and analyzing, however much sociologists may wish to confine themselves to reconstructing the "logos" of communication, however closely they may try to adhere to "the argument itself," removing whatever is *obviously* emotional or political, arguments still must have *starting points* and places where the participants cease to argue. Both of these are, in part, selected through social channels, so that what an inferential structure infers to and from is in part given to it by its social surroundings. This applies in several senses. There is the sense in which, to the extent that academic communication is constructed as a dialogue, one person's argument will begin at some point of vantage vis-à-vis what it is challenging. When one author argues that René Descartes was the father of the Enlightenment, his or her respondent will begin at the predecessor's conclusion and argue that he was someone else—the instigator of cognitivist narrow-mindedness, perhaps. Similarly, ends to argumentation are imposed by partially social criteria. Whereas in the sixteenth or seventeenth century people were prepared to listen to lectures or sermons that stretched over several hours, today news items may be composed of sound bites lasting only a few seconds. Inevitably, what can be said in these highly contrasting periods of time is not identical. Social apprehensions of where to start and stop shape the environments in which arguments take place and hence their contents, as well. In business organizations or in government, arguments may be accepted and decisions taken just at the point where all the disputants have become too bored to communicate any further.

There are other respects in which an argument's situation in social time governs what contents are available for inclusion in it. Consider, for example, Alvin Gouldner's *Patterns of Industrial Bureaucracy* (1954). One of the phenomena discussed in this work, a particular aspect of workers' hopes and expectations for the style with which management should treat them, is called "leniency" by Gouldner. What he calls the wish for leniency includes the desire that managers should accept reasonable excuses for lateness, providing the concession is not too often abused, that managers should allow a certain amount of leeway about taking home material from the factory for home repairs, and that they should provide light work for an injured employee for a period, rather than laying him off.

If this argument were being presented in the 1980s or 1990s, a different set of interpretations would be available for the workers' aspirations. The notion of "leniency" implies something of a grace-and-favor attitude toward management, an acceptance of hierarchical rights and duties. Today, contingently different alignments of social movements would supply more egalitarian terms to cover what the workers were looking for: it might be possible, for example, to describe workers as insisting on being treated as full human beings—aligning them with a worldwide and historically legitimated intellectual tradition. It might have been theoretically possible for Gouldner to produce this type of description at the time of writing, but it was not as ubiquitous, as nonsectarian, in the social air, and it might not have had the same legitimating implication. Gouldner's immediate audience could not have been relied upon to enter unselfconsciously into the language of holistic humanity. However much Gouldner might have wished to use it, it simply would not have had the requisite effect. In the future, we may find that this egalitarian language appears strange; its resonances will alter to convey different intimations. Since attitudes alter in different ways as society changes, available concepts are not set out for our selection in a stable range. What seems to "make sense" fluctuates over time.

Gouldner's text is one that demonstrates well the ravages of time, or more especially the processes of professional socialization, which necessarily take a chronological form. One of Gouldner's research workers, Marcus Stein, added to the work a methodological appendix, describing the researchers' interactions with their subjects and their admiration for some of them. In 1964, he published an afterthought on his appendix. In 1954, Stein, correctly from a rhetorical point of view, had felt that an emotional and political solidarity with his subjects was an appropriate ingredient for sociological work and would not necessarily prejudice its results. His later text distanced itself from this standpoint, apparently perceiving the original work as excessively effusive. This is an example in which, with time, the same set of words can appear to have a new import even to their own author. Stein, writing no longer from the position of a research student but from that of a career academic, wished to embrace a more stringently unemotional position in regard to the contents of sociological texts. It may be possible to perceive in his new position the effects of occupational socialization; after all, to feel embarrassment at having shown emotion is itself an emotional reaction.

From these arguments we can see that texts cannot be freed from the effects of chronology. There are not standpoints and languages enough to include all potentially applicable distinctions in the same text, and of course *there is no time* for writers to go over and over a single account in order to compensate for the likely distortions and omissions that may be perceived in it. Apart from the fact that concentrating on repairing a particular text would mean that its author had no time for anything else—and neglecting other things would appear to indicate that they are not regarded as important—time would still move on. At the end of any such well-meant hermeneutical progression, the first text would mean something rather different from what had seemed to be the case when it was first started. Trying to inject *finality* into a single account is a hopeless task; instead, other guiding criteria for the acceptability of accounts must be sought.

Ethos and Self-presentation: Conventionality and Truthfulness

Thus, what can be said or written, and what can be understood, form a joint and time-dependent process, subject to limitations *from* the social world. Moreover, what can be established or envisaged *about* that social world involves contributions from the recipients of arguments as well as their creators. The intention to limit communication to what is accurate and just has, in the past, resulted in attempts to discover conditions that would limit these interactions. None of these generally static and one-sided attempts appears to have been successful —nor have attempts to establish truthfulness by reference to the ascribed tendency of particular groups of communicators to follow accepted criteria. Guarantees of validity have thus been suggested to emanate from the personnel of those who scrutinize arguments (e.g., the members of a scientific community). Nonetheless, a perusal of those works accepted by the scientific community in Germany only half a century ago, or a reflection on the political complacency encouraged by functionalism in sociology, should dispel any notion that professional consensus can be a *sufficient* criterion for acceptability.

Some writers also have located a certain privilege in regard to accuracy of perception not in the individual status and qualifications of the utterer but in his or her social situation—as a member of Marx's working class "for itself" or of Mannheim's group of free-floating intellectuals, perhaps. Among other features, what these suggestions have in common is that they direct us to pay attention to aspects of the personal situation of the speaker. This completes the classical rhetorical division of argumentative components. After pathos (the sensitization of the hearer) and logos (the argument itself), Aristotle cites the concept of ethos, which concerns the suitability of the speaker to argue, as he or she can communicate it to the hearer.

Given that attempts to form opinions about social matters must always take place in the context of continually shifting positions, and that these opinions are subject to what is communicable to and from particular audiences, it is reasonable to suppose that a last source of safeguards to the reliability of what is said—at least in that particular time and place—should be located in the relationship between speaker and addressed. For Aristotle this was a matter, in the end, of whether the hearer, given mature judgment of what can reasonably be discerned about the speaker, can sensibly trust that person in the capacity of speaker about the matter in hand. If the available evidence shows that the speaker is well-informed, possessed of both moral and intellectual integrity and competence, and well-disposed to the audience, not wishing to mislead it, then it is reasonable to trust this speaker rather than another.

Stated in such a way, this appears almost tautological. Nonetheless, most twentieth-century academic criteria overtly require that the person of the speaker should be ignored in assessing an argument. At the same time, the expansion and increasing specialization of science makes trust in the arguer more crucial than ever: in practice, vast areas of argumentation are borrowed from their original propounders and remain virtually unverified by their subsequent users. Therefore, criteria for relying on those who deliver arguments should not remain undiscussed. In the present state of affairs, criteria relating to ethos are as schizophrenic as those relating to pathos: they are used but their use is denied because it is assumed that *all* such influences must be iniquitous. This is the worst of both worlds in the sense that personal, sociopolitical, and economic criteria continue to impinge on the academic world but are not systematically analyzed. In these circumstances there is no alternative to devising openly appreciable criteria for uses of ethos, pathos—and logos, understood as an aspect of arguing that is not exclusively cognitive. These criteria will certainly involve considerable complexities but recognizing these complexities will allow very valuable components to return to discourse in the human sciences, components that previously have been suppressed.

In this essay I have argued that a search for reliability in accounts should move away from an exclusive preoccupation with the *objects* of discussion and toward the sociopolitical and interpersonal conditions of sayability that conduce to truthful communication. This means that in combination with scientific criteria (as they can be established at any given time), establishing criteria of pathos will involve considering, in individual cases, to what extent the pragmatic considerations inherent in intelligible communication enhance its effects or alter what can be said in that particular situation beyond the bounds of acceptability. Such a search for reliability means recognizing, too, that such questions will need to be decided all over again as communicative contexts change with time. This reintroduction of human values into writing in the human sciences reaches its apogee in connection with ethos. Establishing criteria of ethos in sociological work has the potential to subvert the covert influence of the discourses of power and money, on the one hand, and the discourses of purportedly neutral expertise, on the other. Instead, by paying overt attention to the roles in communication of such characteristics as sincerity, integrity, and benevolence, the human sciences will be able to reintegrate the discourse of virtue.

This account puts forward the claims of pathos, logos, and ethos to furnish partial criteria for truthfulness in communication; at the same time, it emphasizes their interdependence. An excess of pathos would mean too slavish an adaptation to the audience; too much logos would imply insufficient recognition that human beings are concerned with argumentation at all. An excess of ethos would involve placing so much weight on the person of the speaker that other criteria were ignored. A combination of the three allows each to counterbalance the others, though nothing can alter the fact that attempting to be truthful inherently involves risks. These risks may be either increased or mitigated by the fact that looking for statements that approximate truthfulness and are worth defending is a process that develops and changes over time and in which all proponents are dependent on other people.

These considerations affect, first, our idea of the nature of truth itself, and second, our ideas of ourselves as people attempting to tell the truth. If there are reasons for judging a consensus theory of truth as suspect and for seeing a coherence theory as out of the question, there is also ample reason for judging a correspondence theory as the least incomplete. This discussion implies that there will never be a set of words that, once and for all, matches any situation it is required to describe—indeed, the notion of "matching" in this context is misleading. What may be termed, instead, a *rhetorical* notion of truth acknowledges that the truthfulness of any account is a *joint* product of the interaction between speaker and hearer, within the changing opportunities and limitations of their social context. If, given this context, the audience can contribute Y, the speaker may add X if he or she wants to reach a product of the two; if the audience contributes X, the speaker is called upon to furnish Y. If the audience simply refuses to contribute or will only contribute something to which nothing can be added that will result in an authentic outcome, then, at least in the short term, there is nothing the speaker can communicate at all.

As far as people telling the truth are concerned, it seems likely that there is no single set of conditions that establishes one type of discourse as forever superior to others. This is an indication in favor of tolerance in discourse. Loyalty to the truth can coexist with a recognition that one is not always likely to attain it; such loyalty involves recognizing that a particular set of arguments may communicate truthfully with one audience at one time but a different set of arguments may be just as appropriate when advanced by different speakers to different audiences in different local and chronological settings. With this, the attitude appropriate to reporting on social states of affairs could be described as more ecumenical than objectivist: It is an attitude that takes its own attempts at veracity utterly seriously, while at the same time acknowledging, indeed actively seeking, the possible validity in other points of view. Only this can provide for the fact that no set of statements can say the truth about everything, or even anything. It is not possible to mix all metaphors to make one giant metaphor, and it is not feasible to try to say all at once everything that can be said. If only part of what is appropriate can be said in a given situation and if the same truth must be communicated in disparate ways over and over again, many different speakers and audiences are *needed* to attempt this saying in different circumstances and times.

The relation between truth-telling and the people in a particular context who are trying to tell the truth has a further implication: it is partly a *practical* matter to establish conditions conducive to the type of truthfulness of which the inhabitants of a given setting are capable. Rather than attempting the impossible—to devise situations devoid of personality and power from which truthful discourse might be hoped to issue—it should be possible to discover what happens in situations that do appear conducive to truthfulness, at least in some circumstances. In this respect sociological discourse may need to become not less but more like some types of everyday discourse, though I need hardly say that such everyday models must be chosen with care. There are some social situations that have been developed with the intention of conducing to truthfulness—the Humboldt University, jury deliberations, Alchoholics Anonymous, "basic communities" (we may ask whether any of these in practice has produced enactable conventions within which attempts to interact truthfully can be carried out). If we recognize that social surroundings can conduce to conventions that increase the argumentative integrity of their followers, it seems reasonable to attempt to make corresponding changes to the current circumstances of academic communication. Adopting such models would not in itself guarantee truthfulness, but neglecting them might guarantee its opposite.

A perspicuous sociological language along such lines would have the advantage of reflecting rather than hiding its partial methodological dependency on human interaction. At the same time, it would refrain from claiming a proprietorship over the truth that excluded many contrasting contributions to our appreciation of reality. This language would recognize and allow itself to express its involvement in circumstances to which it is only appropriate to show moral or political feelings. There are many states of affairs that cannot reasonably be recounted without some human reaction—for example reports on shantytowns built on rubbish dumps or on the commodification of social affairs. Rather than suppressing reactions to these matters in the interests of an "objectivity" based on unrealistic assumptions about the nature of communication, we should prudently evolve a sociological language appropriate to their moral and energetic disputation.

Notes

For their various forms of encouragement I should like to thank Richard H. Brown, George Taylor, and Markus Wörner.

1. I base this essay on a reading of the first part of Aristotle's *Rhetoric*, from which I believe many of the ideas can be derived.

2. J. L. Austin (1955) not only stresses the extent to which speaking is an *action* but also provides some grounds for being skeptical about common uses of the word "true."

References

Aristotle. 1946. *Rhetorica*. Translated by W. Rhys Roberts. Oxford: Oxford University Press.

Austin, J. L. 1955. *How to Do Things with Words*. Oxford: Oxford University Press.

Bourdieu, Pierre. 1984. *Distinctions: A Social Critique of the Judgement of Taste*. Translated by Richard Nice. Cambridge, Mass.: Harvard University Press.

Brown, Richard H. 1987. *Society as Text: An Essay on Rhetoric, Reason, and Reality.* Chicago: University of Chicago Press.

Edmondson, Ricca. 1984. *Rhetoric in Sociology.* London: Macmillan.

Gouldner, Alvin. 1954. *Patterns of Industrial Bureaucracy.* Glencoe, Ill.: Free Press.

Stein, Maurice R. 1964. "The Eclipse of a Community: Some Glances at the Education of a Sociologist." In *Reflections on Community Studies,* ed. Arthur J. Vidich, Joseph Bensman, and Maurice R. Stein. New York: Harper and Row.

Toulmin, Stephen. 1987. *The Place of Reason in Ethics.* Chicago: University of Chicago Press.

Wörner, Markus H. 1990. *Das Ethische in der Rhetorik des Aristoteles.* Freiburg/Br: Alber Verlag.

Yeats, W. B. 1983. *The Poems of W. B. Yeats,* ed. R. J. Finneran. London: Macmillan.

3 The Poststructural Crisis in the Social Sciences: Learning from James Joyce

Norman K. Denzin

A double crisis of representation and legitimation confronts the social sciences. Embedded in the discourses of poststructuralism and postmodernism (Derrida 1978; Martin 1992; Lather 1991; 1993; Richardson 1992; 1994; Brown 1987; Agger 1989), these two crises are, as Patti Lather (1993) notes, coded in multiple terms, variously called and associated with the "interpretive, linguistic, and rhetorical turns" in social theory. This linguistic turn makes problematic two key assumptions of social theory and interpretive research. The first assumption presumes that theorists and researchers can no longer directly capture lived experience; such experience, some argue, is created in the social text written by the researcher. This is the representational crisis. It confronts the inescapable problem of representation but does so within a framework that makes problematic the direct link between experience and text (Denzin 1991a).

The second assumption makes the traditional criteria for evaluating interpretive theory and research problematic. This is the legitimation crisis. It involves a serious rethinking of such terms as validity, generalizability, and reliability, terms already retheorized in post-positivist, constructionist-naturalistic (Lincoln and Guba 1985, 36), feminist (Fonow and Cook 1991, 1–13; Smith 1992), and interpretive (Hammersley 1992; Lather 1993) discourses. This crisis asks, "How are interpretive studies to be evaluated in the poststructural moment?" Of course these two crises blur together.

In this essay, I examine these two crises and locate them within the history of social theory and qualitative research in the United States (for other histories, in both the United States and Europe, see

Wolcott 1992; Spindler and Spindler 1992; Quantz 1992; Atkinson 1992; Lincoln and Guba 1985; Guba 1990). Then I will use James Joyce's four pivotal literary works, *Dubliners, A Portrait of the Artist as a Young Man, Ulysses,* and *Finnegans Wake,* as vehicles to illustrate how the representation and legitimation crises were resolved in earlier historical moments. Drawing on Joyce's texts, I conclude with a brief discussion of possible new directions for critical, interpretive research and theory. I will argue, paraphrasing Karl Marx, that interpretive social scientists have been living a history that has been handed down to them from the past. Thus, while we make our own history, we do so under circumstances that are not of our own making. Here I attempt to chart a path that will allow us to take greater control over this history.

The Representational Crisis

A single, but complex issue defines the representational crisis. It involves the assumption that much, if not all, social science and ethnographic writing is a narrative production, structured by a logic that "separates writer, text, and subject matter" (Denzin 1991a, 278; for an exception to this conclusion see Richardson 1994). Accordingly, any social text can be analyzed in terms of its treatment of four paired terms: (1) the "real" and its representation in the text, (2) the text and the author, (3) lived experience and its textual representations, and (4) the subject and his or her intentional meanings. The text presumes a world out there (the real) that can be captured by a "knowing" author through the careful transcription (and analysis) of field materials (interviews, notes, etc.). The author becomes the mirror of the world under analysis. This reflected world then represents the subject's experiences through a complex textual apparatus that typically mingles and mixes multiple versions of the subject. The subject is always a textual construction, for the "real" flesh-and-blood person is always translated into either an analytic subject as a social type or a textual subject who speaks from the author's pages. In no case does the "real" subject come to life on the author's pages.

Several questions follow from this formulation (see Denzin 1991d, 61). Who is the subject? Does the subject have direct access to his or her lived experiences? Is there a layer of lived experience that is authentic and real? Is any representation of an experience as good as any other? Are the subject's formulations always the most accurate?

Ethnographers have historically assumed that their methods probe and reveal lived experience. They have also assumed that the subject's

word is always final and that talk directly reflects subjective lived
experience. The literal translation of talk thus equals lived experience and its representation.

Poststructuralism challenges these assumptions. Language and
speech do not mirror experience. They create it and in the process of
creation constantly transform and defer that which is being described.
The meanings of a subject's statements are, therefore, always in
motion. There can never be a final, accurate representation of what
was meant or said, only different textual representations of different
experiences. As Lather (1993, 3) observes, these arguments do not
put an end to representation; they signal instead the end of pure
presence (Lather 1993, 3). The task at hand is to understand what
textually constructed presence means, since there is only ever the
text, as Jacques Derrida reminds us. This leads to the question of a
text's authority.

The Legitimation Crisis

A poststructural interpretive social science challenges neo-positivist
arguments concerning the text and its validity. Neo-positivists interpret validity as the basis of a text's authority and truth and call this
version of validity *epistemological*. That is, a text's authority is
established through recourse to a set of rules concerning the production and representation of knowledge. These rules, as James Scheurich
(1992, 1) notes, if properly followed, establish validity. Without validity there is no truth, and without truth there can be no trust in a text's
claims to validity (Lincoln and Guba 1985). With validity comes
power (Cherryholmes 1988), and validity becomes a boundary line
"which divides good research from bad, separates acceptable (to a
particular research community) research from unacceptable research.
. . . It is the name for inclusion and exclusion" (Scheurich 1992, 5).

In contrast, poststructuralism reads the discussions of logical,
construct, internal, ethnographic, and external validity, text-based
data, triangulation, trustworthiness, credibility, grounding, naturalistic indicators, fit, coherence, comprehensiveness (see Eisenhart and
Howe 1992, 657–69), plausibility, truth, and relevance (Atkinson 1992,
68–72) as attempts to reauthorize a text's authority in the neo-positivist
moment. Such moves still hold (all constructionist disclaimers aside)
to the conception of a "world-out-there" that is truthfully and accurately captured by the researcher's methods and written text.

These words, and the methodological strategies that lie behind
them, represent attempts to thicken and contextualize a work's

grounding in the external empirical world. They represent efforts to develop a set of transcendent rules and procedures that lie outside any specific research project. These rules, if successfully followed, allow a text to bear witness to its own validity. Hence a text is valid if it is sufficiently grounded, triangulated, based on naturalistic indicators, carefully fitted to a theory (and its concepts), comprehensive in scope, credible in terms of member checks, logical, and truthful in terms of its reflection of the phenomenon in question. The text's author then announces these validity claims to the reader. Such claims become the text's warrant to its own authoritative representation of the experience and social world under inspection.

Epistemological validity can now be interpreted as a text's desire to assert its power over the reader. Validity represents the always just out of reach but answerable claim that a text makes for its own authority. (After all, the research always could have been better grounded, the subjects more representative, the researcher more knowledgeable, the research instruments better formulated, and so on.) A fertile obsession, validity is the researcher's mask of authority (Lather 1993, 5) that allows a particular regime of truth within a particular text (and community of scholars) to work its way on the world and the reader.

Poststructural Forms of Validity

Paraphrasing Lather (again) and invoking Derrida, it is now necessary to ask, "What do we do with validity once we've met poststructuralism?" Several answers are possible. The first is *political.* If there is a center to poststructural thought, it lies in the recurring attempt to strip a text, any text, of its external claims to authority. Every text must be taken on its own terms. Furthermore, the desire to produce an authoritative (valid) text is renounced, for any text can be undone in terms of its internal-structural logic.

The unmasking of validity-as-authority now exposes the heart of the argument. If validity is gone, values and politics, not objective epistemology, govern science (see Lather 1986). This is familiar territory, and the answer is equally familiar. It is given in Michel Foucault's concept of subversive genealogy, a strategy that refuses to accept those "systems of discourse (economic, political, scientific, narrative)" (Denzin 1991b, 32) that "ignore who we are collectively and individually" (Racevskis 1983, 20).

An antifoundational social science project seeks its external grounding, not in science, in any of its revisionist forms, but rather in a commitment to a post-Marxism and a feminism with hope but no guarantees (Grossberg 1986, 58). It seeks to understand how power and ideology operate through systems of discourse, asking always how words, texts, and their meanings play a pivotal part in "those decisive performances of race, class, gender . . . [that] shape the emergent political conditions . . . we refer to as the postmodern world" (Downing 1987, 80). A good text is one that invokes these commitments; a good text exposes how race, class, and gender work their ways in the concrete lives of interacting individuals. Lather (1986, 67) calls this *catalytic validity,* the degree to which a given research project empowers and emancipates a research community.

A second solution dispenses with the quest for validity and seeks instead to examine a text's *verisimilitude,* or ability to reproduce (simulate) and map the real. There are two essential levels of verisimilitude—as a group of laws set by convention and as a mask that presents these laws as a text's submission to the rules of a particular genre (Todorov 1977, 84). In its most naive form, verisimilitude describes a text's relationship to reality by asking, "Are the representations in a text consistent with the real? Is the text telling the truth?" Certain actions, for example, are said to lack verisimilitude "when they seem unable to occur in reality" (Todorov 1977, 82). A second meaning of verisimilitude refers to the relationship of a particular text to some agreed upon opinion, for example, epistemological validity, or what Elliot Mishler (1990, 417) calls valid exemplars accepted by a relevant community of scientists. Here it is understood that separate interpretive communities (Fish 1980) have distinctively unique standards or versions of verisimilitude as proof, truth, or validity.

As Tzvetzn Todorov (1977, 83) notes, there are as many verisimilitudes as there are genres (e.g., comedy, detective fiction, tragedy, etc.). In the social sciences there are multiple genres or writing forms: book reviews, presidential addresses to scholarly societies, research notes, critical essays, grant proposals, research reports, committee reports, and so on (see Agger 1989; Richardson 1994). Each genre has its own laws, its own verisimilitude. The validity of a statistical table is different from the so-called validity of a thick description in an ethnographer's report (Geertz 1973). Two separate genres are operating in these two contexts. A work's narrative (textual) freedom is limited by the requirements of the genre itself (Todorov 1977, 83).

Verisimilitude can be described as the mask a text assumes as it convinces the reader it has conformed to the laws of its genre; in so doing it has reproduced reality in accordance with those rules. Every text enters into a relationship with verisimilitude and its laws, including taking verisimilitude, or validity, as its theme (e.g., Mishler 1990), in which case the text must establish an *antiverisimilitude,* that is, a text that appears to lack truth, validity, or verisimilitude. Such moves allow a text to make a separation between truth and verisimilitude, for what appears to be true is false and what appears to be false is true.

Verisimilitude, of course, is the theme of the murder mystery. "Its law is the antagonism between truth and verisimilitude" (Todorov 1977, 86). In a murder mystery the murderer must appear to be innocent, and the innocent person must be made to appear guilty. "The truth has no verisimilitude, and the verisimilitude has no truth" (Todorov 1977, 86). The end of the narrative must, of course, resolve this tension or contradiction. It must show the apparently innocent person to be guilty, and the apparently guilty party to be innocent. Only in the end, as Todorov notes, do truth and verisimilitude coincide. Thus, truth is only and always a "distanced and postponed verisimilitude" (Todorov 1977, 88).

The same law, with an important twist, structures qualitative research and theory. The truth of a text must always be aligned with the verisimilitude it establishes but this verisimilitude will always be deferred, for the text's grounding in the "real" (the site of the true) can always be contested. At the same time, in the qualitative research article structural and causal variables accepted by positivist researchers must be shown to have an antiverisimilitude for the case under analysis. A goal of the qualitative researcher will be to contest, contrast, and challenge these two forms of verisimilitude, the qualitative and the quantitative, while at the same time showing how they supplement and compliment one another. But the better the researcher succeeds, the more powerfully is established the verisimilitude of the genre championed—hence the impossibility of ever escaping verisimilitude. "The more it is condemned, the more we are enslaved by it" (Todorov 1977, 87).

Two questions now emerge. The first doubles back on itself and asks, "Can a text have verisimilitude and not be true? Conversely, can a text be true, but lack verisimilitude?" The recent controversy (*Journal of Contemporary Ethnography,* 1992) surrounding William Foote Whyte's classic work, *Street Corner Society* (1943), illuminates this question, which turns on the status of a text's grounding in the real world. Whyte's work, historically accepted as a truthful text with high verisimilitude, was challenged by the scholar W. A. Boelen

(1992, 49), who claimed Whyte's study, while having some degree of verisimilitude, lacked truth. Boelen argues that Whyte had misrepresented the real structure of Italian street corner life and had perpetuated a false vision of it. Whyte replied that his study was based on member checks and hence had both verisimilitude and truth. His critic, he asserted, had misunderstood his original text and had not penetrated the real fabrics of street corner life in the Italian community.

The implications of this exchange are clear. The truth of a text cannot be established by its verisimilitude. Verisimilitude can always be challenged. Hence a text can be believed to be true while lacking verisimilitude. (The opposite case holds as well.) Challenges to verisimilitude in qualitative research rest on the simple observation that a text is always a site of political struggle over the real and its meanings. Truth is political, and verisimilitude is textual. The meaning of each of these terms is not in the text but brought to it by the reader.

The second question following from this discussion of verisimilitude becomes, "Whose verisimilitude?" for it is the researcher's goal to contest multiple verisimilitudes, multiple versions of reality, and the perceived truths that structure these realities. A text must embody multiple masks as it seeks to unmask the regimes of truth that structure experience in any given situation. As Jean Baudrillard (1983, 12–13, 146) stated, in the postmodern, contemporary moment "the real is no longer what it used to be. . . . There is an escalation of the true, of the lived experience; a panic-stricken production of the real and the referential . . . a strategy of the real, neo-real and hyperreal. . . . The very definition of the real becomes: *that of which it is possible to give an equivalent reproduction*" (emphasis in original). In any situation, then, the researcher can only produce a text that reproduces these multiple versions of the real, showing how each version impinges on and shapes the phenomenon being studied. A text's verisimilitude resides in its ability to reproduce and deconstruct the reproductions and simulations that structure the real. I call this *deconstructive verisimilitude*. Baudrillard's *America* (1988) is an attempt in this direction.

The third answer entertains *alternative forms of validity* poststructurally conceived. Lather (1993) suggests five new forms of validity (reflexive, ironic, neo-pragmatic, rhizomatic, situated) which can be discussed only briefly. *Reflexive validity* describes a text's attempt to challenge its own validity claims. This is done by posing a series of questions concerning the interpretive practices that support the text's attempts to present multiple voices and multiple points of view. Lather cites interpretive sections of her own work, *Getting Smart*

(1991), as attempts to engage in this form of validity work. *Ironic validity,* like deconstructive verisimilitude, proliferates multiple representations and simulations of the real, showing the strengths and limitations of each and arguing that no single representation is superior to another. Lather cites James Agee and Walker Evans's *Let Us Now Praise Famous Men* ([1941] 1988) as an example of a text that deploys this form of validity. Agee and Evans refuse to endorse the authority of any single representation (or interpretation) of the Great Depression on the lives of three white tenant farm families. *Neopragmatic validity* foregrounds disagreement, heterogeneity, and multiple discourses that destabilize the researcher's position as the master of truth and knowledge. Jean-François Lyotard articulates the logic of this position in *The Postmodern Condition* (1984). *Rhizomatic validity* represents attempts to present nonlinear texts with multiple centers where multiple voices speak and articulate their definitions of the situation. Giles Deleuze and Felix Guattari's *A Thousand Plateaus* ([1980] 1987) is an example of a text that enacts this form of validity. *Situated validity* imagines a feminine validity opposed to the dominant male voice that excludes women in their multiplicities—their bodies, their emotions, the maternal world (Lather 1993, 20). Laurel Richardson's (1992) poetic representations of a transcribed interview with an unwed mother situate validity in the intersection of the researcher's and the subject's voices (see also Brown [1977] 1989). As these voices cross paths, multiple feminine versions of sexuality, marriage, motherhood, and family are created.

Into History

None of the above measures are completely satisfactory. They are all reflexive and messy. That is as it should be, for the world we encounter is neither neat nor easy to make sense of. Where do we go next? If the above arguments are allowed, we find ourselves, perhaps like the listener to Bob Seger's song "Against the Wind," "wishing we didn't know now what we didn't know then."

Turn back and look at where we started and where we have come. The history of interpretive theory and inquiry in the twentieth century is coterminous with the history and cultural logics of capitalism and the economic formations that have been connected to these apparatuses. Figure 1 charts this history. Following Fredric Jameson (1991, 400–412), the figure connects the three major phases of capitalism with ethnography's major moments and shows how these moments overlap with the history of cinematic voyeurism in the twentieth

Phases of Capitalism

	Market (1900–World War II)	Monopoly (World War II–1960)	Multinational (1960–Present)

Types of Voyeurism

	Blatant (1900–1920)	Repressed (1930–60)	Transgressive (1960–Present)

Aesthetic Regimes — **Ethnography Phases**

Aesthetic Regimes	Ethnography Phases
Realism	Objective Ethnographies
Modern to High Modernism	———— James Joyce Project ———— Golden Age
Postmodernism to Present	Blurred Genres Poststructural Crisis Writing Culture

Figure 1. Capitalism's Phases, Aesthetic Regimes, and the History of Ethnography and the Voyeur

century, as well as with the dominant aesthetic theories of this century (realism, modernism, postmodernism).[1]

A major thesis organizes this reading of history (see Denzin 1994). The twentieth-century democratic capitalist societies required information from and about their citizens.[2] The social sciences provided this information in the form of social surveys, community studies, and ethnographic, qualitative studies of modern urban life. The introduction of cinema and the cinematic apparatus into American (and European) culture corresponded with this need for surveillance. Cinema introduced new ways of looking and gazing into everyday life. The cinema's voyeur came in several forms, including the journalist, psychologist, psychoanalyst, sociologist, anthropologist, and detective. Cinema's voyeur, like the social science ethnographer, gathered information about society for others and kept alive the central idea of private and public spaces in this culture.

Consider the three major moments and formations of capitalism's twentieth-century history (see Jameson 1991, 400–412): market or local (1900–WWII), monopoly (WWII–1960), multinational (1960–present).[3] Connect these formations to the three dominant aesthetic moments of the twentieth century: realism (a commitment to faithfully reproduce reality), modernism (a self-consciousness that draws on realism), and postmodernism ("which ransacks all the preceding moments for its new forms of 'cultural credit' " [Jameson 1990, 157]). These aesthetic regimes correspond to capitalism's three major formations. This correspondence is not symmetrical. It is, as Jameson (1990, 157) argues, dialectical. The latter stages of each formation build on the accumulated capital of the first stages, rearranging the meanings and formations in the former as they solidify their own representational practices.

Interpretive theory and inquiry divides into five moments. The first moment was the traditional period that lasted until World War II. Ethnographers wrote structural-functional, "objective" accounts of field experiences, concerned, like good scientists, with the validity, reliability, and objectivity of their writing. In this phase aesthetic realism overlapped with the doing of objective ethnographies. The second moment, the modernist and high modernist phase, extended through the postwar years to the 1970s. Ethnographers and sociological participant observers attempted rigorous, qualitative studies of important social processes, often using some version of symbolic interactionism. This was the golden age of rigorous qualitative analyses, such as *Boys in White* (Becker et al. 1961) and *The Discovery of Grounded Theory* (Glaser and Strauss 1967). The third moment, the end of high modernism and the beginning of postmodernism, erupted in 1973 with Clifford Geertz's *The Interpretation of Cultures* and let in a flood of new interpretive theories: hermeneutics, structuralism, poststructuralism. Soon to follow would be constructivist, critical, and feminist theories of discourse and method. This was the period of "blurred genres." The fourth moment (postmodernism) appeared with *Writing Culture* (Clifford and Marcus 1986), *The Anthropology of Experience* (Turner and Bruner 1986), *Anthropology as Cultural Critique* (Marcus and Fischer 1986), *Words and Lives* (Geertz 1988), and *The Predicament of Culture* (Clifford 1988). The fourth moment destabilized everything. It made writing and research problematic in ways that had never been imagined during the first, second, and third moments of this history. We are now in the fifth phase (the present), writing our way out of *Writing Culture*.

Let us take a third look at history to yield one additional sequence of images. Here I borrow from the history of narrative cinema and cinema's voyeur in the twentieth century (e.g., Burch 1990). Cinema's voyeur has passed through three basic stages: the blatant voyeurism of early, primitive (realist) cinema (1900-20), the repressed, anxious, displaced voyeurism of modernism (1930-60, as in Hitchcock's *Rear Window*); and the openly aggressive, transgressive, yet confused voyeurism of postmodernism (e.g., *sex, lies and videotape* and *Blue Velvet*). The cinematic, surveillance society systematically introduced the voyeur into everyday life. This figure maintained the fiction of a private, sacred space that he or she protected. The progressive insertion of this figure into every corner of life systematically opens up the private space to the public gaze. The voyeur, like the ethnographer, provided important functions for capitalism in each of its three phases, spreading the gaze of the state ever more deeply into the private lives of citizens.

These historical formations (cinematic, aesthetic, capitalist), in turn, correspond to the major periods in qualitative inquiry and interpretive theory: realism with blatant voyeurism, ethnographic, and case study objectivity; modernism with repressed voyeurism, and the mixed qualitative-quantitative strategies of grounded theory; and postmodernism with the transgressive voyeurism of the writing culture project. The correspondence, however, is not direct but dialectical. Each stage and each formation builds on the accumulated meanings of the earlier stages and formations. This movement rearranges meanings and fits them to the practices specific to a particular period and formation.

Each of these transformations retains a commitment to a realist epistemology. The early realist moment in qualitative research, like the nineteenth-century realist novel, carried the ideological task of creating a factual realist narrative about the social world (Clough 1992, 6). Modernist qualitative research (e.g., *Boys in White* and *The Discovery of Grounded Theory*) self-consciously enacted and drew its abstractions and generalizations from the older realism of the case studies of the early Chicago school of sociology (Becker 1966). The postmodernist project continues to produce realist and modernist ethnographies, as these works are now being criticized from the post-structural perspective (Clough 1992; Atkinson 1992; Hammersley 1992).

The history of qualitative (and positivist) research in the twentieth century follows the above trajectory. Like cinema's voyeur, we began as blatant observers during market capitalism, under the regime of aesthetic realism. Then we became anxious and furtive in our looking (the repressed voyeurism of midcentury capitalism). Today we are once again blatant, openly acknowledging our own place in the voyeuristic looking and gazing project. Our epistemological aesthetic has moved from realism, to modernism, and now to postmodernism. Today we seek a multinational, multicultural gaze that probes, yet goes beyond, local markets while it challenges the monopoly of the positivists over our inquiring projects.

Where has this history gotten us? The question is rhetorical. The current poststructural crisis in the social sciences articulates this history of capitalism and its cultural logics. A product of this history, the social sciences have embodied capitalism's contradictions in each historical moment, providing, at all times, the kinds of interpretive texts, methodologies, and theories this complex social formation has demanded.

James Joyce's Writing Project

Consider one more history: James Joyce's writing project (see Levin 1978). Remember what Joyce did in his four key works: *Dubliners* ([1914] 1964), *A Portrait of the Artist as a Young Man* ([1916] 1964), *Ulysses* ([1922] 1968), and *Finnegans Wake* ([1939] 1968). In his thirty-six-year writing career (1905–41), Joyce (1882–1941) traversed (as indicated in Figure 1) ethnography's five moments, moved through cinema's three versions of the voyeur and enacted in his texts the realist, modernist, and postmodern (poststructural) aesthetic epistemologies. *Dubliners* is a hard-core, traditional realist ethnography: the lives of ordinary men and women are presented in detailed, realistic fashion as they grapple, from childhood to death, with epiphanic moments in their lives. *A Portrait of the Artist* is a subjective auto-ethnography. The story of a struggle, an attempt to find a voice, and a series of epiphanic moments, the artist questions which way he should turn. In the end he leaves the world of the *Dubliners* and sets off to write the history of his country and its racist, religious, sexist, political, and economic repressions. He leaps into *Ulysses,* an interpretive, modernist, stream-of-consciousness, first-person experimental text. It is a text that insults, provokes, angers, and mocks the writer and his sexuality—the story of one day in the life of an ordinary man. The text turns against everything that has come before, including the major myths that circulate in Western culture. And then he wrote *Finnegans Wake,* an unreadable journey into language and its mysteries—another new text, postmodern and poststructural, reflexive in new ways, always an experiment in and through language, an attempt to create a new language for Ireland, a new, radical way to start anew, free of the categories, tongues, and voices of the past; hence its unreadability, for how can we read what is written in a language that we do not (yet) know?

Joyce's texts (and reactions to them) reproduce the representational and legitimation crises outlined above. *Dubliners* purported to reach out and grab lived experience and bring it into the text. *Portrait* turned the ethnographer's gaze inward and sought its validation and authority on the strength of Joyce's ability to evoke the subjective struggle undertaken by his protagonist. *Ulysses* displays multiple verisimilitudes and each of Lather's five forms of validity. Reflexively the text continually turns in upon itself, as in ironic, neo-pragmatic, and rhizomatic ways it proliferates multiple paths through its own structure. It even dares to capture a feminine validity that later becomes a central topic of *Finnegans Wake.*[4]

In these multiple textual moves Joyce displays a deconstructive verisimilitude and antiverisimilitude. Taken as a totality, his texts mock the real and its representations. Joyce's journey is to fashion a text that creates a new poststructural genre. His lessons may be applied to the history and practices of qualitative research.

Back to History through James Joyce

Return to the key moments of interpretive inquiry and examine these moments, their classical and contemporary crises, and their research practices through the gaze of James Joyce. Taking each phase or moment in order, I will share some observations and propositions. First, the two poststructural crises of representation and legitimation reflect the contemporary moment in which the image has replaced reality and the hyperreal has become more real than the real itself (Baudrillard 1983). The realization that lived experience is a textual (and cinematic) production now produces the crisis of legitimation, for texts no longer have firm external referents as they did during the earlier moments of realism and modernism.

Second, as Jameson (1992, 211–12; 1990, 156–57, 160–61) reminds us in his history of twentieth-century cinema, any aesthetic formation will enact and carry the traces of previous moments. Thus, a postmodern film such as *Blue Velvet* presents themes found in Frank Capra's 1940 realist films, whereas a postmodern work like Lather's *Getting Smart* (1992, especially chapter 7) can be read as a feminist text that builds upon and then deconstructs realist and modernist methods. Third, contemporary qualitative researchers are simultaneously and dialectically located in each phase of this history. Positivist, neo-positivist, and poststructural themes are now brought to bear upon and articulated in contemporary ethnography. At the same time each of the earlier forms of qualitative research continue to be produced (see *Journal of Contemporary Ethnography,* 1992). Fourth, multiple criteria for evaluating the qualitative project now circulate within the postmodern moment, opening any text to criticisms from criteria that operated in an earlier moment. Fifth, four types of hybrid texts are now emerging. They each reflect an attempt to address, either directly or indirectly, the crises of representation and legitimation outlined above. The first type represents texts which are *pro-postmodernist* and *antimodernist.* Such works are located within the traditions and formations reviewed by Lather (1992; 1993) and exemplified by texts such as Richardson (1992), Patricia Clough (1992), and those contained in Carolyn Ellis and Michael Flaherty (1992) and Ivan Brady (1991). These works, which include autoethnographies, ethnographic fictions, and performed texts, are poetic, experimental, and transgressive. They work against the grains of modernist traditions. The second type, termed *pro-postmodernist* and *promodernist* (Jameson 1991, 61), addresses postmodern themes from within the earlier modernist and realist traditions (see Miles and Huberman 1994; Smith 1992). These texts elaborate postpositivist conceptions of validity. The third type represents texts that are *anti-postmodernist* and *antimodernist.* Geertz's work, which represents a rupture with the modernist tradition, is highly critical of the postmodern turn in anthropology. The fourth type represents texts that are *anti-postmodernist* and *promodernist* and are critical of poststructural positions (Altheide and Johnson 1993; Hammersley 1992; Whyte 1992). These works attempt to conceptualize reflexive forms of validity while maintaining a commitment to the modernist project.

A new set of textual aesthetics associated with each of these four types of textualities is emerging. New canons of evaluation for qualitative research loom on the horizon. Promodernist anti-postmodern canons continue to reflect a commitment to a realist epistemology. This emerging canon is sensitive to the textual and contextual effects of research settings, the relationship between the observer and observed, the issue of perspective or point of view, the place of the (reader) audience in the interpretation of texts, and the issue of rhetorical or authorial style used by writers in the production of texts (Altheide and Johnson 1993). The emerging pro-postmodernist, anti-modernist canon envelops the concerns of the promodernist text, while erasing the distinction between fact and fiction and exploring in detail multiple forms of verisimilitude and poststructural validity.

As these canons emerge and take shape they dialectically affect one another, creating modernist texts that look postmodern and postmodern texts that espouse modernist concerns. Four implications follow. First, as Jameson (1990, 166) implies, each aesthetic (research) form constructs its own world of meaning and programs readers to understand and accept that world. Thus, realism (promodernism) teaches readers how to accept the versions of Reality it produces, while postmodernism does the same. The clash between these canons appears on the surface to be incommensurable. In fact, this clash represents a site where the practitioners of these forms are afforded the opportunity to sharpen and clarify the terms of their respective positions.

This leads to the second implication. A new hybrid form of textuality will emerge out of this encounter between the pro- and antimodernist and pro- and anti-postmodernist positions. This can be observed in recent attempts to make postmodern texts modernist (Schmitt 1993; Dawson and Prus 1993) and modernist texts postmodern (Denzin 1992a; 1992b; Clough 1992). Third, until this occurs each position is obliged to continue to clarify the standards and programs that organize its practices. Fourth, each form of textuality should be read from multiple perspectives: the canon it is embedded in (modernist or postmodernist) and the canon that it opposes. This duality of evaluative perspective can only serve to sharpen and clarify the tensions between these competing (but not entirely incompatible) points of view.

Lessons from James Joyce

In 1800, Friedrich Schlegel, the early German romantic student of language and history, contended "that modern literature lacked a centre, such as mythology was for the ancients" (Kiberd 1992, 4). He went on to predict the emergence of a new mythology that "would be less a radical act of creation than a 'collaboration' between old and new. . . . Why should not what has already been emerge anew, and why not in a newer and finer, greater manner?" (Kiberd 1992, 4). This is how we can read *Ulysses,* T. S. Eliot's *The Wasteland* and Pablo Picasso's *Guernica*—as new mythologies, finer and grander mergers of the new with the old (Kiberd 1992, 4).

In this sense Joyce sought to give modern literature a new center, a new language wrestled out of lived experience. He created a new mythology. His new forms of textuality claimed authority to the extent that they broke from the past and worked outward from self-experience to the world as a whole. Joyce created a new form of reflexive and transgressive verisimilitude. A text's authority was now self-referential.

Interpretive theory and inquiry currently lack a center. We confront Joyce's situation anew. We seemingly no longer know who or what the subject is, let alone how to write his or her experiences. We have no agreed upon method, no new text that points the way forward, no unassailed theory. We have lost our myths, those larger-than-life paradigms we did battle with during our earlier historical moments. Even our myths about the social scientist are in doubt, including those old images of the "scientist-as-truth-seeker," the autonomous lone wolf/lone ranger metaphor of the Western "male" working late at night or going off to dangerous, faraway places to discover "truth." The modernist project is itself now under serious challenge, including its attendant notions of ultimate human progress and the belief that the Western world provides the standard for "culture." These doubts are all central to this contemporary crisis.[5] We now seek a new mythology, perhaps not a radical collaboration with the old myths, but a redoing of the old in light of where we have travelled.

Joyce's lesson is that we must invent a new language, a new form of writing that goes beyond auto-ethnography, "teletheory," and "mystories" (Ulmer 1989). This must be the language of a new sensibility, a new reflexivity, a language that refuses the old categories and that reflexively and parasitically, in a rhizomatic manner (Deleuze and Guattari 1982, chap. 1), charts its own course against

Joyce's repressive structures of history, economy, religion, race, class, and gender. This new language, poststructural to the core, will be personal, emotional, biographically specific, and minimalist in its use of theoretical terms. It will allow ordinary people to speak out and articulate the interpretive theories that they use to make sense of their lives. Beyond *Dubliners,* learning from *Portrait,* this new language will express the personal struggles of each writer as he or she breaks free of the bonds that connect to the past. This language will be visual, cinematic, kaleidoscopic, rhizomatic, rich, and thick in its own descriptive detail, always interactive as it moves back and forth between lived experience and the cultural texts that shape and write that experience.

With Joyce we move forward by moving inward. Finding our lost center, we seek to create new forms of verisimilitude and truth—a truth from experience. We seek forms of writing that shamelessly transgress the personal while making public that which modernism kept hidden and repressed (Ellis and Bochner 1992; Ronai 1992). Writing our way out of *Writing Culture,* qualitative research and interpretive theory in the fifth moment discovers what has always been known. We are our own subjects; how our subjectivity becomes entangled in the lives of others is and has always been our topic. This is Joyce's lesson for us.

Capitalism and its cultural logics have had their way with us. We have been living someone else's version of our own history. We linger under old myths and political ideologies: Oedipus, democracy, freedom, the cult of Eros, family, love, intimacy, radical political change (Denzin 1991c). We have submitted for too long to the epistemological and aesthetic logics of realism. If we are to seriously take up the radical challenges of the current moment, then we can do no better than follow Joyce's lead, for in his texts we find anticipated that new center we so urgently seek.

Notes

I wish to thank Ben Agger, Richard Harvey Brown, Patti Lather, Yvonna Lincoln, Laurel Richardson, and Katherine Ryan for their comments on earlier versions of this chapter.

1. Space prohibits the development of these themes, which can only be sketched here (see Denzin 1994).

2. Richard Harvey Brown notes (in conversation) that such information gathering has been central to the rise of the modern nation-state.

William the Conqueror, for example, ordered a census of land, people, animals, and so on for tax and military purposes soon after 1066.

3. As Richard Harvey Brown (and others) have noted, Jameson's storied version of capitalism's twentieth-century history is quite idiosyncratic. For example, some histories of the U.S. economy suggest a local, market capitalism prior to the Civil War, the monopolization and nationalization of the economy from about 1880 forward, and increasing internationalization of capital in spurts since World War I, especially during and after World War II and since 1975. Jameson's periodization is tempting because it enables the other correlations I want to establish, but I am mindful of these problems in his story.

4. Ernest Lockridge (conveyed by Laurel Richardson) raises the issue of Joyce's reactionary views of women. Apparently he believed that Irish women should have more children, especially sons. In this case, a radical text represents reactionary attitudes.

5. I am indebted to Yvonna Lincoln for outlining each of these points.

References Cited

Agee, James, and Walker Evans. [1941] 1988. *Let Us Now Praise Famous Men.* Boston: Houghton Mifflin.

Agger, Ben. 1989. *Reading Science.* Dix Hills, N.Y.: General Hall.

Altheide, David L., and John M. Johnson. 1993. "Criteria for Evaluating Qualitative Research." Pp. 485–99 in *The Handbook of Qualitative Research in the Social Sciences,* ed. Norman K. Denzin and Yvonna S. Lincoln. Thousand Oaks, Calif.: Sage.

Atkinson, Paul. 1992. *The Ethnographic Imagination.* London: Routledge.

Baudrillard, Jean. 1983. *Simulations.* New York: Semiotext(e).

———. 1988. *America.* London: Verso.

Becker, Howard S. 1966. "Introduction." Pp. v–xviii in *The Jack-Roller,* by Clifford Shaw. Chicago: University of Chicago Press.

Becker, Howard S., et al. 1961. *Boys in White.* Chicago: University of Chicago Press.

Boelen, W. A. 1992. "*Street Corner Society*: Cornerville Revisited." *Journal of Contemporary Ethnography* 21:11–51.

Brady, Ivan, ed. 1991. *Anthropological Poetics.* Savage, Md.: Rowman and Littlefield.

Brown, Richard Harvey. [1977] 1989. *A Poetic for Sociology.* Chicago: University of Chicago Press.

———. 1987. *Society as Text.* Chicago: University of Chicago Press.

Burch, Noel. 1990. *Life to Those Shadows.* Berkeley: University of California Press.

Cherryholmes, Celo H. 1988. *Power and Criticism: Poststructural Investigations in Education.* New York: Teacher's College Press.

Clifford, James. 1988. *The Cultural Predicament.* Cambridge, Mass.: Harvard University Press.

Clifford, James, and George E. Marcus, eds. 1986. *Writing Culture.* Berkeley: University of California Press.

Clough, Patricia Ticineto. 1992. *The End(s) of Ethnography.* Newbury Park, Calif.: Sage.

Dawson, Lore, and Robert Prus. 1993. "Interactionist Ethnography and Postmodernist Discourse: Affinities and Disjunctures in Approaching Human Lived Experience." *Studies in Symbolic Interactionism* 15:193-202.

Deleuze, Gilles, and Félix Guattari. [1980] 1987. *A Thousand Plateaus.* Minneapolis: University of Minnesota Press.

Denzin, Norman K. 1989. *Interpretive Interactionism.* Newbury Park, Calif.: Sage.

——. 1991a. "Back to Harold and Agnes." *Sociological Theory* 9:278-85.

——. 1991b. "Empiricist Cultural Studies in America: A Deconstructive Reading." *Current Perspectives in Social Theory* 2:17-39.

——. 1991c. *Images of Postmodern Society: Social Theory and Contemporary Cinema.* London: Sage.

——. 1991d. "Representing Lived Experiences in Ethnographic Texts." *Studies in Symbolic Interaction* 12:59-70.

——. 1992a. *Symbolic Interactionism and Cultural Studies: The Politics of Interpretation.* Cambridge, Mass.: Blackwell.

——. 1992b. "Whose Cornerville Is It, Anyway?" *Journal of Contemporary Ethnography* 21:120-32.

——. 1994. *The Voyeur and the Cinematic Society.* London: Sage.

Derrida, Jacques. 1974-76. *Of Grammatology.* Baltimore: Johns Hopkins University Press.

——. 1978. *Writing and Difference.* Chicago: University of Chicago Press.

Downing, D. B. 1987. "Deconstruction's Scruples: The Politics of Enlightened Critique." *Diacritics* 17:66-81.

Eisenhart, Margaret A., and Kenneth R. Howe. 1992. "Validity in Educational Research." Pp. 643-80 in *The Handbook of Qualitative Research in Education,* ed. Margaret D. LeCompte, Wendy L. Millroy, and Judith Preissel. New York: Academic Press.

Ellis, Carolyn, and Arthur P. Bochner. 1992. "Telling and Performing Personal Stories: The Constraints of Choice in Abortion." Pp. 79-101 in *Investigating Subjectivity: Research on Lived Experience,* ed. Carolyn Ellis and Michael G. Flaherty. Newbury Park, Calif.: Sage.

Ellis, Carolyn, and Michael G. Flaherty, eds. 1992. *Investigating Subjectivity: Research on Lived Experience.* Newbury Park, Calif.: Sage.

Fish, Stanley. 1980. *Is There a Text in this Class: The Authority of Interpretive Communities.* Cambridge, Mass.: Harvard University Press.

Fonow, Mary Margaret, and Judith A. Cook. 1991. "Back to the Future: A Look at the Second Wave of Feminist Epistemology and Methodology."

Pp. 1–15 in *Beyond Methodology: Feminist Scholarship in Lived Research,* ed. Mary Margaret Fonow and Judith A. Cook. Bloomington: Indiana University Press.

Geertz, Clifford. 1973. *The Interpretation of Cultures.* New York: Basic Books.

———. 1988. *Words and Lives.* Stanford, Calif.: Stanford University Press.

Glaser, Barney, and Anselm Strauss. 1967. *The Discovery of Grounded Theory.* Chicago: Aldine.

Grossberg, Lawrence, ed. "On Postmodernism and Articulation: An Interview with Stuart Hall." *Journal of Communication Inquiry* 10:45–60.

Guba, Egon G. 1990. "The Alternative Paradigm Dialog." Pp. 17–30 in *The Paradigm Dialog,* ed. Egon G. Guba. Newbury Park, Calif.: Sage.

Hammersley, Martyn. 1992. *What's Wrong with Ethnography?* London: Routledge.

Jameson, Fredric. 1990. *Signatures of the Visible.* New York: Routledge.

———. 1991. *Postmodernism, or, The Cultural Logic of Late Capitalism.* Durham, N.C.: Duke University Press.

———. 1992. *The Geopolitical Aesthetic: Cinema and Space in the World System.* Bloomington: Indiana University Press.

Johnson, John. 1976. *Doing Field Research.* New York: Free Press.

Journal of Contemporary Ethnography. 1992. "Special Issue: *Street Corner Society* Revisited." 21, no. 1 (entire issue).

Joyce, James. [1914] 1964. *Dubliners.* New York: Viking.

———. [1916] 1964. *A Portrait of the Artist as a Young Man.* New York: Viking.

———. [1922] 1968. *Ulysses.* New York: Viking.

———. [1939] 1968. *Finnegans Wake.* New York: Viking.

———. 1978. *The Portable James Joyce.* Introduction and notes by Harry Levin. New York: Viking.

Kiberd, Declan. 1992. "Bloom the Liberator." *Times Literary Supplement,* Jan. 3.

Lather, Patti. 1986. "Issues of Validity in Openly Ideological Research: Between a Rock and a Soft Place." *Interchange* 17:63–84.

———. 1991. *Getting Smart.* New York: Routledge.

———. 1993. "Fertile Obsession: Validity after Poststructuralism." *Sociological Quarterly* 35:673–93.

Levin, Harry. 1978. "Editor's Introduction." Pp. 1–16 in *The Portable James Joyce,* by James Joyce. New York: Viking.

Lincoln, Yvonna S., and Egon G. Guba. 1985. *Naturalistic Inquiry.* Beverly Hills, Calif.: Sage.

Lyotard, Jean-François. 1984. *The Postmodern Condition.* Minneapolis: University of Minnesota Press.

Marcus, George, and Michael Fischer. 1986. *Anthropology as Cultural Critique.* Chicago: University of Chicago Press.

Martin, Bill. 1992. *Matrix and Line: Derrida and the Possibilities of*

Postmodern Social Theory. Albany: State University of New York Press.

Miles, Matthew B., and A. Michael Huberman. 1994. "Data Management and Analysis Procedures." Pp. 428-44 in *The Handbook of Qualitative Research in the Social Sciences,* ed. Norman K. Denzin and Yvonna S. Lincoln. Newbury Park, Calif.: Sage.

Mishler, Elliot G. 1990. "Validation in Inquiry-Guided Research: The Role of Exemplars in Narrative Studies." *Harvard Educational Review* 60:415-41.

Quantz, Richard A. 1992. "On Critical Ethnography (with Some Postmodern Consideration)." Pp. 447-506 in *The Handbook of Qualitative Research In Education,* ed. Margaret D. LeCompte, Wendy L. Millroy, and Judith Preissel. New York: Academic Press.

Racevskis, K. 1983. *Michel Foucault and the Subversion of Intellect.* Ithaca, N.Y.: Cornell University Press.

Richardson, Laurel. 1992. "The Consequences of Poetic Representation: Writing the Other, Rewriting the Self." Pp. 125-37 in *Investigating Subjectivity: Research on Lived Experience,* ed. Carolyn Ellis and Michael G. Flaherty. Newbury Park, Calif.: Sage.

——. 1994. "Writing as a Method of Inquiry." Pp. 516-29 in *The Handbook of Qualitative Research in the Social Sciences,* ed. Norman K. Denzin and Yvonna S. Lincoln. Newbury Park, Calif.: Sage.

Ronai, Carol Rambo. 1992. "The Reflexive Self through Narration: A Night in the Life of an Erotic Dancer/Researcher." Pp. 102-24 in *Investigating Subjectivity: Research on Lived Experience,* ed. Carolyn Ellis and Michael G. Flaherty. Newbury Park, Calif.: Sage.

Scheurich, James Joseph. 1992. "The Paradigmatic Transgressions of Validity." Unpublished ms.

Schmitt, Raymond L. 1993. "Cornerville as Obdurate Reality: Retooling the Research Act through Postmodernism." *Studies in Symbolic Interactionism* 15:121-46.

Smith, Dorothy. 1992. "Sociology from Women's Perspective: A Reaffirmation." *Sociological Theory* 10:88-97.

Spindler, George, and Louise Spindler. 1992. "Cultural Process and Ethnography: An Anthropological Perspective." Pp. 53-92 in *The Handbook of Qualitative Research in Education,* ed. Margaret D. LeCompte, Wendy L. Millroy, and Judith Preissel. New York: Academic Press.

Todorov, Tzvetzn. 1977. *The Poetics of Prose.* Ithaca, N.Y.: Cornell University Press.

Turner, Victor, and Edward Bruner, eds. 1986. *The Anthropology of Experience.* Urbana: University of Illinois Press.

Ulmer, George. 1989. *Teletheory.* New York: Routledge.

Whyte, William Foote. 1943. *Street Corner Society.* Chicago: University of Chicago Press (editions also published in 1955, 1981, 1993).

——. 1992. "In Defense of *Street Corner Society.*" *Journal of Contemporary Ethnography* 21:52-68.

Wolcott, Harry F. 1992. "Posturing in Qualitative Research." Pp. 3-52 in *The Handbook of Qualitative Research in Education,* ed. Margaret D. LeCompte, Wendy L. Millroy, and Judith Preissel. New York: Academic Press.

4 Trade Secrets:
On Writing Ethnography

John Van Maanen

Once upon a time an ethnography was put forth by its author(ity) as a straightforward, no-nonsense, cultural description. The author simply staked out a group, lived with them for a while, took notes on their comings and goings, and went home to write about it all. It was a little like a peaceful form of journalism and, compared to novel writing, involved lots of travel. All that was required (it seemed) was a steady gaze, a thick notebook, and time to spare.

No more. The work is now pictured as a sort of epistemological trial by fire. For example, Renato Rosaldo (1989) takes ethnography to task for its unwarranted claims of objectivity; Dennis Tedlock (1979) for its inevitable but treacherous subjectivity; Norman Denzin (1989) for its failure to abandon the modernist image of science; Edward Said (1989) for its link to the empire. For all these reasons and more, the cultural representation business has become quite tricky even if one goes no further than the corner tavern in search of "others" sufficiently distinct on the surface from oneself to be ethnographically realized. Just what is required of ethnography is by no means clear and, among its producers and consumers alike, restlessness is the norm.

Such restlessness, however, has not toppled the enterprise. Ethnography still places its living oxymoron, the participant observer, in the field, whether backyard or distant. Yet how this field is, in the first moment of ethnography, rendered intelligible and, in the second moment, passed on in a fashion that persuades readers, in the third moment, of its value and truth are matters of considerable concern and debate. My interest here is more with the second moment of ethnography than with the first or third. It is the account of an individual's learning from the field that marks ethnography as a trade. As is true for all occupational groups, ethnographic practices are not all public. Like bankers and belly dancers, we, too, have our trade secrets.[1]

Prominent among them is the informal but nonetheless powerful injunction always to treat our work as fact, not fiction; real, not imagined; methodical, not spontaneous; and technical, not artistic. Substance, not style, is what supposedly carries ethnography and provides legitimacy for its pursuit.[2] But underneath such posturing lies the realization that we must traffic in communication, and communication itself implies an intention to persuade. Whatever else it may be, ethnography is always rhetorical. We attempt to convince others that we've discovered something of note, made unusual sense of something, or, in weak form, simply put forth an account in good faith. Simply stated, we are in the business of persuading others that we know what we are talking about and they ought to pay attention. We do this primarily by means of text—the written word.

Some writings, however, generate a good deal more interest and response (altered views) than others. Apparently, some ethnographers are able to jump from fieldnotes, lived experience, memory traces, or interview transcripts to published accounts with more success than others in terms of the rhetorical aims of the trade. Of the in(de)finite number of fieldwork-based studies on community schools, for instance, only a handful are remembered or influential in shaping our images of such institutions. Mastering the trade, then, clearly involves a good deal more than topical selection, systematic methods, and the ability to string coherent sentences together. What is so persuasive about certain ethnographies?

One popular account for the production of convincing ethnography is that somehow the persuasive writers load more facts into their reports than the less persuasive. Like literary journalists such as Tom Wolfe or John McPhee, the master ethnographer cannot leave a room or ridge without having first described everything in or on it. Such a view is foolish, however, for this more-is-better ethic pales when confronted with some of our most illustrious and convincing texts—both past and present. If ethnography is cultural representation, the cultures represented in such monographs as E. E. Evans-Pritchard's *The Nuer* (1940), Gerald Suttles's *The Social Order of a Slum* (1968), Peter Manning's *The Narc's Game* (1980), or Sharon Traweek's *Beamtimes and Lifetimes* (1988) are highly selective renditions of group life, concerned more with establishing broad generalizations than with depicting particular settings, occasions, or people. These are works governed by a coherent vision more than by any eagerness to stuff the text with detail.[3]

If not facts per se, then perhaps it is theory that convinces. This is the flipside of the unloading of cultural facts position. Theory convinces because of its elegance, parsimony, problem focus, novelty, sweep, empirical correlates, or any other word or phrase commonly used to elevate the status of one theory over another. In these postpositivist days, this perspective has appeal since facts are no longer seen to speak for themselves. Yet the belief that theory alone convinces is patently false since theory itself is both ephemeral and contentious. Not only does theory come and go with the social tide and the morning mail, but holders of one theory are unlikely to be convinced of another no matter what form an argument takes. Consider the rise and fall of functionalism, structuralism, structural-functionalism, behavioralism, ethnoscience, various strains of psychoanalytic theory, or symbolic interactionism. All have had great success. All have faded with time. Builders of these proud towers of power develop research programs, sponsor journals, speak with authority on the issues of the day, train happy apprentices, and, in general, behave as if Thomas Kuhn were but an annoying figment of the imagination. Invariably, however, new theory replaces the old and we carry on.

Ethnography, as accomplished within both sociology and anthropology, has its tribal circles made up of various theory gangs and method cults. As any given circle grows, it develops a familiar kind of professionally induced blindness in the form of favored topics, celebrated texts, holy facts, sworn enemies, distinctive concepts, beloved approaches, and so on.[4] Each circle generates a litany of proper authorities that litter the writings of members. Work in any one circle is, for example, marked by the textual droppings of famous names (Barthes 1977; Foucault [1969] 1989; Clifford 1983). Obscure in-vogue words fall like bombs in some pleromatic texts, and readers outside the circle are besieged and intimidated while readers within the circle are charmed by the writer's good taste. Over time, however, the writing within a circle grows cold, passive, limp; and it becomes increasingly difficult to know just who is telling the tale, the author or the circle?

This is not to say that theory cannot be instructive or insightful. Theory provides order, and good theories allow the telling of coherent stories that are rich in scope and imagination but held in check by a fresh and precise vision of things. For instance, Erving Goffman's (1961, 1–124) ideas about "total institutions" really enabled us to see old things in new ways. But remember that a good deal of social theory merely confirms what we already accept as true. Stephen Jay Gould's (1981) treatment of the intelligence measurement industry is good on such matters as is George Stocking's (1968) treatment of theories of racial differences. One thing we do know is that theory is not a simple induction from a set of empirical facts.[5] Whether challenging or comforting, theory is a cultural product like any other human invention.

At any rate, theoretically innovative (for their time) ethnographies are not hard to locate. Consider, for example, James Spradley's *You Owe Yourself a Drunk* (1970), Paul Willis's *Learning to Labour* ([1977] 1981), or Roy Rappaport's *Pigs for the Ancestors* (1968). All are strong works and are read despite whatever ill ease a reader may have with the theory woven deeply into each study. Consider, also, the classic urban ethnographies such as William Whyte's *Street Corner Society* ([1943] 1955) or Herbert Gans *The Urban Villagers* (1962). Both are read today even though the functionally driven social exchange and system theory framing each work is no longer very exciting or compelling. What all these authors accomplished in their respective works was to create a narrative using theory to abbreviate, organize, and embed certain features of the account such that a convincing story could be told. Theory was a tool in these studies, a kind of scaffolding device that helped persuade readers good sense had been made of the world.

Such good sense may fall away, however, as new theories emerge to both complicate and challenge the old. Moreover, the failure of theory to persuade and unify across the field allows for discourse and debate on the nature of ethnography to surface. We do not question our aims, methods, or narratives in time of theoretical closure and agreement. Only a sense of difficulty, splintering, unfulfilled promise, and doubt lead to the interrogation of the trade's product. But the awareness of exhausted, limited, or otherwise troubling approaches to ethnography leads also to the promotion of alternative ones.

Candidates for the "new ethnography" are everywhere. Kevin Dwyer (1977) promotes a dialogic, native-focused ethnography in which the other has a say; Paul Rabinow (1977) favors a reflexive, personally explicit one. Marvin Harris (1979) argues for a kind of programmatic ethnography, as rigorous in its demands for the display of behavioral or material data as Oswald Werner and G. M. Schoepfle (1986) are in their pitch for a systematic ethnography and its display of cognitive or linguistic data. Peter Manning (1987) outlines a formal, structural, semiotic ethnography in which the native or native voice is not at the center of things. H. L. Goodall (1989) tries to define a postmodern ethnography as does Stephen Tyler (1986), and so on. The list is long.

Not all of these approaches have resulted in a surge of acclaimed ethnographic texts. Advice, as always, outruns practice. Yet they have stretched our definition of just what may count as an ethnography. Thus, the current questioning and posing of alternatives may well signal a broadened definition and mandate for ethnography rather than its disintegration and decline. If so, the proliferation of the ends and means of the trade suggests ethnographic vitality, not decay.

The secret hidden by all this diversity is that membership in the trade rests not on the mastery of technique, use of a particular analytic scheme, or the pursuit of a common goal, but on the production of a work recognized by others as an ethnography. There is no product shortage in this regard. Therefore, despite the fall of ethnographic traditions, the shrill warnings for having misplaced the signifiers for the signified, the changes in what was once a rather repetitive but cheerful drone, and the worries over theoretical polarization and disciplinary drift, there remains a commitment to produce ethnography. Such affinity surfaces in odd ways but, as Jean-Paul Dumont (1986, 352) observes, no one has yet to be drummed out of the trade for producing bad ethnography: "Even if someone writes what someone else perceives as an abominable ethnography, the latter still recognizes the former's work as an ethnography first and then, only then, interpreting it from that vantage point, empties suitable invectives upon it."

In other words, it is not the objectives, theories, methods, or data that identifies a given work as an ethnography. It is the product—the written representation of a culture or cultural practice. In broad communicative terms, a sign is something that stands for something else. Thus, as a text, an ethnography is a sign (or collection of signs) that stands for a culture or cultural practice (the object). The sign communicates the apparent good sense the author has made of the culture or cultural practice (the interpretant). The text as a sign joins object and interpretant. Together they form a triadic relationship. When split apart, difficulties result.

Consider, for example, the classics of ethnography devoted to the objective description of culture, a practice still carried on in high style by many contemporary writers. The object is always on view in these studies but the interpretant is up for grabs. Or, reversing the equation, consider the newer interpretive ethnographies that focus on how culture is made sensible to the writer. The interpretant is well developed in these writings but the object often fades away. What should be done is to explore the sign itself—the ethnography as text.[6] Here is where the world is put into words as the representative composition or product of our trade.

We have been reluctant to begin this task for a variety of reasons. First, it is not obvious what the close study of ethnographic texts entails. Training in anthropology or sociology rarely, if ever, includes much appreciation for the methods and styles of literary criticism or the analysis of rhetoric, classical or modern. By and large, students are taught to read *through* texts, to appreciate and recall what is represented within them, not to consider how such representations are constructed. The reading of a text for its signature phrases, deployment of tropes, use of language, characteristic voice(s), narrative conventions, allusions and allegories, use of humor (if any), arrangement of facts, authorial gaffes and evasions, placement of snotty quotation marks or italics, barrage of counting-coup footnotes or references, and so forth does not come with formal disciplinary training. On this matter, those schooled in the qualitative arts fare no better than their quantitative brethren even though they may spend more of their student daze pondering narratives instead of numbers.

Second, examining an ethnography as text may well contradict what we think we should be doing—namely, going to the field, collecting data, and writing it up. The student who wishes to sit back and worry about the plots and subplots in police ethnographies, the presence of irony and satire in the collected works of Raymond Firth, or the use of metaphor and simile in field methods texts will be seen, no doubt, as a bit strange if not foolish. The student should be "out there" living and talking with real people, not textualized ones, gathering material from which an ethnography can be constructed.

Third, other ethnographers, perhaps more senior and hence more forgiving of odd pursuits, might still find the study of ethnographic texts as signs off-putting, if not a little embarrassing (especially if the examined texts are their own). To study the allegedly descriptive, interpretive, reflexive, or intertextual writings of ethnography is simply not worth the effort. Writing ethnography is, after all, a matter that rests on fieldwork and it is to this awkward adventure that we should direct our gaze. If we are to improve the art and science of ethnography, surely the first moment of the trade deserves more attention than the second. It is one thing to attempt to decode the narrative structure of fiction which rests (presumably) on nothing but characterization devices, plot lines, use of familiar language, authorial vision, and invented dialogue; it is another matter entirely to worry about the same things in our own works—using words borrowed from the humanities—whose central claim is authenticity.

Fourth, the reluctance to consider ethnography as text may rest on the belief that if we did start looking closely at how our major and minor works are constructed, we might not like what we find. Our silence on these matters results perhaps from the fear that if we examined closely our use of imagery, phrasing, analogy, authority, and voice, we might discover some literary chicanery or authorial trickery that would undercut our ability to make claims about the truth of our writings. If style were shown to play an important role in those ethnographic accounts that linger in the mind, then a corrosive relativism might take over and we would lose whatever advantage and distinctiveness our trade provides. We would become mere players in the game of words, conveyors of personal opinion, trapped in the same prison of language occupied by poets, playwrights, and novelists.

None of these views carry much force. We can certainly all learn to look critically at our texts. Creative underlining is not reserved for just lit crit students. We all know that we spend as much time writing what we think we have learned from the field as we do learning it in the first place, thus dissolving any claims that writing is a minor, mop-up activity done swiftly at the end of a study and therefore not central to the trade. We also recognize the power of the written word in molding our own perspective of the worlds we live in. Indeed, we have a number of persuasive writers within each of our ethnographic circles to blame for recruiting us to the trade in the first place. Finally, claiming that an examination of ethnographies as texts risks the enterprise itself is tantamount to sticking one's head in a hole and suggesting that literary criticism will vaporize the novel. Bringing narrative devices to light and examining how they work does not threaten ethnography any more than the same form of study threatens fiction.

Reading (to Write) the Social Text

There are a number of ways to go about treating ethnography as text. Some are relatively tried and true and need only their disciplined application in a targeted field. Others are experimental, the source of some success but probably more failure. All are ways of expanding our understanding of ethnography and are required if we are to improve the craft.

Perhaps the most familiar approach to ethnographic works is from a sociology of knowledge perspective. To ethnographers, facts are best viewed as values whose truth is dependent on the culture, interests, and historical conditions of those who believe in them. Discerning the social, political, and temporal bases of ethnographic facts is then a worthy pursuit and likely to open ethnographic texts to new interpretations. An exemplar in this regard is George Stocking's magnificent *Victorian Anthropology* (1987) which intimately connects turn-of-the-century ethnographies to the ideas of the day. Another less grand yet instructive effort is Paul Rock's quirky and insightful look at *The Making of Symbolic Interactionism* (1979).

What is apparent in these works (and many others) is that ethnography is mediated many times over by the conventions of the day. These include historical, political, personal, social, institutional, and narrative conventions, and no ethnography can shed them. Such conventions result in an almost limitless set of pretext assumptions—about style, working methods, likely audience, legitimate arguments, language, and so forth—that constrain the ethnography that is eventually produced.[7] Such conventions are no more or less relevant today than yesterday no matter what their form.

Another way of cracking open the text is to treat the process of ethnography as a subject itself thus creating an interpretation of ethnographic work that lies outside the ethnography—a kind of ethnography of ethnography. We have, in fact, a number of fine examples of this work usually created in two-step fashion where the author of a well-received ethnographic text writes another text telling how the first was put together. Jean-Paul Dumont's *The Headman and I* (1978) is in part an account of what stands behind *Under the Rainbow* (1976). Such self-consciousness has become expected (and something of a cliché) since virtually all dissertation and monograph ethnographies include chapters, appendixes, or forwards addressing some of the ways the ethnography itself was developed.[8]

A few ethnographies do not merely tack on a hermeneutic consciousness as an afterthought to the ethnography itself. With more or less grace, some writers have turned cultural objects, including themselves, into subjects. Such a shift in the ingredients of ethnography signals a radical stylistic change (it also raises interesting questions about ethnographic writing, too, but as George Marcus (1980) points out it in no way answers them). This shift occurs in two ways. First, some writers do not bracket themselves out of their accounts or ignore the way their understandings develop over time in the field. The writing then becomes something of an example and examination of the social construction of ethnographic reality (e.g., Briggs 1970;

Read 1965; Johnson 1975). Second, other writers focus closely on the discourse between themselves and those to whom they were talking in the field, thus moving toward an intersubjective ethnography (e.g., Crapanzano 1980; Harper 1987). Both approaches have resulted in highly original work chock-full of textual innovation.

There are troubles still, however, since it is obvious that even in the most self-reflexive or dialogic works, the writer still fashions the final account and has the last word. Cultural members may find no greater comfort in being subjectified rather than objectified. Moreover, the sort of elevated sensitivity that applies to the tentative but hard-earned cultural knowledge represented in such ethnographies does not extend to the representation process itself. Stopping short of the writing process in such personally probing work highlights the irony in our use of the term ethnographer to refer to the one who is immersed in the concreteness of fieldwork, not the one immersed in the concreteness of writing.

Another more distant way to push the analysis of writing is to pursue textual ethnographies in which the writing of others serves as the basis of study. Developing an ethnography of historical people based on surviving texts, for example, draws attention to the period assumptions, textual complexities, and assumptive grounds associated with any piece of writing. Consider the delicate ways Marshall Sahlins puts across his portrait of the Hawaiian people at the point of fatal contact with the West in *Historical Metaphors and Mythical Realities* (1981). Consider, also, the way Anthony F. C. Wallace (1978) reconstructs the *Rockdale* community on the basis of archeological shards and textual materials. Both writers create stunning ethnographies that represent a sharp turn away from the "you-are-there" kind of writing in the ethnographic present.

Another kind of textual consciousness develops among comparativists who must constantly judge the authenticity of the ethnographies they study. Rodney Needham (1985), for example, notes that ethnographic frauds, while rare, are not unknown. George Psalmanazar and Carlos Castaneda serve as his exemplars in this regard. It is always possible that an ethnographer simply makes it all up. Possible, too, is a situation where an ethnographer has been completely taken in by the falsehoods of others, a charge Derek Freeman (1983) levels at Margaret Mead. In either case, this sort of ethnographic detective work begins by suspending or questioning the truth routinely granted to ethnographic accounts. Such work cannot help but remind us of just how dependent we are on our trust in the ethnographer. Yet promises of honesty can be broken (intentionally or unintentionally) and, while it is no doubt quite difficult to deceive on a grand scale, it is not logically or operationally impossible. Ethnography has no ultimate truth test.

Such matters become even more clear when the most direct approach to the analysis of our writings is considered. This approach is represented by current efforts to deconstruct ethnographic texts—a method much loved by some American theorists of literature. Deconstructionists assume ethnographers are neither hoodwinked nor fraudulent but may still mislead readers on the basis of identifiable textual practices of which they may be unaware. Two notable examples are Clifford Geertz's recent pillorying of certain legendary anthropologists in *Works and Lives* (1988) and James Clifford and George Marcus's collection of more felicitous treatments of numerous canonical ethnographic texts in *Writing Culture* (1986). What these authors have shown by their merry deconstruction of text after text is the precise way such texts are put together and how they seem to work as texts. This is clearly helpful and any would-be or practicing ethnographer should pay attention to the literary devices uncovered by the hearty band of deconstruction workers tilling the ethnographic fields.

Such salubrious activity creates some well-known problems of its own. On what basis do deconstructionists rest their respective cases? What allows for such arcane and privileged readings to take place? How are we more prosaic types to treat their claims of unearthing the deep meanings of a text, meanings an author may not have intended to bury within the book and might very well dispute? In times past, ethnographic criticism rested on gauging the relative strength of competing empirical claims and assessing the methodological adequacy of a given work by the standards of the day. But to expect deconstructionists to attend to these matters is to miss the point. Their method is high-church interpretation. It rests on close readings, symbolic analysis, aesthetics, political and ideological critique, cultivated comparative tastes, current semiotic theories, dialectical irony, hermeneutics, and so on.

In contrast to the erudite, head-swirling criticism of this postmodern world, much of contemporary ethnography seems to reside in a posttoasty world. Applying such enigmatic, labor-intensive deconstruction efforts to our own typically mundane, low visibility, restricted, and endlessly qualified research products seems a little like stalking a flea with an elephant gun. Reserved for the highly acclaimed texts of the trade, the effort makes sense and, certainly, the lessons learned by such efforts are not missed by the rest of us. Ultimately, however, as deconstructionists know only too well, there is no external standard with which to test the validity of any given reading of an ethnographic text. Such is the state—and the point—of deconstruction.

This is not to say that deconstruction of ethnographic texts is a futile activity. By reading past explicit claims and surface intentions and trying to make visible what Jacques Derrida (1967) calls the "text within the text," ethnographic authority is questioned and new ways to read old tales emerge. Interpretations multiply. Edward Said's *Orientalism* (1978) provides a splendid example as does Renato Rosaldo's (1986) examination of the pastoral motif in selected ethnographic writings. Like all forms of literary criticism, deconstruction seems, at times, precious and, at other times, profound. At its best, however, deconstruction can only raise questions about the enterprise, not solve them.

A final way of treating ethnography as text is to play with the ethnographic form itself. Perhaps too much attention has been focused on the classic ethnographies of the past and not enough attention given to the ways contemporary writers are going about their trade. Armed with a good deal more textual awareness than their ancestors, some writers are producing fresh, innovative, and altogether convincing work. Consider a few examples. Brad Shore (1982) has written an elegant ethnographic detective story that carries the reader along in a who-done-it fashion. Michael McCall and Howard Becker (1988) have written and performed a theater reading that renders dramatic the ethnographic. Vincent Crapanzano (1985) has authored an emotionally dense ethnography of white South Africans that is stylistically closer to creative journalism than realist ethnography. Douglas Harper (1982; 1987) has produced two engrossing impressionistic ethnographies that make fine use of his talent as a photographer.

Less innovative, perhaps, but nonetheless instructive are those ethnographies strong on historical reconstruction and the evocation of time and place such as Kai Erickson's *Everything in Its Path* (1976) and Renato Rosaldo's *Ilongot Headhunting, 1883-1974* (1980). These unique works may prompt others to experiment. They are texts of knowledge and reflection whose authors did not forget that texts are also literature. Shifts in the reporting practices may be modest or grand but through such changes the manufacture and stylistic aspects of ethnography become visible.

What seems striking about many of the newer experimental ethnographies is the attention their authors place on story.[9] Social dramas, little and big, shape these narratives more than current social theories. And if past work is any guide, stories, not explanations, are what remain in a reader's mind. Who can forget William Whyte's bowling story? Who can recall the theory that justified its telling? Certainly Bronislaw Malinowski's ([1922] 1961) tale of the Kula Ring has outlasted the exchange theory it ostensibly illustrated. Stories are a way of making sense of the world and of passing along that sense. They are both vehicles and vessels of conception (Geertz 1973, 212).[10]

As vehicles of conception, ethnographies open out to an audience. Textual awareness also requires knowing something about how our materials are received; we have been rather quiet on this score. Meanings come from the interaction of reader and text as well as from the author (Fish 1980; Rabinowitz 1977). Ethnographies do not have stable meanings permanently embedded in them at the moment of their creation. A social context surrounds their reception such that distinct interpretations of the same work are possible. Moreover, since social contexts shift over time, the meaning of a text may change. Ethnographies, therefore, have careers. Some fall from grace (e.g., Ruth Benedict's *Patterns of Culture* [1934]) while others enter the elite canon (e.g., Gregory Bateson's *Naven* [1936]).

During any one period, however, the most revered of texts are those able to sustain a relative divergence of interpretation among readers (Levine 1985). Different groups find a work persuasive for different reasons. The good ethnography is neither pat nor pointless. It is located within a set of conventions that are played with and strained but rarely broken. Readers may be intrigued, disturbed, or fascinated but none are utterly mystified or frustrated.

Considering the pleasures and discontents of ambiguity raises a final point about the persuasive and rhetorical power of ethnography. We have come full circle. If ambiguity is central, our task is perhaps more modest than some would prefer. Fundamentally, all we can do is offer an interpretation of and for human conduct. Such interpretations cannot be proved or disproved. They draw their appeal from our use of language, the story we choose to tell, the imagination we display, and our credibility as exhibited in the text. There are no crucial tests or body of axioms on which interpretation rests. Ethnography is bound by time, situation, and the cultural prejudices of those who produce, write, and read the tale.

Whatever direction ethnography takes in the future, it is certain that text will not vanish. Like it or not, writing is our elemental task. We may undertake it with enthusiasm or dread, a sense of pleasure or duty. Our style may be gaudy or sublime, metaphoric or metonymic, encyclopedic or telegraphic, formulaic or experimental. But write we must. As recent work makes clear, we know that we write under erasure and that our texts are signs only partially under our control. Our ink-stained products will always be just short of the mark, always lacking a little something here or there, always saying a bit more or less than what we had planned, and thus communicating in unforeseen ways. If, however, by paying attention to the writing of ethnography—the second moment—we can come closer to understanding what we learned in the first moment and wish to communicate to our readers in the third moment of ethnography, perhaps we will have learned some more trade secrets to pass along.

Notes

This essay was written originally to serve as a short editor's introduction to a special issue in 1990 of the *Journal of Contemporary Ethnography* on "The Presentation of Ethnographic Research." It was not short enough and was cut from the issue. It is revised here with the same basic intent, namely, to take stock of the latest crisis in ethnography. This crisis concerns the problematic ways ethnography is written and has relatively little to do with the fieldwork that may (or may not) inform such writing. At the moment, even the best of our qualitative method texts are rather quiet when it comes to guiding students through the writing process (e.g., Glaser and Strauss 1967; Denzin 1970; Freilich 1970; Douglas 1976; Spradley 1979; Agar 1980; Hammersly and Atkinson 1983; Whyte 1984; Peacock 1986). Rest assured, this won't last long. One can almost hear the word processors whirring and beeping away on revisionist method texts. For guidance on many of the matters covered in this paper, I thank Peter Manning and Robert Thomas.

    1. By trade, I mean merely those who write about the culture of others on the basis of having lived with them for a time. This is not meant to be exclusionary. By secret, I mean merely what those in the trade seem to know but rarely discuss with outsiders or, for that matter, with themselves. I do not expect readers to bang their heads on the desk or otherwise explode with self-recognition at what I have to say. Writing ethnography is not much talked about but that does not mean we do not know much about it. It means only that we are reluctant to hold forth. Becker (1986) offers some playful exercises that help break this silence in seminar rooms.

    2. In days long past, science (small *s*) was the banner under which ethnography operated. Claims that we were doing science helped both to mystify what we did and to elevate our status in the world. It was also a way of limiting the kinds of inquiries made in its good name. We could, for example, deprive others of the right to proceed in alternative ways by

denying them academic promotions (which were still available then even in England). The cry of science is less popular now and the perspective and style of the ethnographies that fly its flag are dated, reflecting a naive era that is no longer epistemologically viable or socially defensible. Ironically, the more scientific we tried to be by revealing our methods, the less scientific we appeared. New understandings now swaddle ethnography but we should not forget that these too are historically relative and, quite likely, exclusionary as well.

3. If traces of the future are to be located in the recent past, ethnography is moving toward ever more spare and lean representations. Part of this may be because so much of it is published in journals and monograph length studies seem fewer in number. Another reason seems to be authors' fear of being charged with (shudder) "haphazard description." To avoid accusation, writers take pains to fit together all details in a tight logic and shed all that may not fit the scheme. Solving this problem produces tidy ethnographies—with all the charm of short funeral orations. See Marcus and Fisher (1986) for a good treatment of what Peter Manning (personal correspondence) calls the "format effect in ethnography."

4. Ethnography is certainly no slouch at the divide and multiply game. We have ethnographic circles attached to just about everything that walks, talks, and chews gum. Domains are carved out along substantive, regional, language, institutional, associational, national, labor process, and topical lines. These domains often overlap, of course, but a list of them would be a worthy addition to Jorge Luis Borges's celestial library: ethnographies of religion, the family, communication, gender, French, police, community, Navajo, West African, astral, and on (and on). Theory differentiates as well. Consider, for example, ethnographies done in the name of practice theory, symbolic interactionism, cognitive anthropology, cultural materialism, cultural ecology, sociolinguistics, structuralism, and postmodernism (whatever that may be). Methods divide as well (e.g., various forms of fieldwork, decision-tree modeling, grid/group analysis, discourse analysis, life history interviewing, and more). With the rise of textual awareness, circles develop around the choice of narrative forms in which to cast ethnography, ranging from the table-thumping, back-to-the-future fundamentalists of ethnographic realism to the risk-taking experimentalists of ethnography perched blindfolded on the epistemological high wire. What all this diversity means is anyone's guess. One thing is clear, however: the objectives of ethnography have exploded. Some see this as something to be mourned, the coming apart of ethnography (Wolff 1985); others see it as cause for celebration, the liberation of ethnography (Dumont 1986). Taking a stance on such matters depends, no doubt, on whether one's own circle is on the way up (and expanding) or on the way down (and shrinking).

5. There are two ways to talk about what it means to be empirical: one is sensible, the other is not. I will address only the former. To be

empirical means mainly to look before leaping, to examine things before drawing conclusions. Being empirical means going to the field to get ideas and going back again to defend them. Everyone is therefore empirical except, perhaps, paranoid schizophrenics. In social research, being empirical usually means we try to offer evidence for our claims, evidence that others can see (if they look) as clearly as we can. This emphasis on sight, however, has tied ethnography in knots for good reason. We are slowly coming around to the view that one can be empirical without being a fanatic since it is but one of many possible bases for truth claims. Observers of this interpretive turn in social science have much to say on the matter (e.g., Geertz 1983; Rabinow and Sullivan 1987; Agar 1986; D'Andrede 1986).

6. This task is well underway; a number of writers are already hard at work (e.g., Boon 1982; Clifford 1981; 1983; 1988; Clifford and Marcus 1986; Crapanzano 1977; Geertz 1983; 1988; Marcus 1980; Marcus and Cushman 1982; Stocking 1983; 1987; Portis Winner and Winner 1976; Wuthnow et al. 1984; Becker 1986; Van Maanen 1988).

7. Such an approach can be pushed to the point of arguing that all ethnographic knowledge is poppycock and fantasy (Sharrock and Anderson 1980; Tyler 1986). Strategically, however, the quest for truth is probably too important to give up on in Western political, cultural, and academic life. Yet we cannot go back to the past in any simple sense since the cat is now out of the bag—the very partiality, self-limitations, and institutional constraints on our work are too well known. Perhaps solace might come from considering ethnographic knowledge as factual (not invention or fiction) and honest (not suppressing evidence), with objective (not relative) truth claims—all of which are historically positioned and generated from a specific research viewpoint. Rosaldo (1989) discusses what we might make of our work in light of the current critique of ethnography.

8. I must put forth a reservation in this regard. A call for confessional ethnography is based on the quite optimistic assumption that ethnographers have a self-consciousness that is, like the Titanic and Andrea Doria, well worth raising. This may not always be the case since there is little guarantee that a raised self-consciousness will be associated with anything more than a sort of modish narcissism. Perhaps this concern about excessive self-centeredness is premature but I cannot help but hope that those for whom self-consciousness is a full-time occupation will take up hang gliding instead of ethnography.

9. Examples on my list of innovative storytelling not yet mentioned in the text include Hebdige (1979), Myerhoff (1980), Crapanzano (1980), Krieger (1983), Latour (1987), Feldman (1989), and Barley (1989). Readers can make their own lists, but I should note that these examples stretch and bend ethnographic reporting practices in wise and sometimes witty ways. All are personal and risk being taken for "light ethnography" as a result. Yet each conveys an essential ambiguity that persists. They

remain open to (re)interpretation, hesitancy, challenge, and contingency in ways that seem to reflect the social experiences on which they are based. While I would not argue for turning ethnography over to the Bedtime Story Association, I do think there is a good deal of self-delusion involved when we think we are doing anything very different than storytelling—as is true(r) also for historians, psychologists, political scientists, and economists (especially economists). All ethnography is shot through with tales anyway, both good and bad, and certainly more attention to their telling cannot help but improve our craft. Good discussions of the working and persuasive power of story and narrative are found in Bruner (1986), Brown (1977), Mishler (1986), and Polkinghorne (1988).

10. Moving toward a narrative rationality does not, of course, alter the truth claims on which ethnography rests for good stories will surely be devalued if they turn out to rest on social fictions, intentional or not. Currently, William Whyte's *Street Corner Society* ([1943] 1955)—something of the sociological equivalent of Margaret Mead's *Coming of Age in Samoa* (1923) in terms of the widespread attention it has received over the years and the place of honor it holds within the discipline—is under scrutiny as to the veracity of its tales. The bowling story I celebrated earlier in the text may well remain memorable but perhaps for different reasons than is presently the case. Michael Agar (1990) provides a cautionary tale in this regard by quoting from a brief item appearing in the *Washington Post* book review section, December 20, 1987: "Earlier this year, Bruce Chatwin's *Songlines* was published and promoted as a travel narrative in the Paul Theroux tradition. Then, Chatwin casually revealed in a *Granta* interview that 'if I had to tot up the inventions, there would be no question in my mind that the whole thing added up to a fictional work.' For some readers, this reduced an excellent travel book to an okay novel."

There are no final answers to the problems such truth questions raise. It is always possible that the pledge of good faith on the part of an ethnographer is no more reliable than the promise not to engage in any insider trading on the part of a bond speculator. The fact is that there are many trade secrets we will never discover.

References Cited

Agar, M. 1980. *The Professional Stranger.* New York: Academic Press.
——. 1986. *Speaking of Ethnography.* Newbury Park, Calif.: Sage.
——. 1990. "Text and Fieldwork: Exploring the Excluded Middle." *Journal of Contemporary Ethnography* 19, no. 1: 73-88.
Barley, N. 1989. *Not a Hazardous Sport.* New York: Henry Holt.
Barthes, R. 1977. *Image, Music, Text.* New York: Hill and Wang.

Bateson, G. 1936. *Naven*. Stanford, Calif.: Stanford University Press.

Becker, H. S. 1986. *Writing for Social Scientists*. Chicago: University of Chicago Press.

Benedict, Ruth. 1934. *Patterns of Culture*. Boston: Houghton Mifflin.

Boon, S. A. 1982. *Other Tribes, Other Scribes*. Cambridge: Cambridge University Press.

Briggs, J. 1970. *Never in Anger*. Cambridge, Mass.: Harvard University Press.

Brown, R. H. 1977. *A Poetic for Sociology*. Cambridge: Cambridge University Press.

Bruner, E. M. 1986. "Ethnography as Narrative." Pp. 139-55 in *The Anthropology of Experience*, ed. V. T. Turner and E. M. Bruner. Urbana: University of Illinois Press.

Clifford, J. 1981. "On Ethnographic Surrealism." Pp. 139-55 in *The Anthropology of Experience*, ed. V. T. Turner and E. M. Bruner. Urbana: University of Illinois Press.

———. 1983. "On Ethnographic Authority." *Representations* 1:118-46.

———. 1988. *The Predicament of Culture*. Cambridge, Mass.: Harvard University Press.

Clifford, J., and G. E. Marcus, eds. 1986. *Writing Culture*. Berkeley: University of California Press.

Crapanzano, V. 1977. "On the Writing of Ethnography." *Dialectical Anthropology* 2:69-73.

———. 1980. *Tuhami: Portrait of a Moroccan*. Chicago: University of Chicago Press.

———. 1985. *Waiting: The Whites of South Africa*. New York: Random House.

D'Andrede, R. 1986. "Three Scientific World Views and the Covering Law Model." Pp. 19-41 in *Metatheory in Social Science*, ed. D. W. Fiske and R. A. Shweder. Chicago: University of Chicago Press.

Denzin, N. 1970. *The Research Act*. Chicago: Aldine.

———. 1989. *Interpretive Interactionism*. Newbury Park, Calif.: Sage.

Derrida, J. 1967. *On Grammatology*. Baltimore: Johns Hopkins University Press.

Douglas, J. 1976. *Investigative Social Research*. Newbury Park, Calif.: Sage.

Dumont, J. 1976. *Under the Rainbow*. Austin: University of Texas Press.

———. 1978. *The Headman and I*. Austin: University of Texas Press.

———. 1986. "Prologue to Ethnography or Prolegomena to Anthropology." *Ethos* 14:344-67.

Dwyer, K. 1977. "The Dialogic of Anthropology." *Dialectical Anthropology* 2:143-51.

———. 1982. *Moroccan Dialogues*. Baltimore: Johns Hopkins University Press.

Erickson, K. 1978. *Everything in Its Path*. New York: Simon and Schuster.

Evans-Pritchard, E. E. 1940. *The Nuer.* Oxford: Oxford University Press.

Feldman, M. S. 1989. *Order Without Design.* Stanford, Calif.: Stanford University Press.

Fish, S. 1980. *Is There a Text in this Class?* Cambridge, Mass.: Harvard University Press.

Foucault, M. [1969] 1989. "What is an Author?" Pp. 978–88 in *The Critical Tradition,* ed. D. H. Richter. New York: St. Martin's Press.

Freeman, D. 1983. *Margaret Mead and Samoa.* Cambridge, Mass.: Harvard University Press.

Freilich, M. 1970. *Marginal Natives.* New York: Wiley.

Gans, H. 1962. *The Urban Villagers.* New York: Free Press.

Geertz, C. 1973. *The Interpretation of Cultures.* New York: Basic.

———. 1983. *Local Knowledge.* New York: Basic.

———. 1988. *Works and Lives.* Stanford, Calif.: Stanford University Press.

Glaser, B., and A. Strauss. 1967. *The Discovery of Grounded Theory.* Chicago: Aldine.

Goffman, E. 1961. *Asylums.* Garden City, N.Y.: Anchor.

Goodall, H. L. 1989. *Casing a Promised Land.* Carbondale: Southern Illinois University Press.

Gould, S. J. 1981. *The Mismeasure of Man.* New York: Norton.

Hammersley, M., and P. Atkinson. 1983. *Ethnography: Principles and Practice.* New York: Tavistock.

Harper, D. 1982. *Good Company.* Chicago: University of Chicago Press.

———. 1987. *Working Knowledge.* Chicago: University of Chicago Press.

Harris, M. 1979. *Cultural Materialism.* New York: Random House.

Hebdige, R. 1979. *Subcultures.* London: Methuen.

Johnson, J. M. 1975. *Doing Social Research.* New York: Free Press.

Krieger, S. 1983. *The Mirror Dance.* Philadelphia: Temple University Press.

Latour, B. 1987. *Science in Action.* Cambridge, Mass.: Harvard University Press.

Levine, D. N. 1985. *The Flight from Ambiguity.* Chicago: University of Chicago Press.

Malinowski, B. [1922] 1961. *Argonauts of the Western Pacific.* New York: E. P. Dutton.

Manning, P. K. 1980. *The Narc's Game.* Cambridge: MIT Press.

———. 1987. *Semiotics and Fieldwork.* Newbury Park, Calif.: Sage.

Marcus, G. E. 1980. "Rhetoric and the Ethnographic Genre in Anthropological Research." *Current Anthropology* 21:507–10.

Marcus, G. E., and D. Cushman. 1982. "Ethnographies as Text." *Annual Review of Anthropology* 11:25–69.

Marcus, G. E., and M. Fisher. 1986. *Anthropology as Cultural Critique.* Chicago: University of Chicago Press.

McCall, M., and H. S. Becker. 1988. "Performance Science." Unpublished script, first performed at the conference "Editing Reality," SUNY–Buffalo.

Mishler, E. G. 1986. *Research Interviewing*. Cambridge, Mass.: Harvard University Press.

Myerhoff, B. 1980. *Number Our Days*. New York: Simon and Schuster.

Needham, R. 1985. *Exemplars*. Berkeley: University of California Press.

Peacock, J. L. 1986. *The Anthropological Lens*. Cambridge: Cambridge University Press.

Polkinghorne, D. E. 1988. *Narrative Knowing and the Human Sciences*. Albany: State University of New York Press.

Portis Winner, I., and T. G. Winner. 1976. "The Semiotics of Cultural Texts." *Semiotica* 18:101–56.

Rabinow, P. 1977. *Reflections on Fieldwork in Morocco*. Berkeley: University of California Press.

———. 1986. "Representations Are Social Facts." Pp. 234–61 in *Writing Culture*, ed. J. Clifford and G. E. Marcus. Berkeley: University of California Press.

Rabinow, P., and W. M. Sullivan, eds. 1987. *Interpretive Social Science: A Second Look*. Berkeley: University of California Press.

Rabinowitz, P. J. 1977. "Truth in Fiction." *Critical Inquiry* 4:121–41.

Rappaport, R. A. 1968. *Pigs for the Ancestors*. New Haven, Conn.: Yale University Press.

Read, K. 1965. *The High Valley*. New York: Scribners.

Rock, P. 1979. *The Making of Symbolic Interactionism*. Totowa, N.J.: Rowman and Littlefield.

Rosaldo, R. 1980. *Ilongot Headhunting, 1883–1974*. Stanford, Calif.: Stanford University Press.

———. 1986. "From the Door of His Tent: The Fieldworker and the Inquisitor." Pp. 77–97 in *Writing Culture*, ed. J. Clifford and G. E. Marcus. Berkeley: University of California Press.

———. 1989. *Culture and Truth*. Boston: Beacon Press.

Sahlins, M. 1981. *Historical Metaphors and Mythical Realities*. Ann Arbor: University of Michigan Press.

Said, E. W. 1978. *Orientalism*. New York: Pantheon.

———. 1989. "Representing the Colonized: Anthropology's Interlocutors." *Critical Inquiry* 15:205–25.

Sharrock, W. W., and R. J. Anderson. 1980. "On the Demise of the Native." Occasional paper no. 5. Department of Sociology, University of Manchester.

Shore, B. 1982. *Sala'ilua: A Samoan Mystery*. New York: Columbia University Press.

Spradley, J. P. 1970. *You Owe Yourself a Drunk*. Boston: Little, Brown.

———. 1979. *The Ethnographic Interview*. New York: Holt, Rinehart, and Winston.

Stocking, G. W. 1968. *Race, Culture, and Evolution*. Chicago: University of Chicago Press.

———, ed. 1983. *Observers Observed*. Madison: University of Wisconsin Press.

————. 1987. *Victorian Anthropology*. New York: Free Press.

Suttles, G. 1968. *The Social Order of a Slum*. Chicago: University of Chicago Press.

Tedlock, D. 1979. "The Analogic Tradition and the Emergence of a Dialogic Anthropology." *Journal of Anthropological Research* 35:387–400.

Traweek, S. 1988. *Beamtimes and Lifetimes*. Cambridge, Mass.: Harvard University Press.

Tyler, S. 1986. "Post-modern Ethnography: From the Document of the Occult to the Occult Document." Pp. 122–40 in *Writing Culture*, ed. J. Clifford and G. E. Marcus. Berkeley: University of California Press.

Van Maanen, J. 1988. *Tales of the Field*. Chicago: University of Chicago Press.

Wallace, A. F. C. 1978. *Rockdale*. New York: Knopf.

Werner, O., and G. M. Schoepfle. 1986. *Systematic Fieldwork*. 2 vols. Newbury Park, Calif.: Sage.

Whyte, W. F. [1943] 1955. *Street Corner Society* (with method appendix). Chicago: University of Chicago Press.

————. 1984. *Learning from the Field*. Newbury Park, Calif.: Sage.

Willis, P. [1977] 1981. *Learning to Labour*. New York: University of Columbia Press.

Wolff, E. R. 1980. "They Divide and Subdivide, and Call it Anthropology." *New York Times*, Nov. 30.

Wuthnow, R., J. D. Hunter, A. Bergensen, and E. Kurzweil. 1984. *Cultural Analysis*. London: Routledge and Kegan Paul.

5 Rhetorical Objectivity in Malinowski's *Argonauts*

Jon W. Anderson

> ... Malinowski endeavors most faithfully to view matters through the eyes of his native informants. Whether or not he has succeeded in entirely eliminating the subjective ... is of course open to question.
> —E. W. Gifford (1923)

Bronislaw Malinowski's Trobriand studies, particularly his first and most famous *Argonauts of the Western Pacific* (1922), have served as exercise books for generations of anthropologists and a point of departure for advancing alternatives to prevailing analytical practices. In that role, Malinowski's work is overwritten so often that its practices have become obscured under later glosses (including Malinowski's own), beginning with "getting the native's point of view." That such overwriting is the fate of "native" cultures is recognized in the rhetorical turn to ethnographies as texts. This turn engages underlying issues about objectification and whose subjectivity is represented, and *Argonauts* may better illuminate that turn than later, more analytical ethnographies that have been its chosen texts.

"To grasp the native's point of view," in Malinowski's phrase (1922, 25), has become iconic for anthropology and has been usually given a contemporary twist with little further reference to his own analytical practice. Native views have been translated into sociology in functionalist searches for values or rules that may be analyzed as variables and diagnosed as reflections or instantiations in the fashions of functionalist anthropology's successors. In the most recent turn fostered by Clifford Geertz ([1974] 1976), where culture-as-text replaces culture-as-values or as-rules, that gloss is proposed to "enlarge the universe of human discourse" by surrounding rather than rendering the other.

But this, too, imagines an analytical context detached from the original, while rejecting such detachment as epistemologically inadequate and ontologically incomplete is the essential step in the transformation of situated practice into transportable text. Neither this interpretive stance nor the text that it abducts develop "native" points of view so much as points of view on native views, and in this objectification they continue to struggle with Malinowski's problem.

Argonauts is a double narrative of Trobriand journeys and of framing how they are traced, and its own movement articulates the tensions of joining these two stories. *Argonauts* brings the reader into another world of experience and its representations conflated together. It is a world of alternative texts and expository practices, but only one of these narratives attracts attention while Malinowski's own is relegated to unrepeatable "style." Yet in its totality *Argonauts* does not develop "the native's point of view" in the representational and sentimental senses that notion has taken on. Native views remain objects until the end when they are allowed briefly to take on limited roles as subjects for purposes of edification. It is the edification and Malinowski's claims for it that is remembered, rather than what he actually accomplishes and how he accomplishes it. The latter, which has more to do with getting native points of view into the analysis, may still be instructive and worth sorting out from the edifications variously claimed for it.

Malinowski's contributions, as he says in the introduction and conclusion of *Argonauts,* and as his contemporaries clearly noted at the time, meant substantially increasing what was to be taken into account in ethnographic description. Above all, Malinowski expands the database with new or newly valued *types* of information, which he came to represent as "psychological" information about the subjective side of customs and beliefs (Malinowski 1931; 1944; 1955). As the example of what that meant, *Argonauts* became both the paradigmatic modern ethnography and, as a "community study," the anthropological discipline most copied in the social sciences.[1] Malinowski intends exactly that in self-consciously bringing issues from other human sciences into encounter with a new database. What is often represented as a "fieldwork revolution" has, in this context, less to do with collection than with reorienting analysis and its subjects.

Much of that reorientation was accomplished through a postgraduate seminar Malinowski held at the new, experimental London School of Economics, which was attended by the generation of social anthropologists who became identified with functionalist studies, including Meyer Fortes, Ian Hogbin, Audrey Richards, Max Gluckman, and E. E.

Evans-Pritchard, among others (Fortes 1978). In this context of discussing and critiquing fieldwork, which often had already been done and was being worked into monographic studies, Malinowski canonized his own practices of working in native languages, of "participant observation," and of two years of fieldwork (which is what he spent) as external indexes of adequacy. By providing *this* context, Malinowski became identified with the "fieldwork revolution" that was actually accomplished by his pupil-collaborators who in their own, often more rigorously developed work used techniques established by his predecessors as much as innovated by Malinowski.

Malinowski originally went to Melanesia on an expedition organized by C. G. Seligmann in the then-conventional manner as a regional survey. Expeditions in Melanesia, northern India, and on the Northwest Coast of North America had been training grounds for the senior generation of ethnologists, such as Alfred Haddon, W. H. R. Rivers, Franz Boas, and others who introduced systematic fieldwork into anthropology. After a brief survey period modeled on the methods of collecting museum specimens, Malinowski spent two periods of a year each in the Trobriand Islands where his exposure to and experience of "native society," as it was called in those colonial days, was altogether different from the touring collector's. That is, it was not guided by the protocol of comparison and distribution that had become established (see Urry 1973), but by everyday life. In addition, unlike the work of the subsequent generation, Malinowski's fieldwork was not *conceived* in what has become the modern convention. That convention derives in part from his rationalization of and claims for his experience.

Malinowski airs that rationalization first in the introduction to *Argonauts* where he defines three strata of information for describing life "in the round and not in the flat," as it was put by J. G. Frazer in his preface to *Argonauts* (1922, ix). We might now say in its living and lived-in dimensions. Those were, in Malinowski's terminology: "concrete, statistical documentation," "imponderabilia of everyday life," and "corpus inscriptionum" (1922, 24). The pomposity of the terms suggests a seriousness of purpose to differentiate kinds of data. Operationally, the first refers not to statistics but to data about form and plan, to schematized abstractions or, in another of Malinowski's metaphors, to social "maps." The second refers to actual cases, observational material that can be decomposed into their conjunctions of motive and means and situated in a chain of events. The third refers to texts of native discourse, both formal compositions and telling phrases. Each of these, but especially the first and third, were established conventions; the innovation Malinowski introduced into ethnographic accounting was the "imponderabilia of daily life," and it disturbed the relations of the other two. The disturbance is manifest in switches between schematization and narrative, which could contain observations of day-to-day practices and unfolding events. Simply put, Malinowski acquired information that the ethnographic conventions of the time could not process (or flatten, to use Frazer's term) as "data," and that continues, in the form of extended case studies, to be the alternative to schematization or "institutional" analysis.

Malinowski's formulas are not clearly drawn because he was less a programmatic theorist than a craftsman and because he chose to address his argument to a professional audience as part of a larger reading public. E. W. Gifford, an American reviewer of *Argonauts*, dismisses his formulations as "matters of method which must be obvious to every properly trained ethnologist" (1923, 102), but concedes that it may be good for the lay reader to see how professionals work, although Gifford does not go into what that is. He was able to grasp the structure and content of *Argonauts* quite apart from Malinowski's instructions; his epithet "subjective" implies a dubious regard for their value as scientific data. Malinowski's formulas do not, in practice, reflect the sources of the method, which is found instead in the layered construction of the text that grapples with *presentations* of objective and subjective witness.

The Text and Its Subtexts

Malinowski's effort to make ethnography a conceptual-analytical method is more a matter of presentation and more transparent when examined in those terms instead of in his own terminology. The scientist collecting his own information had been important in moving anthropology into identification with scientific practice and had already been established in the controlled collection and systematic description of ethnographic data introduced by W. H. R. Rivers and Franz Boas as the then-current academic standards. Malinowski's departure was more one of conveying both the assembly and the integrity of the material or how it fits together. This is what is actually present in the text, in much the same way as the field is present to the fieldworker.

Malinowski's representations of method in *Argonauts* introduce an ethnographic frame more like that of a tour conductor than the museum catalogue that preceded it (see Payne 1981; Stocking 1968);

the ethnographic account employs an analytical stance that persists in ethnography and consists of making substantive or ontological theory ironic and ethnography edifying. Its vulgar form is a simple reversal of the exotic and the familiar, and reversals are the device with which Malinowski constructs his account argumentatively. He displays apparently ("empirically") senseless behavior—sailing in canoes over the open ocean to trade symbolic objects—that has sense or reason after its description is completed. That sense, gained by transcending boundaries of the imagination, then casts another light on more familiar behavior, rather than the other way around, as previously had been the practice. Thus, Malinowski evokes the notion of Economic Man as a foil at the beginning of his account and proceeds to show how it is inadequate as a theory either of Trobriand or of all human behavior. While accepting the general form and the embedded theory of motivations as both unconscious and calculating, he corrects stereotypes that "primitives" are superstitious and magic-ridden irrationalists by disclosing the purposiveness of their behavior and by hinting how our own seemingly purposive actions are themselves superstition-ridden. More positively, he attempts to show how items of behavior and belief hang together as systems whose own integrity is an ethnographic fact of the first instance. But it is an integrity that has to be shown through narration, which fills in what schematization abstracts away.

The core of his treatment is the *kula,* an interisland system of trading valuables known collectively as *vaygu'a.* Instead of interpreting *kula* as rudimentary economics, Malinowski sets out to disclose what its terms are, how ordinary and panhuman they are, and thus how they illuminate the terms we call "economic." The reversal, in short, is from Trobriand behavior read through theories generalized from idealizations of our own culture to making Trobriand behavior the context against which to place our own as text. In this fashion, the case becomes a paradigm (and a parable) rather than a specimen of something already known.

E. R. Leach (1957) labeled this approach pragmatist. What Leach actually shows is not that Malinowski draws epistemologically on pragmatic philosophy but that the result ontologically amounts to a doctrine that the primitive-as-pragmatist is not a failed version of ourselves (i.e., employing a mistaken epistemology as was commonly argued at the time). The figure that emerges is something more like the Enlightenment notion of nature's nobleman updated for the twentieth century. That is, *primitive* pragmatism illuminates the human condition by exemplifying its naive version—thus, the edifying tone of the concluding chapter where Malinowski writes of how we may know ourselves better by coming to know others.

This sort of turnabout became a stock routine in the anthropological repertoire that obscures Malinowski's own. His work represents a real change in anthropology from a late Victorian science of human progress in the service of progress (Tylor 1871) to the more contemporary view of diversity in the service of another edification, one that replaces notions of Enlightenment as progress with a twentieth-century rewriting of Enlightenment as expanded rationality,[2] and eventually of doing better as knowing better. But if this is where his successors and exegetes stood, it is not so simply where Malinowski stood on the professional divide between an anthropology of manners-and-customs and one based on everyday behavior and common institutions.

Malinowski studied and wrote in a period when nineteenth-century ideas were being revised and so appear confusingly like, but also oddly unlike, earlier paradigms. On this cusp, he appears paradoxically romantic and skeptical, at turns rationalist and antirationalist to Leach (1957), who associates Malinowski's stance with pragmatism. Andrzej Pankula (1981) and Ivan Strenski (1982) reject this identification (with Anglo-Saxon philosophies) in favor of another with the so-called "new" romanticism and "new" positivism of turn-of-the-century Central European epistemological and linguistic thought that were Malinowski's background. Strenski argues that both strands are present in Malinowski's work: the *Neuromantik* rewriting of Johann Gottfried von Herder's earlier nineteenth-century romanticism of the unique into a more dour methodological individualism, originally a rationalist doctrine, and the incorporation of romanticist notions about the primacy of values in action into rationalist views of action. Mirror images of each other, together they amount to holding means as rational but ends as extra-rational and sharedness of values as the basis of society. The paradigmatic or underlying praxis is the new social contract of the bourgeois arrival, updated with the individualist glosses of nineteenth-century liberalism and surviving in twentieth-century doctrines of cultural relativism. Society, in this view, is made by extensions of the will rather than by giving up freedom—hence, (1) methodological (2) individualism. This, Pankula and Strenski suggest, Leach confounds with philosophical pragmatism, to which it is similar but to which it has no connection as a doctrine. In other words, Leach confounds period with provenance in his overwriting of Malinowski's text with his own.

The tension—of romanticism and a realism renewed in individualist garb salvaged from an even older rationalism—helps to put into perspective the tension between narrative line and schematization in the construction of *Argonauts*. It is not that Malinowski brought fieldwork into the ethnographic report: one of the complaints of contemporary reviewers was that he did not narrate his fieldwork, and *Argonauts* contains no sustained account of where he went or procedures he followed. The narrative he employs is specifically a narrative of native behavior to which he also progressively subordinates his own. This is the difference between travelogue and ethnography: moving the frame for his observation out of the main narrative into interpolated schematic asides, Malinowski's log of Trobriand travel is the expository structure of his account, at the expense of a log of his own "voyages" among Trobrianders, as both contemporary (Gifford 1923) and subsequent critics have pointed out (e.g., Payne 1981). Reconceived after the fact as "grasping the native's point of view," this substitution, which subordinated ethnographic priorities to those of native cultures, was the major thrust of his method as well as the basis for doubts about it.

From Rhetoric . . .

Malinowski's narrative of the *kula* system is periodically broken by asides that explain the action in a schematic fashion as it might be selectively abstracted in some other-than-native terms. Those asides serve to fill in what Trobrianders know, rather like Herman Melville's diversions on whaling provide the technical setting of *Moby Dick*. The whole ethnography is constructed by weaving narrative and schematizing modes of exposition into a single composition. Thus, he begins schematically with two chapters on the country and its inhabitants that set the scene and the players, followed by one on "Essentials of the *Kula*," which describes the plot. He then turns to a narrative account of building canoes and the ceremonies of launching them with a schematic aside on how both are financed (in a subchapter, "Essentials of Trobriand Economics") and moves on to sailing. This leads into a narrative of the *kula* expedition that becomes more and more specific (the voyage to the Amphlette Islands). Then a counterpoint discussion of *kula* mythology provides the Trobriand context (a "corpus inscriptionum") that fills out the setting of the "imponderabilia" of case studies. Narration resumes with an account of the arrival of an expedition, is broken by a schematic discussion of exchanging *vaygu'a*, and resumes with an account of returning home.

Within this initial counterpoint of action and plan, narration and schematization are woven together ever more tightly as the account proceeds, until his discussion of the reciprocal expedition is his most schematized narrative, followed by an odd collection of chapters on spells and "linguistic aspects" of spells, which are his most narrative schematizations (or "corpus inscriptionum" in his terminology). By comparison to the previous part of text, they are virtually lists and they depend on the story/history already laid out. The "story" is then used to frame a brief account of inland *kula*, a Dobuan expedition for comparison, various additional branches of the *kula*, and other odds and ends, which are even more schematic narratives. As the account proceeds, the distinction between narration and schematization progressively narrows and, indeed, is reversed; it takes less to tell the later parts of the story, and the accounts accordingly become abbreviated in comparison to the earlier parts. Such compression is, of course, a narrative device itself; the expository efficiency of selection to heighten relevance is the vehicle by which Malinowski arrives at the concluding chapter, "Meaning of the *Kula*," which he finds to illuminate rather than to be illuminated by more familiar behavior codified at the time in notions of Economic Man.

This ironic denouement is most telling about the analytical exposition employed. Malinowski did not, as subsequently became the practice, set about doing ethnography in order to write *this* ethnography. The form did not exist, at least for him, when he embarked on his research; it could not therefore serve as his goal in the way that producing an ethnographic monograph subsequently became the goal of ethnographic field research. The form that existed, at least for him, was that of the survey; its model was collecting specimens for museums or according to an index or protocol.[3] The form that we know as "an ethnography" was invented afterwards, very largely in the London School of Economics seminars where he sought to rationalize and canonize his practice in a "scientific" setting that included other people working field materials into ethnographies of peoples rather than ethnologies of customs.

Unlike monographs written in its shadow that argue "scientifically" to conclusions from amassed evidence, *Argonauts* harks back to a more general format of presentation described by Hayden White (1973). The format moves from metaphor (establishing likenesses to identify a type), metonym (taking apart the components that define the instance as a specification), synecdoche (reassembling the composition from the viewpoint of its parts), to irony (inverting the relation of text and context to illuminate the latter with the former). Its narrative progression develops and then releases an expository tension in order to create an edifying effect. White (1973; 1978) describes this format as the "classical" rhetorical structure of exposition that served in the nineteenth century as the common form of intellectualizing discourse, or the grounds on which different discourses could be displayed and examined, much as, for instance, legal argumentation provided a common form in its specialized realm. *Argonauts* follows this structure: it begins in metaphor, finding what *kula* is like and not like. Unlikenesses are more prominent at the beginning: *kula* is not like an economic system; it is more like a psychological system. It does not satisfy material wants or requirements or goals but emotional and spiritual ones. At the same time, it is accomplished technically and thus not like religion. It is like each of these in some respects, an observation that Malinowski lays out in the initial chapters and then examines in later ones for how those respects are combined.

As he proceeds, Malinowski lays out the parts of *kula* less in terms of genera to which its parts can be assimilated as specifications or types (i.e., the then-current mode of comparative ethnology) and more through an exposition of how the parts relate to one another. Thus, for example, magic (spells) completes technical actions; both are indivisible parts of a whole. Throughout the account, he links practical activities to the ceremonies that surround them, moving from the form to its behavioral context to the textual-discursive settings (his three kinds of data). The discussion shifts to metonymic properties in order to clarify the domain descriptively after first (typological) approximations provide guides. Then it sifts the domain to *kula* proper for parts that encapsulate the whole or exemplify it, its synecdoches. Here he finds magic and spells that tell what *kula* is about, so to speak, or contextualize it indigenously *as kula* instead of treating it as a version of something else, thus establishing its objective character (i.e., literally, as an object).

Having accomplished the exposition of such connections by moving between voyaging and casting spells, Malinowski turns ironic in the last chapter by telling what *kula* means not uniquely to Trobrianders but to him with his new knowledge of what being Trobriand is about. This knowledge is what he as an ethnographer and what we as readers did not have at the outset, and its problematic qualities as "data" are hardly to be underrated, as Gifford (1923) noted. What was "objective" has been made subjectively a matter of perspective by making what was subjective ("native" perspectives) into part of the object. Anthropologists were already doing this by collecting tales and spells, but by drawing this additional data, which Gifford called "psychological as well as . . . ethnological," into the same frame with canoe building and rules of exchange, he drives toward a synthesis that turns the whole endeavor inside out. The argument becomes that a fuller understanding of *kula* illuminates our own institutions instead of the opposite. Text becomes context, and the tension of the initial conundrum—sailing in canoes across the open ocean to exchange trinkets—is released in a paeon to the edifying outcome of ethnography in seeing ourselves more clearly for having made the effort to see another without either excessive skepticism or excessive gullibility, which were the charges leveled against the "old" realism and "old" romanticism.

Satisfying as the demonstration is in those terms, we are left ambivalent about how satisfying those terms are. This is still a rhetoric for domesticating wild thoughts and making them presentable, while expanding consciousness is not quite the transcendence promised. Methodologically, the problem resides in how to deal with the additional kinds of data of relations uncovered by this highly constructive method.

. . . To Method

How the analytical organization into object and subject, or subject and frame, is dissolved involves Malinowski's own departures from this rhetorical format into a new one. This movement is from the literary genre he employed toward what became the ethnographic rhetoric of case study and institutional analysis in Raymond Firth's *We, the Tikopia* (1936) or, in its mature form, in E. E. Evans-Pritchard's *The Nuer* (1940). Malinowski does not find a single or simple part that stands for the whole, a synecdoche, upon which his format was predicated and that its successful employment required. He does not find labor (as Marx did) or sexuality (as Freud did). What he finds is a complex systemic unity—but one in which some parts encompass others without standing on their own. What comes closest analytically is what is most Trobriand about the *kula* system, its ceremonial and magic, which are both technical and "emotional" in Malinowski's terms;[4] they have a pragmatic purpose, but that purpose is not just comforting. Instead, they comfort because they define through classification. Those odd and discursive chapters on magic and spells, followed by a truncated narrative of another *kula* expedition, hark back to older compendia but with a difference. Malinowski refers to this difference as the "native's point of view," and his chapters for getting the point of those views are in fact the most important in developing the "scientific" rhetoric of his ethnography.

In *kula* magic and myth, which he discusses throughout as asides or diversions until these penultimate chapters, Malinowski finds behavior that is most like belief and belief that is most like behavior, and in these confounded states he finds the means for relating them as data of the same sort. It is telling that he does not make a clear distinction between *kula* myths and spells. He cannot, for they are versions of the same thing: they are differentiated, in both words and actions, more by context than by their formal properties. Malinowski distinguishes them functionally. Both myth and spell enable *kula*: myth as its "charter," as Malinowski termed the verbal abstractions we might consider to be discourse about its terms and technique, and spells as part of the technique, in which the medium of grouping things together becomes the message. Each is both performative *and* discursive; and performance (rendered through narrative) and discourse (rendered schematically) converge, in Malinowski's analysis, to be the "emotional" satisfaction that completes the action. By leaving the implication that this is an indigenous satisfaction, method becomes ontology; hence the odor of subjectivity to which Gifford points. There was nothing unusual in recording spells and myths or in theorizing these as indigenous settings of native conceptions. What was unusual was the weight, the rhetorical objectivity, given them by an expository method that more commonly found a different ontology behind talk.

Malinowski sits on the cusp of this shift, but it cannot be said that the shift to a new ontologic of culture is realized in his treatment. That treatment is interrupted by a substitution of functional distinctions for those dissolved on formal grounds—such as distinctions between myths (as charter) and spells (as technique)—and by a psychological gloss on functions that will account for their identity at a more basic level. These moves break away from immediate settings of the data to another analytical setting in which their relations serve as parables. Malinowski gropes toward a method which captures the sort of identity that the new romantics found in methodological individualism and that philologists found with notions of protolanguages in which divergent expressions were united. In those protolanguages is a secularist vision of redemption through knowing human nature uncorrupted, and beneath the edifying tone of his conclusion is a powerful sense of Trobriand humanity as nearer than our own to an original one. This looks backward, not forward, and for that Malinowski's contemporary Paul Radin (1933) detected a lingering evolutionism in his anthropology.

Malinowski is also post-Durkheim and was a close student of Émile

Durkheim's sociology. In Malinowski's anthropology thesis on the Australian family (1913), he sought to do for family relations what Durkheim had done with Australian religion ([1912] 1915). Durkheim's method in *Elementary Forms* was to reduce the distance between analytical variables instead of drawing their distinction sharply (or essentially) and to find an analytical setting in which they were most alike, or differentiated by *only* the difference that one wanted to illuminate. Durkheim's model was the controlled experiment, and he expounded this method, somewhat opaquely, as explaining some social facts with other social facts ([1895] 1938). By that, he meant explanation without recourse to other presumably more "base" or more "essential" components from which social phenomena might be constructed (most especially, for Durkheim, the facts of individual psychology). On such grounds, he opposed methodological individualism and insisted that social phenomena be treated as "caused" by other social phenomena. In practice, this meant finding things that were similar by virtue of being *placed* in the same context.

This is what Malinowski, more clumsily than Durkheim, is doing in those odd chapters on spells and by incorporating descriptions of magic into descriptions of the pragmatic settings where it occurs. He is not emphasizing how magic as practical action differs from other practical, instrumental actions, such as science, so much as he is emphasizing how magic and science are *alike* as practical, technical, instrumental actions because they occur together in the same contexts. Magic is part of the *kula* toolkit, so to speak; or, ironically, tools have a magical quality that in Malinowski's terms is supererogatory to their purpose until it is realized that their purpose includes what he calls "emotional" or "psychological" ends. Moreover, those are part of the action itself, without which *kula* would be nothing more than it appears initially (externally) to be (building canoes, voyaging, and exchanging valuables) without any sense of those values. These additional data thus identify what an action is rather than only what (else) it is merely *like*. At this point, Malinowski withdraws into the "psychology" that Gifford notes and that Durkheim had avoided by insisting on the social logic and ontology of myth and ritual. This move recontextualizes Malinowski's findings in a frame on "human nature," which he sought to critique and correct by adducing additional data to that frame, where Durkheim sought to establish a new frame.

Malinowski flounders about terminologically to conceptualize or capture such extra qualities in terms of "psychology," "emotion," "feeling," and "spirit" and to hold those as equally "real" by the test of being equally as compelling as the mundane qualities of actions. Primitive pragmatism unites the two, but it is clumsy, and in the end Malinowski must admit that even in these terms there is much for which he cannot account.

Still, Malinowski's attempt is ingenious and far more carefully crafted than is often credited. What he did was to combine narrative with schematization, first, by focusing on the "voyage" that Trobrianders take instead of on his "voyage" among them. His own voyage is reduced to a list of places visited dropped into his discursive introduction (1922, 16). The overall structure of the ethnographic account subordinates schematization to this narrative. But it is a peculiar, mixed narration that carries along a schematic story. The *kula* becomes an object: it is not a *kula* voyage that is described but the *kula's* system, abstracted and no longer *kula* except for its parts. Malinowski is aware of the ambiguity and tension in this intermediate product. He emphasizes that no Trobriander shares his view, and he briefly compares it to alternative "ethnological" (i.e., comparative) perspectives (1922, 510-14, 517). The significance of his view is to encompass the various specific views that specific Trobrianders have of their part in the Trobriand drama and thus, in a sense, is neither here nor there. But then he backtracks: narration serves to connect the schematization with "emotional life," which is squeezed flat by the intellectualizing thrust of schematization, any schematization, on its own. Gifford's cautious, skeptical appraisal points to this problematic turn in the text that would connect Trobriand perspectives with Malinowski's, or with analytical perspectives that he has disowned.

Ethnography Recast

Malinowski subtitles *Argonauts* "An Account of Native Enterprise and Adventure in the Archipelagoes of Melanesian New Guinea" to signal that the account and ethnography in general are about both the action and its loading. While schematization is adequate to enterprise, narration is required for capturing the adventure, the "emotional" loading of experienced enterprise. Schematization retrieves the rational structure, narration the adventure; and the overall subordination of scheme to narrative on which he begins and ends in order to locate his account is melded in its course into an increasingly schematic character in each succeeding narration. Eventually and practically, this is the difference that dissolves, rather than that between enterprise and adventure. Malinowski never quite resolves their tension into a new unity. His devices of collapsing synecdoche into metonym and irony into metaphor, or of combining them into complementation within a frame, only partially succeed. Indeed, his narration begins to unravel in the conclusion, which is rushed to a close just as he seems to realize that having turned the tables he has opened a whole new analytical problem that has him theoretically in the position from which he started, only facing in the opposite direction of now "knowing ourselves better" (1922, 516, 518). Thus, the edification of his method intrudes.

The drift at the end is away from epistemology and into ontology. Ontologizing puts him in the uncomfortable position of having to adjudicate interpretations not in terms of how he knows but in terms of what he knows. Analytically, he has proceeded by creating tensions between partial accounts. In the introduction, he describes the process of ethnography to include "cross-fertilization" of constructive work and observation (1922, 13). He proceeds by making an outline of native institutions as a guide to research ("statistical documentation") and filling that in (with "imponderabilia"). But his distinctions of constitution and content, legal and intimate, technical and emotional—for getting beyond the mere register of details to penetrate "the mental attitudes addressed in them" (1922, 20)—actually pull his analytical terms apart rather than bring them together. These distinctions repeatedly create a dilemma out of the relations that constitute the forms of native institutions and that he observed. Malinowski never escapes this point of entree, in behavior, and behavior remains his essential view of custom: "there is the routine prescribed by custom, then there is the manner in which it is carried out, and lastly there is the commentary on it" (1922, 22). This is a more revealing stratification of data (into routine, setting, commentary) than his formal terminology of organization, imponderabilia, and corpus inscriptionum. This analytical stratification of information describes an ontology of behavior almost out of consciousness (routine) encasing metabehavior (situations) itself encasing subsequent representations continuous with it, and his method follows from this ontology. He progresses toward mentality from action and from there to "corpus inscriptionum" or discursive native representation. Each provides the context for the next more general level of behavior. He is interested in Trobrianders as actors in Trobriand society and not in their specific institutions, which he can locate ultimately nowhere else than in psychological service.

The fragility of weaving narrative and schematization together is indicated by how rarely it was repeated and how quickly it came apart. Probably the most successful repeat performance was Raymond

Firth's *We, the Tikopia* (1936), published a little over ten years later. Firth's text opens with his arrival and proceeds as a narrative but one fitted to the specificity of particular individuals, including his intercourse with them, which is far less problematic than the base-to-superstructure completeness of institutions Malinowski addressed. Filled with specific persons, Firth's ethnography is almost biographical: it emerges as a composite biography of a specific society in a particular time and place. Firth's subsequent monographs on politics and religion also depend on this conservatism, which makes Firth's Tikopia corpus an exemplar that Malinowski's failed to be for being, by comparison and paradoxically, too reflective.

In other hands, the synthesis came apart into its components. Schematization became the mode of the structural-functional analysis and narrative the mode of what became the extended case-study method. The former takes as its task the unpacking of a structure of interrelationships, the latter the unpacking of an event, each in order to retrieve a wholeness as part of the data. The difficulty of their synthesis was shown by Gregory Bateson's effort to focus ethnography on its epistemological difficulties, which he flagged by subtitling his monograph, *Naven* ([1936] 1968), "A Survey of the Problems Suggested by a Composite Picture of the Culture of a New Guinea Tribe Drawn from Three Points of View."

A Perspective on Malinowski's "Ethnography"

While Malinowski did, indeed, take anthropology off the veranda and into the village, as he put it, he also brought it into the study, which is no less important because that is the other context of the story (Anderson 1986). We have come to recognize that mode as inadequate because ultimately it does what it studies: it elaborates significance. As Malinowski recognized in his conclusion, the "Meaning of the *Kula*" is its meaning for someone who wants to know something other than what Trobrianders know. The irony is edifying the first time, but alternative points of reference multiply with Tikopian ironies, Nuer ironies, Iatmul ironies, and Zulu ironies, each depending on an ethnographer not just going but also returning. Paul Radin, the arch skeptic among Malinowski's American contemporaries, highlighted the problem when he criticized Malinowski's method for overvaluing the ethnologist's role in fixing and arranging the record, especially for assigning native texts a tertiary position and arranging data around his own problems of comprehension. To Radin, contextualizing data in this fashion distorts instead of letting them "speak for themselves." Insofar as social facts do not so much "speak" (on their own) as they are "read" (in some context), Radin's radical empiricism puts Malinowski's composite empiricism into perspective. Ethnography comes home as ethnographies, each one less edifying than the last, and in the end reproduces the babble of voices it sets out to harmonize.

Malinowski's *Argonauts* is a transitional work and its strains are both apparent and hidden. What is most apparent is its unformedness as modern ethnographic method; what is most hidden are rhetorical practices in which Malinowski was struggling to free a sensibility about what counted as "data" about customs and how those data should be stratified. Theorized (e.g., Malinowski 1944), his stratification of routine, situations, and commentary was a failure. The speedy disintegration of his synthesis into its component narrative and schematic elements in subsequent social anthropology reminds us that in practice what counts as data is an epistemological rather than an ontological problem. Keeping that epistemological accent in the study is a problem, when the challenge of examining how one knows gets subordinated to the challenge of examining what one knows and when the disciplines of human encounters are replaced by those of inner dialogue, where doubt rather than contradiction is the characteristic challenge.

Malinowski's study reflects life: his experience and observations of Trobriand practices and how Trobrianders explained and justified those to him were all brought together—but not just in life. Instead, these data are brought together in a rhetorical form for eliciting edifying lessons from new information. This is not, and does not give, the native point of view; but it does take such views seriously by attempting to treat them as a single type of data that is of a piece with other data about them, such as their usage and consequences. The project has both theoretical (e.g., Giddens's theory of "structuration" [1982; 1983]) as well as methodological dimensions. The success of method is, in part, measured by its edifying purposes to expose what has been hidden or gone unrecognized. Such a method was also employed by Durkheim to establish and explore the relations of what he called "social facts" (and similarly by Freud to explore the grounds of neuroses and by Marx to explore relations of production).

Argonauts of the Western Pacific is perhaps the last early modern ethnography that employed a nineteenth-century rhetorical format, which it shared with the works of Marx, Freud, and Durkheim, and which Malinowski's own mentor, James G. Frazer, employed in *The Golden Bough*—in each case bringing a new kind of data into the center of analysis. It also uses one of the core early-modern devices:

the fabulous journey at the end of which one meets oneself, which links it with *Candide* and exhausts that form by making the form itself ironic. It is also "modern" for addressing the central epistemological issue of objectivity and subjectivity in ethnography; and it illustrates how that issue comes to turn on representation, simultaneity, and a gap narrowed but not closed between ways of knowing.

Second, and perhaps more instructive, the study has been made transitional by later use. *Argonauts* is still used because it speaks to ethnographers' experiences before those get formulated. In their formularization, however, ethnographic study itself is subordinated to additional analytical agendas beginning with Malinowski's own and overwritten by a surrounding narrative. In the narrative around the narrative, and in additional layers of commentary on it, is the ironic presence of the reflexive turn's principal point about the subordination of native cultures; the fate of this most ethnographic of texts is a far better representative than stronger versions of that claim. Here, it is Malinowski's that is subordinated to another, more accessible textualization that, like his, disguises its own practice and, in failures to close the gap, is afflicted with guilt and disappointment.

Notes

1. Malinowski's model was explicitly adopted by Robert and Helen Lynd in their *Middletown* (1929), which spawned the approach in sociology.

2. This was exemplified, for example, in Margaret Mead's almost coeval *Coming of Age in Samoa* (1923) and given its strongest expression as substantive theory for anthropology in Ruth Benedict's *Patterns of Culture* (1934).

3. For example, a protocol was formalized later for comparative purposes in the HRAF *Outline of Cultural Materials* (1955); for Malinowski's own time, see James Urry (1973).

4. In these terms, Malinowski follows James Frazer's view that magic (in its ceremonial aspects) is either intermediate between religion and science or partakes of the properties of both while being wholly neither.

References Cited

Anderson, Jon W. 1986. "Reinventing the Shape of Meaning: Ambiguities in the Ontology of Ethnography." *Anthropological Quarterly* 59:64–74.

Bateson, Gregory. [1936] 1968. *Naven*. Stanford, Calif.: Stanford University Press.

Benedict, Ruth. 1934. *Patterns of Culture*. Boston: Houghton Mifflin.

Durkheim, Émile. [1895] 1938. *The Rules of Sociological Method*. Chicago: Free Press.

———. [1912] 1915. *The Elementary Forms of The Religious Life*. London: Allen and Unwin.

Evans-Pritchard, E. E. 1940. *The Nuer*. Oxford: Oxford University Press.

Firth, Raymond. 1936. *We, the Tikopia*. London: Allen and Unwin.

Fortes, Meyer. 1978. "An Anthropologist's Apprenticeship." *Annual Review of Anthropology* 7:1–30.

Geertz, Clifford. [1974] 1976. " 'From the Native's Point of View': On the Nature of Anthropological Understanding." Pp. 221–37 in *Meaning in Anthropology*, ed. K. H. Basso and H. A. Selby. Albuquerque: University of New Mexico Press.

Giddens, Anthony. 1982. *Profiles and Critiques in Social Theory*. Berkeley: University of California Press.

———. 1983. *Central Problems in Social Theory: Action, Structure, and Contradiction in Social Analysis*. Berkeley: University of California Press.

Gifford, E. W. 1923. Review of *Argonauts of the Western Pacific*, by Bronislaw Malinowski. *American Anthropologist* 25:101–2.

Leach, E. R. 1957. "The Epistemological Background to Malinowski's Empiricism." Pp. 119–37 in *Man and Culture*, ed. Raymond Firth. New York: Harper Torchbooks.

———. 1971. "Concerning Trobriand Clans and the Kinship Category *Tabu*." Pp. 120–45 in *The Developmental Cycle of Domestic Groups*, ed. Jack Goody. Cambridge: Cambridge University Press.

Lynd, Robert, and Helen Lynd. 1929. *Middletown*. New York: Harcourt, Brace.

Malinowski, Bronislaw. 1913. *The Family Among the Australian Aborigines*. London: University of London Press.

———. 1922. *Argonauts of the Western Pacific*. New York: Dutton.

———. 1931. s.v. "Culture." *Encyclopedia of the Social Sciences* 4:634–42.

———. 1944. *A Scientific Theory of Culture, and Other Essays*. Chapel Hill: University of North Carolina Press.

———. 1955. *Magic, Science, and Religion*. New York: Doubleday.

Mead, Margaret. 1923. *Coming of Age in Samoa*. New York: William Morrow.

Pankula, Andrzej K. 1981. "The Polish Background to Malinowski's Work." *Man (n.s.)* 16:276–85.

Payne, Harry C. 1981. "Malinowski's Style." *Proceedings of the American Philosophical Society* 125, no. 6: 416–40.

Radin, Paul. 1933. *Method and Theory of Ethnology*. New York: McGraw-Hill.

Stocking, George W. 1968. "Empathy and Antipathy in the Heart of Darkness." *Journal of the History of the Behavioral Sciences* 4:189–94.

Strenski, Ivan. 1982. "Malinowski: Second Positivism, Second Romanticism." *Man (n.s.)* 17:766–70.

Tylor, E. B. 1871. *Primitive Culture.* London: John Murray.

Urry, James. 1973. "*Notes and Queries on Anthropology* and the Development of Fieldmethods in British Anthropology, 1870–1920." Pp. 45–58 in *Proceedings of the Royal Anthropological Institute for 1972.* London.

White, Hayden. 1973. *Metahistory.* Baltimore: Johns Hopkins University Press.

———. 1978. "Interpretation in History." In *Tropics of Discourse: Essays in Cultural Criticism.* Baltimore: Johns Hopkins University Press.

6 Constructing the Soviet Other: Reputation and Representation in Western Sovietology

Thomas Cushman

Struggles by Western intellectuals to interpret and understand the former Soviet Union are, in one sense, struggles against the webs of representation which they themselves have spun in the course of their historical confrontation with the Soviet other. These webs, as much as any of the historical and contemporary complexities of Soviet or post-Soviet society and history, are a formidable barrier to new understandings and interpretations of this most important of the world's others. In this essay, I propose a theoretically grounded framework for the study of the process of representation in Western studies of the Soviet Union in the post–World War II social context. Next, I present an empirical analysis of the rhetorical construction of intellectual reputation within the field of Soviet studies. To the reader who has little interest in Soviet studies per se, it is important to stress that this field represents a unique case history in the politics and poetics of representation. Forged during the Cold War, funded by immensely powerful political and economic interests, and characterized by a passionate and poetic discourse on totalitarianism, tyranny, freedom, survival, and hope, the field of Soviet studies offers a unique microcosm in which to explore the construction and legitimation of representation. The cultural construction of the "truth" about communism, in general, and the Soviet Union, in particular, has decisively affected the lives and consciousnesses of all who have lived in the post–World War II era.

Over the last decade, scholars in various academic fields, most notably in anthropology and literary criticism, have begun to analyze the general process of representation and the roles that scholars themselves play in constructing images and ideas about external social realities (Said 1978; Clifford and Marcus 1986; Clifford 1988). Such attempts to explore the presence of the scholarly self in depictions of the "other" have drawn much theoretical sustenance from recent developments in literary theory. While there are a diversity of perspectives that comprise this position, the central thrust of this movement calls into question traditional subject-object dichotomies of positivistic social science and focuses on how scholars construct "narratives" and "texts" about "objective" social and historical phenomena. The focus in analyzing this process is not so much on ascertaining facts about an external, objective, noumenal world as on the textual practices with which scholars render their phenomenological experience of the world into legitimate and credible representations of reality.

The central conclusion that emerges from such a perspective—that the world is a world of constructions, a world of phenomena rather than a world of noumena, and that perhaps nothing "real" or "certain" exists outside representations—is a potentially chilling one, especially for intellectuals who produce knowledge about the Soviet Union. For many of these scholars, the most vitally important task of the intellectual in the postwar era was to know the "reality" of the Soviet Union, for only with such knowledge could the free world be protected from communist tyranny and illusion. Yet many of the most central, hegemonic "realities" about the Soviet Union, which were crafted over the last forty years, were so deeply entrenched in the minds of those who created and shared them that, upon hearing the news of the dissolution of the Soviet Union, they stood gaping and breathless with disbelief. Most Western intellectuals quite rightly recognized the repressive aspects of the Soviet social system. Yet there was a tendency for the repressive dimensions of Soviet society to assume a centrality in Western ontologies of communism that precluded the possibility of seeing the Soviet Union as anything but repressive, much less as a reformable or dissolvable entity. Unlike many other societies, the Soviet Union was constructed in the West—by scholars, politicians, and the public at large—as the embodiment of evil. To study the Soviet Union was to confront not only a society but a particular form of evil embodied in the form of the nation-state. Because the Soviet Union became a central metaphor of evil in the Western mythos, its death would seem unlikely: evil, after all, dies hard. Before the dissolution of the Soviet Union, prognostications about its demise were often greeted with derision and, in some cases, as out-and-out heresies within the community of Sovietologists.

It is for these reasons that now, more than ever, questions about the social construction of knowledge and the process of representation of the Soviet other must be asked and answered. Western intellectuals who study the Soviet Union have been remarkably "unreflexive." Only a few scholars have displayed any tendency to engage in critical reflection on the social and cultural forces that influenced the production of knowledge in the field (e.g., Dallin 1973; 1986; Meyer 1991; Cohen 1986). Indeed, it is possible to say that within the intellectual field of Soviet studies (which includes what is now called post-Soviet studies), there is virtually no discussion on how realities and truths are constructed by scholars within the field. Thus, the field of Soviet studies presents a remarkable case study for the sociology of knowledge. In this essay, I propose a two-pronged approach to the study of knowledge about the Soviet Union. This approach blends together recent developments in the critical analysis of rhetoric and in the sociology of intellectuals and knowledge.

Intellectual Reputation and Representation

Following Richard Harvey Brown (1992, 48), I propose that it is analytically useful to view knowledge production as a process similar to other forms of economic production; the production of knowledge is a particular "subprocess" of a more general process of the organized and institutionalized production of culture that is characteristic of the modern world. Within certain institutional contexts, representations of the world are created, defined, legitimated, and shared (Knorr-Cetina 1981; Mulkay 1979; 1984). Representations are the constructed products of human beings and their interactions and are shared with others in texts. Focusing on these texts, the practitioner of critical rhetoric attempts to understand how the representations in texts are legitimated through the use of rhetoric. The focus of critical rhetoric is on how truth and reality are constructed and legitimated in specific texts that appear within specific social and historical contexts (Schapiro 1988; Brown 1992, 47). From the standpoint of critical rhetoric, the truth value of propositions is not a function of the degree to which they correspond to some objective, taken-for-granted, noumenal reality. Rather the degree to which a proposition is "true" depends on how it is *constructed* and *argued* as true: who argues for or against it? How do they do so? For what reason and toward what end? This holds true for propositions in all realms of knowledge production: the natural sciences, social sciences, and humanities. Even a proposition such as "$E = MC^2$," a proposition that may accurately describe a noumenal reality about the nature of energy, is not accepted by other scientists as "truth" until communities of scientists agree among themselves to accept it as such. In sociology, concepts such as "social structure" or "modernity" have no resonance as the "truth" about the social world until a community of sociologists decides that they do. Ironically, even new perspectives in literary theory that proclaim that "there is no meaning outside of the text"—the central claim of so-called deconstructionist and postmodern viewpoints—must be agreed upon as "true" by members of the community of literary theorists, a fact which suggests that it is possible to view even postmodernist and deconstructionist discourse as a discourse that can be understood sociologically (Lamont 1987; Mestrovic 1992).

Critical rhetoric is valuable for understanding how reality is constructed within texts. Yet proponents of a purely text-centered approach to the study of representation ignore a more fundamental reality underlying the texts that they critically interrogate. That reality is the culture (the norms, values, beliefs, sentiments, rituals) of those who produce such representations. In addition to rhetorical practices that construct legitimate, actual representations of the world—or knowledge—there are also practices that construct and legitimate the identity, character, and reputation of those who create representations of the world. In some recent literature, this process is referred to as the "politics of reputation" (e.g., Rodden 1989). The politics of reputation is perhaps better understood sociologically as the social construction of the intellectual reputation and identity. Among groups of intellectuals, the process of constructing reputation underlies the process of creating representations and rendering them as true or false, good or bad, accurate or inaccurate, insightful or ordinary. "The reputation of the artist and his art are not simply matters of individual achievement and intrinsic value, respectively. Value and repute are relational phenomena, shaped according to the dynamics of interpersonal and institutional histories" (Rodden 1989, 51).

The assessment of representations depends to a large extent on the cultural construction of the reputation and identity of those who create, disseminate, or adjudicate such representations within a given institutional context. Cultural categories such as reputation, character, identity, and status are created, maintained, or destroyed through a wide variety of cultural practices ranging from everyday interaction rituals (Goffman 1967), such as two intellectuals gossiping in a hallway, to large-scale, formal, commemorative events, such as banquets at meetings of professional associations in honor of a field's luminaries. Such interactions and events are reported in texts as an important buttress to knowledge claims within a field. In other words, texts include not only knowledge but also ideas about those who produce knowledge. The latter constitutes what might be called the "poetic of reputation." This poetic offers us a glimpse into the social relations of intellectuals and their appraisals of and feelings about each other and is an important aspect of the legitimation of knowledge.

My argument in this essay is quite simple: in addition to studying the rhetorical strategies through which representations are legitimated and "made truthful," it is equally important to study the practices used by knowledge producers in constructing the reality of each other's identity and reputation. In this essay, such practices are viewed as *rituals* that work to enhance or "sacralize" the status, reputation, and identity of selected agents within a field of study. As rituals, such practices literally make sacred or sacralize certain qualities of an intellectual's life and persona. The sacralization of identity and reputation is fundamentally related to the degree to which the representations (or "knowledge") produced by those who are the subjects of such cultural practices are considered factual or truthful depictions of the noumenal world. In short, *the process of the construction and sacralization of intellectual identity and reputation is fundamentally related to what will be accepted as the Truth about the world.* The two processes—of constructing reputation and of legitimating representations—are inseparable. This essay, then, is a study in the social construction of the "truth" about those who construct the "truth" about the Soviet Union and communism. Concepts or representations, *a modem* Wittgenstein (1968), have no "truth" without community. Communities always have cultures and, in order to understand a community's concepts, we must understand its culture. In order to understand the culture of the community of intellectuals working in Soviet studies and the relation of that culture to the social construction of the reality of the Soviet union, I propose that the critical analysis of rhetoric be more closely tied to existing frameworks in the sociology of knowledge and the sociology of intellectuals. In this task, Pierre Bourdieu's sociology of intellectual life is an important complement to understanding the cultural processes that buttress the creation and legitimation of representations.

Theoretical Context: Pierre Bourdieu's Reflexive Sociology
and the Analysis of Intellectual Fields

The central starting point behind Bourdieu's sociology of knowledge
is, in his own words, "to objectify the objectifying subject," which is
"the intellectual working within a particular intellectual field" (1988,
xii)."[1] An *intellectual field* is comprised of agents who assume different positions, concrete bodies of thought, their networks of inter-
relations, patterns of power and dominance relations between agents,
patterns of resource allocation, and forms of knowledge. Bourdieu
notes that within intellectual fields, scholars "compete for the right
to define or to co-define what shall count as intellectually established
and culturally legitimate" (quoted in Ringer 1990, 270). Intellectual
fields are competitive arenas in which agents who occupy the fields
engage in symbolic "combat" with each other. The aim of this combat
is to win the right to define what will be considered legitimate
knowledge. Such knowledge is useful in gaining and maintaining
locations within the space of the field and is referred to by Bourdieu
as *symbolic capital.*

A most important aspect of Bourdieu's conception of intellectual
fields is his argument that fields are autonomous, that is, they have
their own particular structural organization and ways of doing things,
their own culture. This does not mean that the dynamics of intellectual fields are not influenced by processes and practices from outside
the field. Rather, it means that the influence of external forces on the
internal operation of a field is a matter of degree and that the
struggles within a field are primarily among that field's agents over
the symbolic resources specific to the field rather than over resources
outside the field. Thought within a field is "interested" but it is
interested primarily in the forms of symbolic capital, status positions,
and material resources that the field has to offer. Thus, scholars may
compete for grants, which are a material resource allocated to an
intellectual field from the outside, but they must acquire such grants
by producing or acquiring those forms of symbolic capital that are
hegemonic within an intellectual field. Similarly, agents in a field may
seek positions of status or power outside the intellectual field but
such positions are hard to acquire without prior claims to symbolic
resources and status within the intellectual field.

It is through struggles between agents within an intellectual field
to define reality that divergent and competing bodies of thought
emerge. Within any intellectual field, dominant forms of knowledge
emerge that occupy a central location within that field. These are

referred to as *orthodoxies*. Because they are shared by the largest number of scholars within a field, orthodoxies are the most important forms of symbolic capital in terms of securing a stable, high status position within the field. Alternative meanings that present points of view which contrast with orthodoxies are known as *heterodoxies*. While orthodoxies are the most valuable forms of symbolic capital, heterodoxies often aspire to displace them; when heterodoxies are successful they often assume the status of a new orthodoxy within an intellectual field. Yet heterodoxies are always carved out in relation to orthodoxies: they emerge, so to speak, in the shadow of orthodoxy. Within any given intellectual field, even the most heterodox and innovative positions must be carved out under the influence of the past traditions, ways of thinking, and dominant orthodoxies. Thus, intellectual fields are characterized by a confrontation between agents who struggle to maintain and reproduce orthodox representations and agents who seek to counter orthodox representations by constructing new definitions of reality.

In this dialectical struggle between orthodoxies and heterodoxies, the former are privileged in two ways. First, orthodoxies are hegemonic, that is, they have a taken-for-granted, natural quality that makes them appear incontrovertible. Orthodox representations become what Bourdieu call the *doxa* of the intellectual field. The doxa is thought conceived of as "natural," "the way things are." The world contained within the doxa simply could not be any other way. Second, orthodoxy is privileged in that it is strengthened by challenges to it: a heterodox position that attempts to displace an orthodox one mobilizes the forces behind the orthodoxy to meet the challenge of heterodox thought and, in the process, the centrality and hegemony of an orthodoxy within a field is actually strengthened.

Soviet Studies as an Intellectual Field

In the twentieth century and increasingly since World War II, we have seen the rise and institutionalization of various institutions for knowledge production that we refer to as "area studies." In addition to affiliations with standard academic disciplines, intellectuals affiliate, interact, create, and share representations with other intellectuals based on a common interest in a particular geographical part of the world. Thus, interdisciplinary fields such as Asian studies, African studies, European studies, American studies, Latin American studies, and so on have emerged. Particular types of knowledge are produced by intellectuals who work within the epistemological and ontological frameworks of various disciplines but who are also united by a common concern with producing knowledge about a particular geographical area.

Following Bourdieu (1988; 1990), I find it useful to view area studies as *geographical intellectual fields*. The boundaries of geographical intellectual fields are defined according to the geographical location or national identity in the space of the world system of the object of study rather than some substantive area of interest or traditional disciplinary boundaries. It is important to delineate geographical intellectual fields from other types of intellectual fields, because the dynamics among nation-states in the world system are likely to affect the form and content of knowledge production within them. French studies in Germany during the Franco-Prussian war, Middle Eastern studies during the Persian Gulf War and, as we shall see, Soviet studies in Cold War America and Britain were decisively affected by the historical relations between the particular nation-states in the world system.

In analyzing the construction and legitimation of knowledge within geographical intellectual fields, there are two important tasks. The first involves an examination of the structure and operation of the field itself and of the social and cultural characteristics of agents within a field. What are its sources of material and symbolic support from outside the field? How are material and symbolic resources allocated within the field? How are orthodoxies reproduced within the field? Such questions are useful starting points for an understanding of the political economy of knowledge production. Yet, another aspect of the study of geographical intellectual fields involves the analysis of the cultural practices within fields. This might be labeled the analysis of the poetics of intellectual fields. The task here is to understand how such practices *create* and *legitimate* representations that are the dominant forms of symbolic capital within a field and that appear as knowledge in the texts of a field. Thus, an understanding of how representations are legitimated depends fundamentally on how reputations of intellectuals are constructed through the cultural practices within a given field. What do intellectuals say and do to each other by way of constructing and defining each other's identity and reputation? How are such constructed definitions of reputation and identity related to the process of legitimating and making truthful representations within an intellectual field? How, when, and with what consequence do intellectuals together as a community ratify certain concepts and build the identities and reputations of each other? How is such reputation building related to concrete systems of economic and political power and interests?

These are questions that a sociologically based interpretation of the politics and poetics of representation in the field of Soviet studies must address.

Post-World War II Representations of the Soviet Other: Early Orthodoxies in the Intellectual Field of Soviet Studies

It is beyond the scope of this essay to discuss all of the competing representations in the field of Soviet studies over the last forty or more years. Rather, I will focus on the representations of the Soviet Union and communism that emerged during the Cold War period. The dominant and most powerful representation of Soviet society in the early Cold War period was the totalitarian model of Carl J. Friedrich and Zbigniew Brzezinski (1956). This model of Soviet reality became the hegemonic theoretical representation of Soviet society in the 1950s and early 1960s; indeed, the model provided an ontology of the essence of the Soviet Union. Briefly stated, the model assumed the existence of a new type of society, a "totalitarian" society, characterized by five elements:

1. a strong dictatorial leader, who
2. exerted complete control over a party apparatus that was
3. united by a single ideology and that
4. enforced its edicts by means of mass terror and fear and
5. exerted complete control over the means of mass communication.

The totalitarian model contributed to the forging of a widely disseminated cultural idea of fundamental difference between the United States and the Soviet Union.[2] The model provided intellectual legitimation to the fundamental Cold War dichotomization of the world into forces of "good versus evil," "right versus wrong," "hope versus despair," "capitalism versus socialism," and so forth. There has been a great deal of discussion about the hegemony of the totalitarian model in studies of the Soviet Union and of the homologies between the rhetoric of the totalitarian model and the rhetoric of the American political sector during the initial period of the Cold War. Few would disagree that from the late forties to the late sixties the totalitarian model was the master theoretical principle in Soviet studies (Cohen 1986; Meyer 1991). Like all orthodoxies, the totalitarian model relegated any challenging heterodoxies to a marginal status within the intellectual field of Soviet studies. Even later, as new positions that rejected the dominant ontologies of the model began to emerge, authors could not break away from the language of the model, a fact that belies both the pervasiveness of the model and its status as a form of symbolic capital. Even more than twenty years after the decline of the model's hegemony, it was still considered an act of deviance within this intellectual field to discuss the hegemony of the totalitarian model and its marginalization of competing discourses. Moreover, the relative facility with which Cold War metaphors of Soviet otherness and the evil of the Soviet Union and communism were resurrected in the 1980s suggests that the ontology of the totalitarian model was never fully excised from Western culture, even though quite serious challenges to its orthodox status were made throughout the postwar period.

What I am most concerned with in this essay—holding aside all considerations of the motivations and interests of scholars and questions about the truth of representations—are the ways in which cultural practices of the Cold War Sovietological community conferred truth, facticity, and legitimacy on the reputations of agents within this field and, by way of this, also on their representations of the Soviet Union. The idea of the Soviet Union as a totalitarian society is legitimated through a wide variety of rhetorical practices in the discourse of Soviet studies. Yet underlying these practices is the rhetorical construction of the reputations of those who held and promulgated such views. The latter constructs the "truth" about those who construct the truth and is found most clearly in the cultural practice of the *intellectual obituary.*

The Rhetorical Construction of Identity, Reputation, and Truth in the Obituaries of Western Sovietologists

Other than losing or being denied tenure, getting fired, or quitting voluntarily, death is a major means of exit from an intellectual field. Indeed, it is the way out of an intellectual field that those scholars who manage to avoid the first three must inevitably experience. Death signifies many things to those within an intellectual field: the loss of an important source of knowledge about the world, the possibility for the living to increase their own status or reduce the status of others, the necessity to find someone who can fulfill the function of the deceased within the intellectual field, and so on. Death is also an important rite of passage and rites of passage are always attended by numerous ritual events (Van Gennep [1909] 1960; Turner 1969). Within intellectual fields, death provides an opportunity for a ritual "taking stock" of the identity, character, and reputation of the deceased and for championing (or challenging) his or her contribution to the field. The intellectual obituary is part of the culture of an intellectual field, an important ritual that constructs and sacralizes the reputation of the deceased and thus lends legitimacy to the credibility and truthfulness of the representations of the deceased. This ritual event sacralizes one last time the identity and reputation of the deceased. "What the obituary restores, as does the professorial report at a different stage of the career, is the *academically constituted social representation of the person,* which is the principle behind all academic operations of appreciation and cooptation" (Bourdieu 1988, 213, emphasis added).[3] This "academically constituted social representation of the person" confers a postmortem legitimacy on the truthtelling capacity and representations created by the deceased; the intellectual obituary ensures that even after death, their representations will be treated as accurate and truthful depictions of the noumenal Soviet Union. The intellectual obituary is part of the poetic of an intellectual field and it is this poetic that plays a part in rendering representations hegemonic within a field.

The obituaries analyzed in this essay appeared in a Soviet studies journal from the late 1950s until the mid-1980s. The journal was founded as *Soviet Survey: An Analysis of Cultural Trends in the Soviet Union* and then changed to simply *Survey: An Analysis of Cultural Trends in the Soviet Orbit. Survey* was highly important in the emerging field of Soviet studies after World War II. The journal was founded and supported by the Congress of Cultural Freedom, an organization with close ties to both the American government (including the CIA) and American foundations, especially the Ford Foundation (Berman 1982, 50ff).[4] The explicit purpose of the Congress was to fend off a perceived Soviet ideological and expansionist threat in the post–World War II era. It did so through the covert funding of numerous overseas agencies (especially in the "vulnerable" Third World), the sponsorship of conferences and other intellectual gatherings, and the subsidy of a number of journals and magazines that promoted anti-Marxist, anticommunist, pro-capitalist, and pro-Western views. These journals included *Encounter* in England, *Preuves* in France, *Tempo Presente* in Italy, *Cuardernos* in Latin America, and *Survey,* which was originally published in Paris and then in London. *Survey* included numerous articles by American intellectuals and had a wide readership in both the United States and Europe. It published articles on general intellectual themes that were broadly critical of communism, on substantive aspects of the Soviet Union and its satellite states, and on Western Marxists, Soviet sympathizers, and fellow travelers.

Unlike some of the Congress's other journals, *Survey* was conceived and designed on the model of other scholarly journals and in keeping with an effort to convey a sense that the knowledge contained in it was objective; its ideological affiliations, especially after 1960, were increasingly enthymematic.[5] The majority of articles published in *Survey* were by intellectuals working in academic institutions in Western countries. Many of these intellectuals formed the core of a new intellectual field of Soviet studies, but many had already established their reputations in other intellectual fields such as economics, sociology, philosophy, and political science. Even though *Survey* was a British publication and Soviet studies had its own specific development in America, Great Britain and its intellectuals were close allies of America in the struggle against communism. A large number of authors published in *Survey*, as well as a large number of the subjects of obituaries, are Americans. Americans' writings and obituaries appeared with articles by and obituaries about British, French, Polish, Italian, and Spanish scholars. *Survey* was clearly a global effort, a repository of the representations of a global community of intellectuals. The criteria for inclusion in this group had little to do with nationality but emphasized instead a common commitment to anticommunism.

For purposes of this essay, I assume that journals such as *Survey* were a major component of what I call, to paraphrase Clifford Geertz (1973, 89ff), the Cold War cultural system. The articles in *Survey* constituted a discourse that resonated strongly with the discourse of politics, economics, and mass-mediated public opinion. The knowledge that found its way into the pages of journals such as *Survey* was simply presented as the hegemonic "truth" about communism and the Soviet Union without any explicit acknowledgment of either the political or economic forces underlying its production. Articles in the journal worked to create a hegemonic conception of the nature of the Soviet Union and communism and the "proper" role of the Western intellectual in relation to communism. Representations of communism, the Soviet Union, Soviet satellite states, and Western fellow travelers, published by Western intellectuals, became central orthodoxies and major forms of symbolic capital in the emerging, postwar intellectual field of Soviet studies.

There are two important aspects of the intellectual obituaries found in *Survey*. First, not all of the obituaries are of Sovietologists per se. Some offer appraisals of those whose major reputations were outside the field of Soviet studies but whose writings were nonetheless influential in this field for a variety of reasons that are usually made clear in the obituary. In my analysis, I have chosen not to make distinctions between such intellectuals and others who were more central to the intellectual field proper. Secondly, I have chosen not to "name names" as I elaborate and analyze the rhetoric of these obituaries. In the exegesis of the discourse of the obituary, I have indicated the deceased with the symbol X and related names with a Y. While the subjects of obituaries will be clear in some cases and while I have listed their names in the appendix, it is important that the personal identity of the deceased not be confused with their socially constructed identities in the obituary. Bourdieu (1988) has argued that the sociology of knowledge is not about naming specific people but of identifying practices that occur among particular *types* of people who share particular cultural practices and definitions of reality and thus constitute a community of interpretation. I have chosen to see the subjects of the obituaries as well as those who write about them in this Simmelian sense as *social types*, that is, as intellectuals who occupy high status positions in an intellectual field and who are engaged in the process of constructing and legitimating representations.

Intellectual Epiphanies: Struggle, Suffering, and Victimage as a Means to the Truth

One of the more prevalent themes in the obituary is the dramatization of the transformation of intellectual identity and worldview that took place among intellectuals as a result of their biographical experiences with communism. The vivid documentation and sacralization of such "intellectual epiphanies" is a central component of construction of reputation within the obituary and is fundamentally related to the ability of the deceased to know the "truth" about communism and the Soviet Union. There are two basic types of epiphany documented in the obituary; those who have experiences can be separated into two groups. The first group is composed of those who suffered personally under totalitarian regimes or because of the machinations of communist politics. This group includes those who were incarcerated, tortured, harassed, ruined, or expelled from the Communist Party or from their country. As the manifestation of personal suffering at the hands of communists, they are in the best position to speak the truth about totalitarianism because they have borne witness to it—they are its victims. As with all those who have undergone epiphanies, the representations of those who have suffered as a result of actual confrontation with the Soviet Union or with communism are in a better position to know the truth. A second group is composed of those who did not suffer personally at the hands of communists but who at some point in their career realized the essence of the Soviet system and modified their representations in light of a reformed idea about the nature of communism and the Soviet Union.

In the aftermath of World War II, emerging facts about the Soviet Union weighed heavily on the conscience and consciousness of Western liberal intellectuals (e.g., Longstaff 1989). The most direct consequence of the postwar revelations about the Soviet Union was a massive "sea change" in the consciousness of Western intellectuals on both the left and right. The swift defection took place with a concomitant and virulent denunciation of former positions and the Soviet Union, and those who continued to support Trotskyite positions or any communist alternative were seen as seriously deluded and mystified. Within this context, an ironic prerequisite for claiming the right to produce knowledge about the Soviet other was status as a former communist, communist sympathizer, or even communist leader. Within the emerging field of Soviet studies, it was as if intellectuals of the time felt that "exposure to communism was the only effective 'inoculation' against it" (Lasch, 1969, 66).

A central rhetorical theme of the obituaries reaffirms struggle with communism as the means to deeper and more enduring truth about the evil of the communist system and its ideology. Consider, for instance, this construction of reputation as a survivor and the linking of such a reputation to the veracity of representation: "His special talent was to move along the outer margin of life (as he called it) and to see the world complete; this was the course of his poems, his strength and laughter. There was another aspect to him, *one that seemed to contain all others*: the survivor; for he made it through the nightmare of our century, with his skin and his spirit intact. And if those years of war and prison had broken his health, they had also given him things few men ever get to touch, let alone hold—a measure of genuine authority and the good cheer of the wise" (66 [1968]: 160). Struggle confers upon this poet's own poetic the air of a fundamental truth; this is what *must* be sacralized in the obituary so that such poetry will be rendered truthful long after the deceased is gone. It is worth noting that, unlike the practices of many social science journals, *Survey* places the obituaries of poets, politicians, and social scientists together. This fact indicates that in the discourse of Sovietology, the boundaries between social scientific knowledge, politics, and poetry are obscured: all three are seen as means to the truth about communism and each has its particular function within the Cold War cultural system. Poetry, in particular, is seen as a particularly poignant and insightful representation of truth; indeed, the obvious poesis of the poet resonates with the poetic which is less obvious but nonetheless present in more scholarly analysis. Poets in this area are forthcoming with their poetics, indeed, their business is poetics. The poetic of representation, however, has to be extracted from what otherwise presents itself as the objective truth about the essence of the Soviet Union.

This obituary is an example of a modal pattern in *Survey* obituaries in which *courage in the face of suffering or adversity* is sacralized as an essential component of intellectual reputation. One of the most positive qualities of the intellectual is his or her perseverance and emergence from adversity with a newfound capacity to see some permanent and enduring truths about the world, in general, and the Soviet Union and communism, in particular. In most cases, struggles with communism or the Soviet Union are most strongly sacralized. Yet the deceased also fought against fellow travelers at home and other intellectual mediocrities who, because of their inferior methods or insights, could not produce truthful or insightful analyses of the Soviet Union, its satellite states, or communism. In many obituaries, the deceased are held to have special intuitive capabilities that allow them to transcend normal, rational, epistemological standards of truth. Such standards are often constructed as a domestic structural impediment to their special insight; thus, "he also suffered, and bitterly resented, the careerism and intellectual timidity that characterized too many of those in the middle and upper reaches of the bureaucracy and that imposed violent excisions on critical analysis of public policy" (20 [1974]: 180). Another author, a Russian émigré to America, was "distressed" at the "superficial understanding of the Soviet economy" and in light of this embarked on what were seen as iconoclastic studies of the economy. In this endeavor, he was bolstered by his personal courage, which gave him a special insight: "During the early and middle 1950s he was involved in bitter controversy with those who used more refined and slower procedures in American academic work, which outraged his sense of realism and urgency. . . . '[*His most*] *outstanding characteristic was his courage*—which was apparent in many disputes with editors and publishers. He was incapable of any superficiality or, despite the maze of figures which much of his work involved, of dullness'" (1986, 186, emphasis added). The deceased is constructed by the author of the obituary as somehow "above" normal methodological procedures in the intellectual field; the wellspring of his knowledge is no ordinary adherence to the mundane methods of economic research but comes instead from a pool of intuition located within the individual. This scholar was an economist who stood above the epistemological canons of his field, and his courage in the face of this seems justification enough for the facticity and truthfulness of his representations. Indeed, "most of his work was done before the immense improvement in the quantity and honesty of Soviet statistical and other information, [a fact which] has confirmed his conclusions to a remarkable extent" (186). The deceased's personal intuition allowed him to transcend the normal procedure for producing knowledge. When the slow and cumbersome procedures of normal social science "caught up," this deceased hero and his knowledge stood vindicated. The obituary stresses and sacralizes, "in the end," personal vision and genius over ordinary and mundane epistemology.

The quality of courage and determination in the face of adversity is also sacralized by making reference to occurrences in the life of the deceased that were relatively unrelated to ideology, the intricacies of world politics, or the foibles of the deceased's colleagues. While such battles have little to do with the ability to understand the truth about communism, they are constructed as if they do and are linked with the ability to see reality and truth for what they really are. In such cases, there are no references to any rational criteria for why readers should believe that the deceased should be trusted to tell the truth. The authors convince us that it is qualities such as courage in the face of personal adversity that conferred upon the deceased a special ability to see the truth. Thus, the subject of one obituary was a person who suffered from cancer, a fact which she took great pains to hide from others, and a fact which, in the eyes of the writer, defined her as a person of immense courage: "Characteristically, X did not disclose this fact [that she had cancer] till the end, even to her closest friends, and this made conversation with her in the last year of her life particularly poignant. The truth about her condition reached me soon after publication of her review but it was never mentioned in our conversations, although at some point she must have realized, endowed as she was with an extremely sensitive intuition, that I knew, just as she did, the gravity of the situation. . . . Yet such was the strength of her will that almost to the last moment, when she still had some energy left, she continued to work on the translation of a book by Y" (73 [1969]: 197). The author continues to construct the courageous identity in terms of X's unwillingness to share the truth about her medical condition with friends and family: [this] "epitomized two facts about her character: she was always more concerned about others than about herself and she was determined. . . . She was deceptively mild and unassuming but was always ready to work day and night for the things she believed in. She was amazingly single minded when she decided that a given cause deserved her support. She was indefatigable in her effort to promote it and she was usually very successful" (ibid.). The deceased was also a translator of Alexander Solzhenitsyn's *Cancer Ward,* a fact that the author finds extremely meaningful. He notes that in her translation, "she avoided giving any indication of self pity, although Solzhenitsyn's book offered not one, but many mirrors of her own predicament. She concentrated instead on the wider, more impersonal issues raised in the book. . . . Ultimately, the human illness, cancer, and the social illness, dictatorship, raise the same question of the need for spiritual courage. X had this courage. She also knew that it had to be based on a vision which reaches for the significance of the human, and not just of the social condition" (73 [1969]: 198). Thus, through a recognition of the link between personal illness and "social illness" in the work of Solzhenitsyn (one of the most important heroes of the Cold War cultural system era and in her own life) she is conferred with those personal qualities that afford her the capacity for truth and wisdom.

In another obituary of a rather famous figure from the Bolshevik Revolution, the same type of linkage between courage and truth is constructed with a great deal of hyperbole. This obituary was not actually composed by an intellectual working in Soviet studies, nor could the role of the deceased be seen as a knowledge producer within the field. In fact, the deceased was an important Russian revolutionary politician and a major adversary of Lenin and the Bolsheviks. Nonetheless, *Survey* does not distinguish between different types of knowledge, and the political knowledge of this famous figure is now considered part of the historical record on what "really" happened during the Bolshevik revolution, as well as a subject for historical analysis. While this obituary was not written directly for *Survey,* it is reported in the journal together with other obituaries and its themes resonate widely with those obituaries. Of particular note is the sacralization of this individual's capacity for survival, strength, and courage:

> We are met to say goodbye to a great man whose spirit is moving
> from us to a kinder world than ours, a man who toiled ceaselessly
> for his fellow men, with selfless devotion, high purpose and bound-
> less courage. Eighty-nine heroic years have drawn to their close,
> years of prodigious achievement, splendid adventure, often, indeed,
> mostly years of peril, "with darkness and peril compassed round,"
> years that span far back into the struggle for the soul of Russia, a

struggle in which he played such a momentous role. It is a miracle
that he lived physically unscathed through the manifold hazards
that they brought, with his contemptuous disregard for his personal safety, a disregard which became almost legendary. Morally
unscathed, he, of course, came through it all as even his severest
critics would admit. (77 [1970]: 207)

The ritual continues:

He remained unswervingly loyal to the ideal of civilized democratic
behavior, and never for a moment condescended to the methods of
the ruthless despots who came after him. . . . Civilization must
always be grateful to him and his Ministers and if, in the end, they
could no longer stand, almost alone, against the blizzard, that
should not be accounted failure, but rather they should be honored
for their iron will and dauntless courage, a shining beacon light for
the future conflicts between the rule of reason and the yoke of
dictatorship which may yet afflict mankind. (77 [1970]: 207–8)

To those to whom his memory is precious, apart from his brilliant
talents, and stupendous courage and willpower, perhaps the quality in him on which they would think with most pleasure was his
perfect integrity, his utter inability, as his public career, ever to
stoop to a mean or underhand action. (77 [1970]: 208)

Finally, in a rhetorical move that illustrates the way reputation is
linked with representation, the author asks us to think about the
knowledge of the deceased in light of the sacralized qualities of
reputation, which appear throughout the text leading up to the final
paragraph: "It is so that we would like to think back on him, when in
future we read his thoughts in his own words in his books or in the
words of historians who write about him" (77 [1977]: 209). As with
other obituaries, there is no appeal to any rational standards of
verification of truth statements but rather an appeal to personal
qualities as the most important standard of veridicality.

In another obituary we again see the sacralization of the link
between intellectual capacity and personal suffering:

[His forthcoming work] will demonstrate . . . the quite unrivalled
grasp which he had not only on the history and culture of Russia,
but on the histories and cultures of the rest of the west, and the rest
of the world. *It was matched too, by the broadest experience, from
labor camp to lecture room.* For, when it comes down to it, it is only
by the profoundest knowledge and feeling, the most powerful exercise of the intellect and the imagination, the broadest combination
of erudition and common sense, that the modern world, or any part
of the modern world, can be fully understood and presented. Many

people have possessed one or another of these qualities, without sufficient admixture of the others. This total grasp is an extreme rarity: it is also an urgent necessity. For those of us who cannot attain it, it is the greatest good fortune that there was a man who could, and whose wisdom will soon be available in its completest flowering. (19 [1973]: 213, emphasis added)

This obituary sacralizes the identity of the subject on the eve of the posthumous publication of his book. We are advised to read it and adjudicate its truth claims in light of decidedly nonrational criteria, according to the experiences that constitute the phenomenological world of the deceased, rather than to rational criteria of veridicality. Interestingly, the author of this obituary acknowledges the difficult task of "presenting" (or re-presenting) the modern world in all its spectacular intricacy. Yet he notes that those with special qualities such as that possessed by the deceased can do so, and in a meaningful way. The experience of a prison or labor camp, which is mentioned in so many of these obituaries, is seen almost as a rite of passage that confers upon the individual a special faculty for understanding the reality of the world.

In spite of the fact that the suffering of the deceased is seen as a major qualification for seeing the world as it really is, there is nonetheless within the discourse of the obituary room for anomaly, for those whose lives did not fit the modal script of life from early communist commitment to anticommunist rebirth. One of the deceased (one of the few females with obituaries in *Survey*) is presented as an enigma, a person who, for all the suffering endured because of the Soviet regime, could never quite exorcise the animus of communism from her soul:

She was an extraordinary person, this *comrade*. She was the embodiment of political inconsistency. On odd days an old fashioned communist would suddenly come to life in her, on even days quite contrary passions moved her. Freud would describe it as a love-hate relationship. The police to the east of the Elbe branded her as a "deserter" and a "renegade." The police in the West scratched their heads. Eight years in the slave labor camps, Kolyma and Magadan, the deaths of her father and mother, who perished in the dungeons of the NKVD where they were thrown on the personal recommendation of Stalin as "Trotskyites," the loss of a child who disappeared in some Soviet orphanage, *such and similar painful personal experiences couldn't somehow cure her of her illusions. If only Stalin, this regrettable freak of history, had not spoilt pure communism. . . .* She was not the only one among the *victims* who thought against all the empirical evidence that communism is no more responsible for the "excesses" of Stalinism than the Catholic Church for the "distortions" of the Inquisition. Utopia "as such" deserves, despite anything, eternal loyalty. (24 [1979]: 173, emphases added)

Here communism is reconstructed rhetorically as a "disease," an "illusion," or a "delusion" which can, in most normal, empirically astute individuals be "cured." The metaphor of disease is a powerful rhetorical device that can be used to resolve what seems to be an irrational and unintelligible act: the refusal to disavow communism in spite of the horrors one has suffered because of it. Within the overall discourse of the *Survey* obituary, the inclusion of a deceased who refused to disavow communism is potentially disruptive of the central narrative that thematically unites the obituaries and makes them cohere. Such disruptions are normally "repaired" rhetorically and enthymematically. The decision to remain stubborn in the face of what every intelligent person now knows to be true—that is, that communism is evil—is a result of positive personal qualities: "Ever since her youth . . . [she] was smuggling arms and revolutionary literature as a courier between Berlin, Prague, and Moscow, from this epoch of conspiracy and later from her experience in prisons and concentration camps, *what remained in her was a permanent hunger for friendship and a very impartial habit of personal kindness*" (24 [1979]: 173, emphasis added). The paradox of commitment to communism is resolved rhetorically by stressing the deceased's existential human needs. Such needs make her fallible and susceptible to the "germ" of communism and, because of her "even days" of sanity, she has at least some opportunity to see the error of her previous ways. She thus ensures a place for herself in the intellectual field that survives her and in which her reputation will continue to live. Even if she cannot see the light, we can feel sorry for her as a victim of communism and as a fallible human being. It is worth noting another story about the character of the deceased, a story that depicts an event at the deceased's funeral and is reported in her obituary:

At the end of the ceremony, to the great surprise of all present, we suddenly heard from the loudspeaker a Russian revolutionary song.

"She's incorrigible," whispered into my ear an elderly gentleman in a threadbare coat, "even after death she can't give up her revolution."

It was an old communist who had lost all his illusions a long time ago (he spent eight years in a Nazi camp in Buchenwald and 12 years in the Soviet camp in Vorkuta), and who, once upon a time, let the 16 year old schoolgirl talk from the platform at a worker's meeting in Berlin in 1927. Forty-five years later he travelled from Hamburg to Munich to put a few red carnations on her grave. (24 [1979]: 174)

The above is a ritual of absolution in which the old, anonymous, former communist who suffered under the communists and is now an anticommunist—it could be anyone and his anonymity is important to the story—travels across Germany to forgive the deceased for her communism and, perhaps for a moment, to reflect on her as a metaphor of innocence and utopian idealism retained in the face of evil. This ritual and its forlorn imagery is incorporated into another ritual, the intellectual obituary, in which the identity of the deceased is sacralized. X's persistent belief in the original spirit of communism and revolution, while ultimately a delusion, is seen in one sense as quaint: she is defined in the obituary as "incorrigible" (the title of the obituary touts her as an "incorrigible girl"), a rhetorical move that constructs a childlike quality of excessive or incurable naughtiness and immaturity.

It matters little, however, if "in the end" the subjectivity of the deceased does not fall into line with the anticommunist subjectivity of other agents in the field. The obituary still serves as an occasion for the dramatization of how communism can delude even the most intelligent of people. It serves as a pretext for the reconstruction of elements of a demonology that would be decidedly out of place in the more "objective" pages of the journal proper (e.g., the portrayal of Stalin as a "regrettable freak of history" or communism as a "disease"). In spite of the inability of X to give up utopian ideas, it is ultimately the anticommunist side that wins. It can only be so if her obituary is to appear in *Survey*. The attribution of personal qualities as the source of her delusion, though, is rather inconsistent within the field, since it is those same personal qualities that legitimate anticommunist representations in other obituaries.

Further sacralization of the capacity of the deceased to know the truth about the world occurs through the presentation of mythical anecdotes about the deceased's interactions and confrontations with powerful or important people. These stories are somewhat apocryphal; their purpose is not to convey truth but to use allegory, hyperbole, and other tropes to rhetorically construct an identity. The following account of a meeting shows how an ordinary confrontation between two people is constructed as allegory and drama in the ritual of the obituary:

A few weeks ago at a meeting of Russian and German writers in Bonn, the following dialogue took place: "This is X," somebody whispered into the Soviet Ambassador's ear, "the one who writes about Russia. . . . "

"Does she say good things or bad things?" asked the Ambassador.

"I praise good things and I criticize bad things," said the ex-comrade [X, who has obviously overheard and intervened in the conversation].

"And how can you know, living in Germany, what is good and what is bad in our country?" remarked His Excellency.

"My conscience tells me!" came the answer.

"The conscience can be capitalist or it can be socialist!" snapped the Ambassador.

"It can simply be human!" she said, her voice slightly too loud.

The embarrassed host quickly changed the subject. (24 [1979]: 174)

The above story is apocryphal, for the conversation between the deceased and the Soviet Ambassador, in all likelihood, could never be reported with the alacrity with which it is related in the obituary. Yet it matters little whether or not the story is constructed, since the very purpose of reconstructing, embellishing, and dramatizing events is to sacralize the reputation of the deceased in order to legitimize their role as the producers of truth. The brave voice of conscience who is the protagonist in the above allegory is the same X discussed earlier who was unable to transcend her communist leanings. But in this allegory, the persona of X is able to serve as a metaphor for the triumph of humanity and conscience over evil communism, pressing the Soviet Ambassador until he recognizes that the discussion is about humanity and conscience (two things in short supply in the Soviet Union) and terminates the conversation.

Local Heroes

One quality that distinguished the capacity of intellectuals to define the reality of the Soviet Union or communism was the fact that they had suffered personally during their lives from either personal misfortune or some aspect of the communist system. The intellectuals discussed above were mostly those who had lived in Soviet society; this class of intellectuals played and continues to play an important role in the field of Soviet studies. Yet there is another class of intellectuals in Soviet studies: namely, non-émigré Western intellectuals who were comfortably ensconced in high status academic positions and who had learned from their own experience with communism, others' mistakes or the suffering of others. In the context of the postwar cultural system, the entire infrastructure of the new intellectual field of Soviet studies was constituted by individuals who had experienced intellectual and political epiphanies in the form of "leaps from communism." Almost as a prerequisite for inclusion in the field, one had to prove one's experience of disillusionment by ritually recanting earlier foibles and beliefs as naive and misguided. This experience of personal transformation and intellectual epiphany among "local heroes" is sacralized very strongly in the *Survey* obituaries.

The modal pattern in the obituaries presents the deceased as seers of truth in the face of others who were deluded or blinded by the Soviet Union and communist ideology. Note the construction of the righteous individual in the face of a compliant mass: "At a time when many socialist intellectuals and politicians had abdicated in the face of the Soviet myth, X was among the few who saw that the USSR was not 'a counterpoise to the regimes of capitalist reaction that we are enduring in the many European and American countries, but an element of this reactionary constellation, sustaining itself within it and by it'" (24 [1979]: 209-10).

As in all obituaries, not only intellectual but personal qualities are strongly sacralized: "It was an untimely death for a dedicated and revered teacher, a compassionate and generous human being, and a noted scholar. He was endowed with so many remarkable qualities and accomplished so much in his lifetime that the imprint of his keen mind, wide ranging knowledge, and warm personality lives on in many fields of scholarly and practical endeavor and in the lives of many people." Even in the wake of the pre-detente Cold War, in the face of the emergence of a new one, and in the general swirl of anti-Soviet rhetoric within Soviet studies, the subject of one obituary is respected and trusted not only by his own students and colleagues, but by the enemies themselves: "One further tribute to the quality of his mind and heart should be noted: he had the respect and the trust not only of those who knew him in the West but of the Soviets as well. They speak with the same admiration and warmth of 'Filip Arturovich' as Americans speak of 'Phil'" (24 [1979]: 218).

Personal and intellectual qualities are fused together in support of veridical ability; quite often the discourse of the obituary takes on striking religious tones. In many obituaries, the identity of the deceased is constituted in distinctly religious terms. Personality is reconstituted as "spirit," interactions with the deceased are reconstituted as "communion," and the writers of obituaries, like all people who com-

mune with sacred figures, left such "communions" dramatically transformed: "We spent together a full afternoon in the heart of New York,
comparing notes, after a long interval, on the recent developments in
Russian émigré literature and politics. What a pleasure it was to have
one's hunches confirmed, one's lingering doubts resolved! What a joy
it was to commune once again with that generosity of spirit, that
unfailing rightness of tone and judgement, with the firm sense of
commitment totally immune to fanaticism, the low key wisdom that
was X!" (24 [1979]: 217). As in many obituaries, the sacralization of
personal qualities follows what often seems like an obligatory listing
of intellectual achievements. Such a practice indicates that "in the
end" it is the personal qualities of the deceased that are most
important for constructing truth, and it is precisely those qualities
that legitimate the truth of the representations created by the deceased
during his or her lifetime.

A modal pattern throughout the obituaries of these former "fellow
travelers" is a reconstitution of their biographies in terms of a "script
of life." The lives of the deceased follow a trajectory from early and
passionate devotion and sacrifice to the communist cause, through
disillusionment with communism in practice, to a new level of capacity for understanding the true nature and dangers of communism. As
with émigré intellectuals, struggles in the name of communism are
touted as the very credentials that qualified the deceased in his or
her later fight against communism: "X lived for most of the next 13
years the fitful, tangential existence of an underground revolutionist.
He was familiar with the faction fights, the agitation of party conferences,
the wanderings in foreign capitals, the tactical duels with the secret
police, the camouflage of false names, the sparse rations of food and
shelter" (23 [1977-78]: 194). At some point, usually after undergoing a
plethora of trials and tribulations due to life in the communist underground, the deceased experiences an epiphany in the form of a revelation about the true meaning of the evil of communism and the perils of
revolution. This epiphany is usually presented as the triumph of an
inner, personal "will to truth" against a more insidious "will to
power" that permeates twentieth-century communist-revolutionary
politics. The "underground revolutionist," having struggled for years
as a communist, finally realized—through strength of personality and
will—that communism was evil; the author constructs this image in
the discourse of his obituary: "It was probably during this time that X
came to realize his own personality was not adaptable to the
dishonesties and intricate maneuverings of international communist
politics" (23 [1977-78]: 195). In this case, personal disillusionment

and sometimes even direct conflict with Stalin led to a stark reversal of position and a transformation of the deceased into an anticommunist.

The anecdotal recounting of direct confrontations with most demonic elements of the Soviet system are worth noting, for they sacralize the triumph of communists who have repented the error of their ways at the same time as they profane elements of the communist cultural system. Communist ideology, cultural practices, and even the identity of Stalin, who is seen as the *personal* embodiment of totalitarian irrationality and evil in the postwar world, are strongly desacralized in the obituary. Indeed, such direct confrontations with communism were the actual driving force behind the collective transmogrification of intellectuals from communists into anticommunists and it is in the obituary that this transmogrification and its sources are recollected and sacralized. In speaking of the involvement of the revolutionist-turned-anticommunist, the writer of the obituary notes the impact of the deceased's personal experience with Stalin. He had been head of an American mission of communists to Moscow to discuss the future of the American Communist Party: "Stalin met with the Comintern's 'American Mission,' and laid down the condition of the Americans' capitulation; not satisfied with the simple acceptance of party discipline, he demanded the ouster of Y and X from the leadership and that they should stay on indefinitely in Moscow. Stalin's outburst against the Americans during the main session was so violent and threatening that X never forgot it. *The memory of it hovered over the pages that he later wrote concerning the social system of Soviet despotism*" (23 [1977–78]: 195, emphasis added).

Stalin's irrationality rips the deceased from his own irrational belief in communism; the outbursts of demons have much more valence in converting those who are fundamentally righteous than do the outbursts of those who are already on the side of truth. In a later part of the obituary, the same imputation of personal vision, experience, and genius as the driving force lending legitimacy to representation is seen: "The ordeals of his own life imparted to his political knowledge the ingredient of human wisdom that gave a timeless aspect to his work. In its pages, the *'truth of the defeated' stood alongside and indeed superior to the 'official truth' as truth itself emerged*" (23 [1977–78]: 198, emphasis added). For many of the subjects of these obituaries, life after communism entailed a painful process of self-examination and self-repudiation: "Slowly, he began to turn the searchlight on himself and his comrades to understand the laws of ideological commitment, the laws of the pack, for only by understanding could he achieve freedom" (23 [1977-78]: 196). Thus, personal experience and suffering—confrontation with an irrational despot, the experience of defeat and disillusionment—buttress the claim of seeing the reality of the world, in general, and the reality of communism, in particular. One does not have to clarify the relation between the credentials that such transmogrification yields and the ongoing process of constructing representations about communism or the Soviet Union: the connection is enthymematic within the text. As the author of the above obituary notes, the experience "hovers" over such representations, bathing them in the glow of veracity and legitimacy.

A central enthymeme in the obituaries is that the knowledge (i.e., representations) of the defeated, disillusioned, and victimized is somehow superior and more truthful to the knowledge of those who "run with the pack" and spin "official truths" which are, in reality, lies. In terms of content, the thought of many of the deceased, by virtue of their advanced ages, represents the first wave of knowledge legitimated through suffering. These intellectuals were the first generation of anticommunists; the sacralization of their previous experiences was meant to lend a degree of permanence to their ideas so that mistakes would not be made by future generations who were fortunate enough not to have suffered the misfortunes of communism. No one who came after them, no matter how intelligent, could ever know the truth like they did because their truth was based on experiences that could not be reproduced. Such a rhetorical construction of immortality ensures the deceased and their acolytes a kind of epistemic power that is meant to last well beyond death.

The relation between previous experience and epiphany is often related in terms of mythical anecdotes that sacralize the profundity of the insight of the deceased in the face of either direct enemies or those who are making grave mistakes that will enable enemies: "X remained sceptical, however, of the prospects for Soviet-American detente, and no doubt saw the new Euro-communism as an attempt to do all over again, and probably with equal futility, what he had tried to do with American exceptionalism. A couple of years ago, he [and his wife] happened to encounter in Mexico City the American Secretary of State, Henry Kissinger. The Mexican police became agitated when they saw this tall, thin, wan, old man, with a smiling countenance, wending his way towards Kissinger, but the Secretary of State, hearing who he was, said: 'I want to meet that man. I've read every one of his books.' So the Mexican police let X pass, and he told Henry he admired him, but that his detente policy was 'for the birds'" (23 [1977-78]: 199). Or consider the following, which sacralizes the

courage of the deceased in the face of evil incarnate, Hitler and
Stalin: "I recollect my last visit to his apartment in Rome. I went to
see him with an Italian friend and some Polish dissidents. He was
already very weak; time and illness had taken their toll. Yet he was
interested in the struggle of East European dissidents and was moved
to tears when his visitors spontaneously sang for him the Polish
counterpart of 'For he's a jolly good fellow.' I remember a remark by
one of them, addressing his friend (both were scions of prominent
Polish communists) with the words: 'I particularly respect X because
while our fathers were licking Stalin's boots, he had the guts to stand
up to both Hitler and Stalin!' " (23 [1977-78]: 218). Note the fusion of
qualities of age and wisdom and the ironic correlation between
physical feebleness and intellectual clarity. Such a fusion of components into a coherent whole is a central element of ritual (Tambiah
1985) and a central aspect of the ritual recollections that constitute
the discourse of the intellectual obituary. This is to be expected since
many of the deceased were in their later years when the obituary
writers knew them. Yet the linking of age and wisdom is also an
important poetic device that confers upon the aged intellectual the
capacity to see things that members of younger generations simply
cannot see. The imputation of wisdom based on age is simply one
more example of the way in which the obituary relates the validity of
representations to nonrational categories of identity. Thus, the obituary sacralizes age as a font of wisdom (and never a source of senility
or crankiness), not only about life but about the nature and essence
of the Soviet Union, communism, foreign policy, and so on.

The lives of other deceased Sovietologists are reconstructed according to the script of life that runs through the obituaries. One, a
personal friend of Lenin and a member of the Comintern, was notable
for his prescience in understanding some of the evils of communism
long before many Western intellectuals. This person suffered not only
at the hands of communists—he was expelled from the Comintern
and the French Communist Party in the 1930s because of his affiliations with Trotsky—but also at the hands of a deluded, "leftist,"
Western intellectual establishment that refused to listen to him because
he criticized Stalin as well as Trotsky's policies in the 1930s. Again,
the character of the deceased is lionized at the expense of the
"ordinary" deluded intellectuals who ostracized him and refused to
take his work seriously. As with other intellectuals, X saw the error
of his earlier communist ways and spent his later years fighting
against the persona of his earlier years: "In the 1920s, X, attracted by
the mirage of Utopia, went with the current—deceiving himself and

quite innocently deceiving others—in the stream of Western intelligentsia who 'saw the light from the East.' And then, for the rest of his life, X went against the current, exposing the illusoriness of the communist mirage" (28 [1984]: 201). Furthermore, "X, after understanding the illusions and errors, became the first French anticommunist, bearing to the struggle against Falsity not only a remarkable intellect, high culture, and brilliant writing talent, but a *tremendous knowledge of the enemy 'from the inside' and the courage necessary to do battle*" (28 [1984]: 204, emphasis added).

The transmogrification of X is rhetorically constructed in terms of a battle between Truth and Falsity. Falsity (capital F) is the hallmark of the current that X must battle. As the voice of Truth against Falsity, X invariably suffered at the hands of intellectual mediocrities and fellow travelers who refused to listen to the truth about Soviet communism: "Very few people listened to X when he exposed the falseness of the Moscow trials or revealed the unbelievable scale of the Stalinist terror of the 1930s. On 7 May 1939, he published an article in *Le Figaro* in which—alone in the world press—he warned about the preparations being made for an agreement between Stalin and Hitler. The French Foreign Ministry swiftly took measures: *Le Figaro* was firmly recommended not to publish similar commentaries by X. Having left occupied France for the USA, X could not find work there in his profession, for his anti-communism turned out to have no place in the atmosphere of universal love for 'Uncle Joe' which erupted after Hitler's breach of the pact of friendship and non-aggression with the USSR" (28 [1984]: 201).

Thus, the whole world conspired against this quintessential anticommunist to repress his special truth about the Soviet Union "from the inside" as an "enemy" of the West. The Western liberal intelligentsia is reconstituted as an unthinking and obeisant collective, and the reputation of the deceased takes on a special positive valence by virtue of his repression by such mediocrities. In spite of such repression, the deceased ultimately won. According to the author of the obituary, X was vindicated by the special report of N. S. Khrushchev to the Twentieth Congress of the Communist Party of the Soviet Union, which contained facts that the deceased had proclaimed all along. Almost forty years later, his biography of Stalin (which had been "repressed" by Western procommunist intellectuals in the 1930s), was reissued to the accolades of like-minded Western anticommunist intellectuals.

The sacralization of the transmogrification of identity from communist to anticommunist in the obituary offers an important glimpse into a key condition for the allocation of status within the field, especially in the early postwar years, but probably throughout the history of the field. From the point of view of such transmogrified intellectuals, any expression of socialist commitment would be immediate grounds for the disqualification of such knowledge and the intellectual who produced it from the intellectual field. This firm Manichean belief that the world is divided into forces of good and evil no doubt played a role in the ongoing conflicts between former communists and members of younger generations who had not witnessed firsthand the horrors of Stalinism and who subsequently remained committed to "naive" positions such as socialism and even liberalism.

Ritual, Representation, and the Construction of the Fact and Reality of the Soviet Other

The discourse of the obituary is an important ritual that sacralizes the identity of key, high status intellectuals within Soviet studies. An important aspect of ritual is its ability to fuse different elements, some of which may have very little to do with each other, into a coherent whole that sacralizes a cosmology, worldview, or definition of reality (Tambiah 1985). In almost none of these intellectual obituaries are the dead adjudicated on their adherence to epistemological standards of any of the social scientific disciplines that comprise the intellectual field of Soviet studies. Indeed, qualities quite unrelated to empirical realities about the Soviet Union are sacralized, thus rendering the *personae* of the deceased sacred and conferring upon their representations a corresponding degree of sacredness. In the discourse of the intellectual obituary, the passions and sentiments of intellectuals and their feelings about each other and each other's work bubbles to the surface of the text in ways that are quite rare in a social science discourse imbued with the rhetoric of objectivity. Such passions and sentiments are an important influence on the process of the social construction of reputation and intellectual identity. This process lends legitimacy to the constructed representations of the field. In the intellectual obituary, knowledge—that supposedly most rational of all phenomena—is not immune to the nonrational forces: love, hate, friendship, ideological commitment (in short, a host of emotional factors) are involved in the construction of reputation and are seen as primary qualities that legitimate representation. It would be a mistake to view the cultural construction of reputation as the "cause" of the legitimacy of representations; rather, the construction of reputation occurs in an ongoing way in the everyday cultural practices of intellectuals and appears in the texts in which intellectuals present their visions of the world. It is in these texts that reputation confers facticity and truth-value on representations within fields.

What is most striking about the intellectual obituaries in *Survey* is their dramatic and poetic quality. Indeed, seldom are the truth claims of the fallen heroes grounded in relation to any rational epistemological, methodological, or conceptual standards. Dead Sovietologists are considered especially adept at understanding the realities of communism because they are endowed with special qualities that have little to do with the capacity to do social science or write poetry: capacity to endure struggle, courage, love of children, friendliness toward others, intuition, and insight. These qualities are sacralized most strongly in the obituary; these symbolically constructed and sacralized reputations of deceased intellectuals grant the deceased, even after death, the right to have their perceptions of experience treated as factual and truthful knowledge about a noumenal world. The intellectual obituary in *Survey* renders unto dead Sovietologists the right to tell the Truth about communism and the Soviet Union. Within all intellectual fields, there is a strong poetic behind the process of representation, which melds together "truths" about persons and "truths" about things in order to lend legitimacy to both. In the light of an identity sacralized one last time, we have no need to subject their truth claims or representations to any other epistemological or ontological criteria: they stand as Truth and fact because those who created them, like all heroes, possess special qualities that make what they say simply true.

The poetic of Soviet studies is best seen in cultural forms such as the obituary. This poetic was itself a form of power, for it defined the very essence of the Soviet Union and its communist ideology in ways in which normal academic discourse could not, without betraying its ideological commitments. In a global context in which the very *raison d'etre* and self-definition of the advanced capitalist societies of the West depended on the prevailing definitions of their major adversary, the construction of representations must be seen as an immense form of power. Indeed, in relation to the present *fin de siecle* in which the power of intellectuals to shape public and political discourse has waned considerably, Sovietologists must be seen as having wielded a great deal of power. For their representations literally shaped the entire cultural discourse on the Soviet other from the end of World War II until the startling events of 1990. The dramatic poetic of this "discourse on the dead" was remarkably supportive of the more general political discourse of the Cold War period. Homologies between academic and political rhetoric indicate the existence of a fundamental relationship of mutual legitimation, of a resonance of the habitus, between two central discourses of the postwar cultural system. The forging of a Cold War cultural consensus between different sectors of advanced industrial society relied on forging a resonance between the forms of poesis found in intellectual fields and those in the discourse of conventional politics. Homologies between metaphors, similes, and the propensity to dramatize and engage in hyperbole are all indications of a fundamental habitus that leads agents in different fields to construct representations in a similar way. All of this would be rather benign if the political and economic consequences of such homologies were not so great. The power of poesis is a real form of power.

Some of my conclusions in this essay—that truths about the Soviet Union are constructed and that the truth of such constructions is itself related to a construction of the reputation and identity of intellectuals—are likely to be read as subversive and even heretical statements within the field of contemporary Soviet and post-Soviet studies. As we have seen through the discourse of the obituary, a dominant rhetorical theme in the field is that the Soviet Union and communism always represented a clear and present danger to the rest of the "free" world and that we needed to know it empirically and factually as such. Imagine, then, how such statements are likely to be taken in a field that, historically, has even disallowed simple *theory* as a dangerous obfuscation. The intellectuals who are the subject of this essay may have been right or wrong about the essence of the Soviet Union; what is most important for a sociology of representation, however, is the ways in which their culture aimed at convincing and persuading us, through forms of poetic discourse such as the obituary, of the veracity of their visions.

Appendix 1
Obituaries from *Survey* Used in the Analysis

Title and author	*Survey* volume, date, and page numbers
"In Memorium, Alfred Rosmer," by Gustav Stern	53 (1964): 98–106
"Naum Mikhailovich Jasny, 1883–1967" (no author)	64 (1967): 186–87

Appendix 1 (*cont.*)

Title and author	*Survey* volume, date, and page numbers
"Obituary for a Futurist: In Memory of Aleksander Wat," by Richard Lourie	66 (1968): 159-61
"Manya Harari," by Leo Labedz	73 (1969): 197-99
"Alexander Kerensky," by Lord Stow Hill	77 (1970): 207-10
"Tibor Szamuely, 1925-1972," by Robert Conquest	19 (1973): 213-14
"Jane Degras, 1905-1973," by Leo Labedz	20 (1974): 164-65
"Morris Watnick, 1914-1974," by David Spitz and Bernard S. Morris	20 (1974), 180-81
"Bertram David Wolfe, 1896-1977," by Lewis S. Feuer	23 (1977-78): 194-201
"Farewell to an Incorrigible Girl" [Obituary of Wanda Bronska-Pampuch]	24 (1979): 172-75
"Nicola Chiaromonte," by Gino Bianco	24 (1979): 209-13
"Max Hayward, 1924-1979," by Leo Labedz	24 (1979): 216-17
"Andrei Amalrik, 1938-1980," by Leo Labedz	25 (1980): 217-21
"Raymond Aron: The Sage of a Generation," by Alain Besancon	27 (1983): 304-5
"Leonard Schapiro: Sovietologist Extraordinary," by Leo Labedz	27 (1983): 305-7
"Boris Souvarine, 1895-1984," by Michel Heller	28 (1984): 198-204
"Zauberman, Alfred, 1903-1984: A Scholar and a Gentleman," by Peter Wiles	28 (1984): 227-28

Note: Until 1972, issues of *Survey* were published without reference to volumes. Individual issues were referred to as numbers. Thus, all citations up until 1972 refer to issue numbers. Beginning in 1973, *Survey* individual numbers appeared in volumes. Thus, all citations from 1973 on refer to volume numbers.

Notes

Preliminary versions of this essay were presented at the 1992 Conference on Academic Knowledge and Political Power at the University of Maryland, College Park, and at the 1993 meetings of the American Sociological Association in Miami Beach. For their helpful comments I would like to thank Richard Harvey Brown, William H. Sewell, Jr., Arthur Vidich, James Tucker, John Herrmann, David Swartz, Carol Hartigan, and an anonymous reviewer. The essay remains an expression of my own reflexive thinking about the field of Soviet studies and the agents who operate in it.

1. The following discussion draws as well on Ringer's (1990) work on German intellectuals in the early twentieth century. Ringer finds many of Bourdieu's concepts useful for understanding the decline of the German intellectual class (or mandarins) through the early part of the century.

2. The concept of totalitarianism was not purely a creation of Friedrich and Brzezinski; it had been brewing for decades in Europe in response to the early triumphs of Mussolini and Franco and, later, Hitler and Stalin (Armstrong 1973, 579). Nonetheless, Friedrich and Brzezinski's model seemed to crystallize the various senses of the concept regnant in European and American intellectual discourse on twentieth-century dictatorships.

3. Bourdieu (1988, 210-25) provides an empirical analysis of discourse in the obituaries of his own fallen comrades, the *normaliens,* graduates of France's most elite academic institution, the *Ecole Normal Superior,* which demonstrates convincingly the important link between the discursive practice of writing about the dead and the legitimation of representation within intellectual fields. By writing about their dead with passion, irony, and force, the *normaliens* were engaging in a ritual sacralization of their comrades, themselves, and the *Ecole Normal.* In doing so, they reaffirm the status within French society of themselves and their institution and claim the right to define truth and reality.

4. The following discussion of the Congress for Cultural Freedom is based on Lasch (1969), Kramer (1990), and Berman (1982).

5. I am using the notion of enthymeme as it is used in rhetorical studies to refer to the unspoken or unstated premises underlying a discourse. On the analysis of the enthymematic nature of ideologically laden cultural discourse, see Guerrero and Dionisopoulos (1990).

References Cited

Armstrong, John W. 1973. "Comments on Professor Dallin's 'Biases and Blunders in American Studies on the USSR.'" *Slavic Review* 32:577-87.

Berman, Edward H. 1982. "The Extension of Ideology: Foundation Support for Intermediate Organizations and Forums." *Comparative Education Review* 26, no. 1: 48-68.

Bourdieu, Pierre. 1977. *Outline of a Theory of Practice.* Cambridge: Cambridge University Press.

———. 1984. *Distinction: A Social Critique of the Judgement of Taste.* Cambridge, Mass.: Harvard University Press.

———. 1988. *Homo Academicus.* Stanford, Calif.: Stanford University Press.

———. 1990. *In Other Words: Essays Towards a Reflexive Sociology.* Stanford, Calif.: Stanford University Press.

Brown, Richard Harvey. 1992. "Poetics, Politics, and Professionalism in the Rise of American Psychology." *History of the Human Sciences* 5, no. 1: 47–61.

Clifford, James. 1988. *The Predicament of Culture: Twentieth-Century Ethnography, Literature, and Art.* Cambridge, Mass.: Harvard University Press.

Clifford, James, and George Marcus. 1986. *Writing Culture: The Poetics and Politics of Ethnography.* Berkeley: University of California Press.

Cohen, Stephen. 1986. *Rethinking the Soviet Experience: Politics and History Since 1917.* New York: Oxford University Press.

Dallin, Alexander. 1973. "Bias and Blunders in American Studies on the USSR." *Slavic Review* 32: 560–76.

———. 1986. "The Uses and Abuses of Russian History." Pp. 181–94 in *Soviet Society and Culture: Essays in Honor of Vera Dunham,* ed. Terry L. Thompson and Richard Sheldon. Boulder, Colo.: Westview Press.

Friedrich, Carl J., and Zbigniew Brzezinski. 1956. *Totalitarian Dictatorship and Autocracy.* Cambridge, Mass.: Harvard University Press.

Geertz, Clifford. 1973. *The Interpretation of Cultures.* New York: Basic Books.

Goffman, Erving. 1967. *Interaction of Ritual.* New York: Anchor Books.

———. 1973. *The Presentation of Self in Everyday Life.* Woodstock, N.Y.: Overlook Press.

Guerrero, Laura K., and George Dionisopoulos. 1990. "Enthymematic Solutions to the Lockshin Defection Story: A Case Study in the Repair of a Problematic Narrative." *Communication Studies* 41, no. 4: 299–310.

Knorr-Cetina, Karin. 1981. *The Manufacture of Knowledge: An Essay on the Constructivist and Contextual Nature of Science.* New York: Pergamon Press.

Kramer, Hilton. 1990. "What Was the Congress for Cultural Freedom?" *The New Leader* 8, no. 5: 7–13.

Lamont, Michele. 1987. "How to Become a Famous French Philosopher." *American Journal of Sociology.*

Lasch, Christopher. 1969. *The Agony of the American Left.* New York: Knopf.

Longstaff, S. A. 1989. "The New York Intellectuals and the Cultural Cold War: 1945–1950." *New Politics (new series)* 2, no. 2: 156–70.

Mestrovic, Stjepan. 1992. *Durkheim and Postmodern Culture.* New York: Aldine de Gruyter.

Meyer, Alfred G. 1991. "Politics and Methodology in Soviet Studies." *Studies in Comparative Communism* 24, no. 2: 127–36.

Mulkay, Michael J. 1979. *Science and the Sociology of Knowledge.* London and Boston: Allen and Unwin.

———. 1984. *Opening Pandora's Box: A Sociological Analysis of Scientists' Discourse.* Cambridge: Cambridge University Press.

Ringer, Fritz. 1990. "The Intellectual Field, Intellectual History, and the Sociology of Knowledge." *Theory and Society* 19, no. 3: 269-94.

Rodden, John. 1989. *The Politics of Literary Reputation: The Making and Claiming of "St. George" Orwell.* New York: Oxford University Press.

Said, Edward. 1978. *Orientalism.* New York: Pantheon Books.

Schapiro, Michael J. 1988. *The Politics of Representation: Writing Practices in Biography, Photography, and Policy Analysis.* Madison: University of Wisconsin Press.

Simmel, Georg. 1971. *On Individuality and Social Forms: Selected Writings.* Chicago: University of Chicago Press.

Tambiah, Stanley Jeyaraja. 1985. *Culture, Thought, and Social Action.* Cambridge, Mass.: Harvard University Press.

Turner, Victor. 1969. *The Ritual Process: Structure and Anti-Structure.* Chicago: Aldine.

Van Gennep, Arnold. [1909] 1960. *The Rites of Passage.* Chicago: University of Chicago Press.

Wittgenstein, Ludwig. 1968. *Philosophical Investigations.* New York: Macmillan.

7 Realism and Power in Aesthetic Representation

Richard Harvey Brown

The victory above all will be
clearly at a distance
To see everything near at hand
And may all things bear a new name.

—Guillaume Appollinaire (1980, 341)

Now we come to the concept of *realism*. This concept, too, must first
be cleansed before use, for it is an old concept, much used by many
people and for many ends. This is necessary because the people can
only take over their cultural heritage by an act of expropriation. . . . With
the people struggling and changing reality before our eyes, we must
not cling to "tried" rules of narrative, venerable literary models, eternal aesthetic laws. We must not derive realism as such from particular
existing works, but we shall use every means, old and new, tried and
untried, derived from art and derived from other sources, to render reality to men in a form they can master.

—Bertolt Brecht ([1967] 1977, 81)

Realism is that mode of painting or writing that is taken to
represent the world directly as it is. As J. P. Stern (1973, 2) notes of a
diversion in a Charles Dickens novel, its "fullest purpose . . . is to add
and superadd to that sense of assurance and abundance and reality
that speaks to us from every page and from every episode of the
novel." But why this particular mode of representation and not another?
How did various modes of representation, each in its time, come to be
taken as truly representing the real? How do modes of mimesis,
paradigms of propriety, and professionalism, property, and privilege
interact?

In addressing these questions, I assume that there is a radical entanglement between aesthetic and political practices, between the formalization of discourses, the privileges of their practitioners, and political and economic power. By untangling these relationships, we can gain insights into the ways in which the real not only has been fashioned through aesthetic practices but also how it has been imposed historically, structurally, and discursively.

To understand such interchanges between political and aesthetic representation, the key question no longer is *what* is the universal real, beautiful, or true. Instead, the focus is on *how* reality and truth are constructed, both aesthetically and socially, in specific historical contexts. In this view, realistic representations become true descriptions not by correspondence to their noumenal objects but by conformity between the dominant ontology and the conventional methods of aesthetically representing it. Representations are regarded as realistic when their socially orthodox practices of writing and reading or painting and viewing have become so familiar that they operate transparently (Shapiro 1988, xi). For example, if we show a painting by Canaletto and say, "This is the Grand Canal," we assume that the Grand Canal and Canaletto's image of the Grand Canal have a certain equivalence. That is, we see the realism of the image as independent of our conceptions of painting, perspective, architecture, history, and metaphysics that guide our way of seeing and reading that image.

Since its emergence in the seventeenth century as a discrete category of objects and experience, "aesthetics" has been mostly about beauty, and beauty has been largely defined in terms of harmony and order. Since harmony and order were also political ideals, for many centuries the aesthetically fitting work, in its very character as "beautiful," also served as an allegory for state power. This particular linkage continued into modernist art, which "privileges . . . purity as an end and decorum as an effect" (Foster 1987). As the painter Brice Marden said, "The idea of beauty can be offensive. . . . It doesn't deal with issues, political issues or social issues. But an issue that it does deal with is harmony" (quoted in Danto 1992, 418).

Today the situation is more complex. Part of this complexity lies in the de-essentialization or de-ontologization of the Beautiful (as well as the Good and the True). All such concepts have lost their grounding in Reality and, hence, are no longer ultimate. Antifoundationalism has invaded moral philosophy, theory of knowledge, and aesthetics. This de-ontologization and consequent fragmentation of standards of beauty render it seemingly impossible to establish consistent relations between aesthetics, politics, and reality. Instead, all such efforts are seen to have an ideological content. At the same time, however, the derealization of canons of beauty allows us to view them as social and historical constructions and to ask how "reality" is crafted in art, not only aesthetically but also politically.

In this essay, I do not attempt to test empirically a model of realism and power. Instead, I hope to develop one speculatively with discussions and examples. These include the construction of realism within aesthetic paradigms, the social and historical relativity of realism in literature and painting, the French Academy's strategy and success in creating a national culture, the "scientific" aesthetics of realism in the nineteenth century and the resultant effort to professionalize artistic production, the novel as a sourcebook for textual realism, and the status of realism in the late capitalist or postmodern period.

On the Construction of Realism within Paradigms[1]

The "realism" of any representation cannot be determined solely on the basis of the reality of its objects or contents (Harms 1986, 13; Brinkmann 1976, 76, 310). Instead, realism is greatly shaped by the maker's use of the resources of the aesthetic paradigm within which he or she is working. Whether they are doing stained glass windows or styrofoam sculptures, all artists confront certain choices that are inherent in the act of aesthetic making. These choices include the degree of consistency in the use of narrative structure or historical allusions, in the deployment of aesthetic distance and point of view, in the allocation of textual, temporal, or visual space to various subjects or narrators, and in the use of tropes, such as metonymy or irony. One such stylistic choice under which those above may be subsumed is that of genre. In which genre (or paradigm) should one write, or paint, or sculpt? How closely should one adhere to or depart from its canons?

There are as many verisimilitudes as there are genres; the limits and freedom of any work are encoded by the generic rules through which it gains intelligibility (Todorov 1977, 83; see also Denzin in this volume). Hence, realism is achieved in part through strict adherence to the rules of an aesthetic paradigm and to the redundancy and repetition of their application. This may be called *genre thickening*. The opposite, a weaker application of genre rules and a reaching toward other or newer genres, might be called *genre stretching*. Works that are thinly encoded or that stretch their genres have a lesser degree of realism than those that are thick. If a new genre becomes more sedimented and established, of course, its representative works may acquire a greater degree of realism. As Pablo Picasso said to a viewer who claimed that his portrait of Gertrude Stein did not look like her, "Never mind, it will."

Genre thickening involves tightly coded descriptions, a semiotic denseness. The genre's rules of representation are applied literally and strictly in order to display a reality that is taken as pregiven. Genre thick discourse reproduces or elaborates a paradigm that is well established and taken for granted (Riffaterre 1984, 159). By contrast, subjectivity or relativism is yielded by stretching, making ironic, or mixing genres and their rules. Genre stretching puts the polysemous properties of representation in the foreground; new meanings or relationships are suggested by shifts in point of view, ironic reframing, or metaphoric leaps. Genre stretching or mixing fosters artistic revolutions, the shaping of new paradigms, the creation through articulation of a reality-in-formation.

Objectivity or realism is yielded by consistency or thickness of representation according to the rules of a paradigm or genre. Such realism is achieved textually through thick encoding according to that genre's rules and, indeed, through elaborating, formalizing, and codifying these rules. As we experience art that is thickly encoded in a dominant paradigm, we tend to see the reality that is projected aesthetically as being self-subsistent and exterior to our practice as makers or viewers, auditors, and readers. Thus, "the recognition of realism depends conventionally precisely on fidelity to a given mode of representation, or repetition" (Heath 1986, 144). As Roland Barthes wrote, "Realism . . . cannot be a copy of things, but the knowledge of language; the most 'realistic' work is not that which 'paints' reality, but which . . . explores as deeply as possible the *unreal reality* of language" within a given genre (Barthes 1964, 165, my translation).

By thickening representations within an accepted paradigm, artists and audiences also define as errors those activities that stretch the paradigm or mix it with others. When sufficient anomalies arise, competing perspectives challenge the dominant one, or shifts occur in the reigning habitus, then both old and new genres appear as metaphors for, rather than copies of, a reality that can now be known differently through different aesthetic evocations. At such moments the conflicts between the old and emergent artistic paradigms can be more easily seen as political struggles between representatives of opposing definitions of the correct artistic tradition (Brown 1987, 164–69; MacIntyre 1980; Fisher 1987). The dominant genre may ignore the new perspectives and representations and thereby limit its relevance and range. It thus may remain internally consistent but will be able to credently represent an ever diminishing portion of the relevant reality. Conversely, the dominant paradigm may be stretched to accommodate new experiences, techniques, or viewpoints. But practitioners thereby run the risk of rendering their paradigm internally inconsistent, thinly encoded, and thus bereft of the thick consistency of representation that was a source of its realism and objectivity and, hence, of its authority. Finally, the old image of the world will be reaffirmed or a new one will replace it. After such sea changes, when the waters again are calm, the revived or newly dominant paradigm will once more become the taken-for-granted code for realistic representations. Artists will again start thickening the new genres that they have created through stretching and mixing. An aesthetic half-truth, invented through genre stretching, will be thickened into an institutionalized discourse as a whole reality and doctrine, not only accepted but *indispensable* to further representations made under its aegis. Paradigm enforcement will become valued and necessary to create professionals who will profess that paradigm and continue to elaborate it.

The Historical Relativity of Realism

All mimeses carry a surplus of possible meanings. Realistic art tries to narrow such potential meanings to a single monological one. Too much of this, however, is counterproductive to artistic innovation. In conveying new ideas or even elaborating old ones, some deviation from the norm is indispensable, because it is impossible to say something new in artistic language that has been invented all at once. To do this we would have to know everything about a domain before we have represented it. By stretching genres, however, we can apprehend something new before we fully comprehend it. We use borrowed or stretched images to represent the emergent domain until the new artistic language or the new usage of the old language becomes sedimented and thick—a genre of its own.

Thus the logical distinction between genre stretching and genre thickening is also dialectical and temporal. Each of these modes of mimesis presupposes the other, and each may *become* the other over time. This is partly because genre thickening creates realism only if the genre itself is homologous with the dominant ontology of its public. As Stern (1973, 89) noted, "Every age . . . has its own realism." Realism is always realism for someone from some point of view. "Realism appears as rationality to classicism, as irrationality to romanticism, [and] as objectivity to nineteenth-century naturalism" (Hauser 1982, 720). Thus, Dostoevsky could say, "I love realism in art beyond all measure, the realism that approaches the fantastic. . . . What can be more fantastic and unexpected for me than reality? In fact, what can be more improbable than reality?" (quoted in Hauser 1958, 155).

Representation is not only a portrayal; it is also an argument, a deputation, a representation not by but of and for the viewer, an attribution of identity, a case for the intelligibility of the world (Heath 1986, 110). For example, religious art is realistic only to a public of literal believers, whereas Renaissance painting could be realistic to its elite public to the extent that they had come to share a mechanistic, geometric conception of the world, a view that itself was fostered by neo-Platonic aesthetic conceptions of mathematical harmony, symmetry, and form (Hallyn 1990). Similarly, the realism of the nineteenth-century novel *became* realistic as a secular and scientific ontology entered the consciousness of the new middle-class reading public. Different peoples in different times and places have different ontologies and aesthetic paradigms and different forms of realism. "To see (*voir*) is a function of the knowledge (*savoir*), or concepts, that is, the words, that are available to name visible things, and which are, as it were, programmes for perception" (Bourdieu 1984, 2). Thus, realism is not *the* correct form of perception, but rather an historically relative function of changing aesthetic paradigms, collective ontologies, and social structures (Eisenstein [1929] 1963, 35).

A genre whose representations are literal and realistic for one public may be seen as metaphoric and imaginary by another. Consider, for example, how conceptions of realism have changed over the centuries for literary and pictorial representations. In both these fields, those who adhere to older paradigms call new modes of representation subjective, arbitrary, or decadent. They see the new modes as deformations of the old canons, a rejection of verisimilitude and realism. They insist that the established paradigm is the only one that yields realistic representations and, hence, that speaks the truth.

Thus, realism in various media and cultures tends to be aesthetically conservative, produced through a semiotic consistency or density within an existing paradigm or genre. Though practitioners often seek to extend the frontiers of their paradigm, the specific rules of any mode of representation are fully intelligible only in terms of local contexts of use; moreover, these rules are often incommensurate with those of other paradigms. Thus, no one realism can encompass all others. Whoever senses truth to life in Racine is unlikely to find it in Shakespeare. Whoever finds Michelangelo's human forms to be realistic will likely find no realism, or a different kind of realism, in Lucas Cranach's nudes.

Judgments of realism change over time. Paintings like Paolo Uccello's battle scenes were not taken to represent reality "the way it is" until much later, after the paradigm of perspective and a mechanistic world image were established (Panofsky [1927] 1991, 66). Similarly, the realism of Canaletto is not the same as the later realism of Gustave Courbet. Canaletto invited the viewer to dominate the scene whereas Courbet sought to negate or neutralize the presence of the beholder (Hulse 1990; Fried 1990). Just as the invented has the prospect of becoming the literal, so the literal, in retrospect, can become the invented. Thus, "a contemporary critic might detect realism in Delacroix but not in Delaroche; in El Greco and Andre Rublev, but not in Guido Reni. . . . A directly opposite judgment, however, would have been characteristic of a pupil of the Academy in the previous century" (Jakobson 1971, 472). Some critics even banish from art those representations that do not fit the dominant canon.

Thus, deviant representations may be officially forbidden. Indeed, such paradigm enforcement is a major function of academies, institutes, graduate programs, and other institutions that license or censure practitioners. For example, about 2600 B.C. the authorities in ancient Egyptian began dictating the colors, designs, and conventions that artists could employ. The representation of the human figure had to be "ankle on the first horizontal level, knee on the sixth level, shoulder on the sixteenth level" (Clapp 1972). Contemporary aesthetic conservatives now defend the modernist paradigm against postmodernism, much as former conservatives once defended classicism against modernism. For example, in the editorial of the first issue of *The New Criterion* (really the *old* criterion), Hilton Kramer (1984a) rejected postmodernism as an "insidious assault on the mind" and called for a return to modernist criteria of representation and truth. Daniel Bell (1979) extended this argument to politics, arguing that postmodernism "undermines the social structure itself by striking at the motivational and psychic-reward system which has sustained it." Instead, said Bell, art should be autonomous, resist the decline of standards, and convey high modernist values.

The extreme cases of such orthodoxy were socialist and fascist realism or, rather, the fantasies of reality whose intention was to curtail understanding of how the real is created aesthetically and politically. Such orthodoxies tend toward academicism or kitsch. They "triumph over the experimental avant-garde by slandering and banning it, and by providing the correct images, the correct narratives, and the correct forms which the dominant group commissions and propagates" (Lyotard 1985). When the attack on artistic experimentation is launched by its political apparatus, a regime's reactionary aesthetics are generally a good clue to its actual politics—but not necessarily. Honoré de Balzac was a royalist; Ilya Repin, a Tolstoyian Slavophile (Valkenier 1990). At the least, however, aesthetic judgment will be restricted to decisions on whether any given work is in conformity with the established rules of the beautiful, and the work of art will no longer be permitted to investigate what makes it an art object and how it creates its audience and effects.

Those who favor aesthetic innovation take the opposite position. They consider as art only that which is invention, which stretches or even breaks the existing paradigm or genre. As Arnold Hauser (1982, 725) put it, every work of art "is historically and aesthetically unique, tied to the instant of its creation, and . . . different from every other product of the genre. If it identifies with a prototype, it is no longer a work of art." In this spirit Henri Matisse insisted that "the importance of an artist is to be measured by the number of new signs he has introduced into the language of art" ([1943] 1972, 110-11). Even more strongly, José Ortega y Gasset in *Velázques* (1956, 34, 135) conceived of art as derealization and was convinced that realism is "the negation of art." His defense of Velázques was that the artist's alleged realism was but a variety of the irrealism of all great art. Similarly, in *Idea del Teatro* (1977), Ortega discussed transmigration into the unreal worlds of fun and joke and stressed that a great novel does not refer to anything outside itself. Of course, this is an extreme position since what it advocates is an impossibility: a fully original, autoreferential novel (or theory, etc.) would be unintelligible, a private code that even its would-be maker could not break.

In sum, every realistic representation is always a re-presentation from some point of view, within some frame of vision, and these frames of vision tend to be embedded ontologically and politically. Realism is that mode of representation that has "made it" socially and, thence, denies its necessary partiality. Realistic representation is therefore inherently ideological because it excludes from consciousness the possibility of alternate valid versions of things as they are. Bertoldt Brecht stated this most strongly: *"Realistische Kunist ist Kämpferische Kunst"* ([1954] 1967, 547). If the point is not to describe reality but to change it, then realistic art is a form of combat. Thus, to reveal the practices by which representations become realistic is to disclose the ideology that is encoded in the modes of production of reality—those processes of human inscription that are collapsed into and held captive by a static mimesis that is the product of these very processes.

The French Academy: Creating a Modern Public Culture

Standards of realism, objectivity, or aesthetic adequacy are often homologous across fields such as architecture, painting, and literature. Such standards also may display parallel political processes of institutionalization. But the question remains as to the relation between specific forms of cultural representation and the representation of authority in specific political institutions. The French Academy provides a good example of such an interaction because it was the major force in fostering a new kind of aesthetic representation, in professionalizing artistic producers, and in shaping the public culture that helped legitimate the French nation-state.

The kings of France began to foster an official culture in order to aggrandize the state and their power at a time when no concentrated commercial sector or culture existed to compete with their efforts. In effect, they created the only available nonascriptive, secular, national culture. This was a "civilizing process" that involved changing not only art styles but also people. That is, part of the population acquired a new national identity by adopting the manners and language of the Academy and the court (Zolberg 1989; Elias 1978).

The French Academy spearheaded this process. It was created by successive monarchs at the urging of artists, whose own cohesiveness and privilege was reinforced by the patronage of the Academy (Williams 1981; Clignet 1990). The Academy was the major institution that operated theaters and museums, directed educational institutions, offered competitions and prizes, and comissioned art for public purposes. It selected and educated talented aspirants, fostered creativity, established and maintained standards of quality, legitimated selected art forms, subject matters, and styles, and developed rationales that drew on classical scholarship (White and White 1991).

The aggrandizement of the French state through cultural mobilization from the center also had an international dimension. In the age of Louis XIV, divinely appointed ruler of the wealthiest and most populous state of Europe, the French language seemed likely to replace Latin as the international language of diplomacy and culture. This project was led by writers whose patronage was controlled by the Academy. For example, in January 1687 Charles Perrault read before the Academy his poem, "The Age of Louis the Great," in which he suggested that the literary glories of the Sun King's reign would outshine those of all earlier epochs, including the great ages of Greece and Rome (Levine 1991).

As the canons and control of art and life became more centralized, regional or provincial cultures, such as those of Brittany and Provence, were pushed to the edges of networks of artistic power and patronage centered in Paris. Thus, exemplary events in the creation of the French nation-state include the deliberate destruction of the culture of Languedoc in the Albigensian Crusade and the suppression of autochthonous regional languages in favor of the French of the Ile-de-France (Zolberg 1989, 6; Clastre 1987; Mousnier 1984).

The Academy propagated hierarchic distinctions between art and craft, high and folk art, and aesthetic and religious objects. Voltaire's dictum, *"le superflu, chose très necessaire,"* underlined the importance of nonutilitarian, aesthetic objects and activities as status markers for new national elites as leaders of an international hegemonic cultural movement (DiMaggio 1987; Elias 1978; Veblen 1979). Artists and art forms that were excluded from official recognition were consigned to relative oblivion and separate development as "little cultures," marginalized as clients of the Catholic Church rather than the state, or abandoned to the market. The works of such artists were not admitted to official salons where they could be viewed by high status clients or officials with funds to purchase art for private collections or public buildings. Such non-Academic artists displayed "their paintings at outdoor markets and fairs, to an indiscriminate clientele of lesser standing, and with much lower financial reward. During the nineteenth century they might be obliged to eke out a living as writers or illustrators for the growing publishing market or the commercial advertising world" (Zolberg 1989, 6; see also Corvisier 1978). Although a few became rich and famous as creative artists, such as Alexandre Dumas, Eugène Sue, or Émile Zola, most were exploited by the commercial press.

Many of the ideas embodied in the new public culture turned out to be extremely durable (Zolberg 1989, 5). Even after its dissolution along with the *ancien régime* and its re-creation in an altered form after the Revolution, the academic system shaped culture for the French nation with or without a monarch throughout most of the nineteenth century. The frontiers on the Rhine and the Pyrenees became sacred, public education came under state control, the central administration was vastly expanded, and much regional particularism was assimilated or suppressed. In altered forms, official culture continues to serve as a gauge of quality and reward for the arts (Zolberg 1989, 5; Mesnard 1974), as is recognized in the ministries of Education, Culture and Communications, Tourism, and Foreign Affairs.

The Academy was able to create an aesthetically unified and

politically useful paradigm. This historical institutionalized character of academic rules of representation is highlighted by the diversity of modes of representation during the same period outside of France. To be sure, artists everywhere elaborated the basic rules of their disciplines, while guilds and local academies sought to standardize art markets and limit competition among artists. Yet outside of France there generally was no unified body of principles governing the choice of the objects of aesthetic research and of the appropriate symbolic languages.[2] Further, these communities did not have the power or stature to authoritatively rank individual practitioners, much less cultures, in some order of merit and to distribute resources accordingly. In some places there was active hostility toward academic art, often in the service of anti-French nationalism. Supported by a growing middle class that bought his prints, William Hogarth equated naturalism in painting with British beer, British roast beef, and British common sense. He rallied against tastes for foreign art among London elites and scorned the orthodox methods imposed after 1663 by Charles LeBrun at the Academie Royale in Paris (Paulson 1991; Dorment 1993, 17). David Hume gave a philosophical justification to such sentiments when he argued that "Beauty is not quality in things themselves: It exists in the eye which contemplates them; and each eye perceives a different beauty" (1882).

In the visual arts, private sponsors outside of France kept asserting their right to define the subjects to be treated and the size of the canvas, as well as the colors and the rules of composition to be used (Haskell 1963). For example, "Pope Clement did not only command Michelangelo to paint *The Last Judgment,* but he also determined it should be a masterpiece" (Gablik 1985, 23). Similarly, at a later date, "John Sebastian Bach was expected by his local prince not only to play the organ for the consistory of Darnstadt, but also to maintain the instrument in working condition, to compose scores agreeable to his employers, and to associate only with people held to be socially acceptable. Like mathematicians, astronomers, or writers, composers of the period were often obliged to sell their labor rather than their works" (Clignet 1990, 231).

Thus, unlike the situation in France, the demand for culture that governed artistic transactions elsewhere tended to be personalized and particularistic (Baxandall 1986). In France as in other countries, those who commissioned or purchased works of art were also those empowered to define them as beautiful. What is salient here, however, is that in Europe outside of France, it was usually a pope or prince or merchant, or perhaps the artist, who called the tune or tone or trope, which engendered different and often competing codes of representation, thus yielding diverse and therefore mutually subverting forms of realism. Multiple codes of realism may have permitted greater artistic freedom but they also undermined the monopoly on modes of mimesis that is a prime basis for the privilege and prestige of artists. From the Renaissance to the Enlightenment and to some extent beyond, this was not the case in France. On the eve of the bourgeois era, however, the hegemonic power of the crown to represent society within society had broken down. Henceforth, as Simon-Nicolas-Henri Linguet (1778, quoted by Luhmann 1987, 103) put it, "the monarch calls himself the nation; the parliaments call themselves the nation; the nation can't say what it is, nor even if it is. Waiting for this point to be clarified, everything stays confused; everything serves as material for claims and disputes."

Property Rights, the "Scientific" Aesthetics of Realism, and the Professionalization of Producers of Art

By the time of the French Revolution, producers of culture in Europe had achieved a certain autonomy. Entrepreneurs came to believe that economic development was driven by technological innovations and that the free trade of commodities had to be accompanied by the free circulation of ideas. Princes and prelates lost power and prestige, on the one hand, to states that were empowered to impose more general standards of law, exchange, and representation and, on the other hand, to citizens, business people, and free laborers who had new rights and powers to make their own decisions. Finally, academies had established control over the production and sale of culture. As a result, they were able to offer their individual members greater economic and social protection.

The notion of the "author" also came into being at this time. As Michel Foucault (1980, 141, 159) noted, this constituted "a privileged moment of *individualization* in the history of ideas.... Since the eighteenth century, the author has played the role of the regulator of [the relationship between] fictive ... and private property." Art and forms of knowledge became private property and the individual author became the principle by which such property could be regulated (Hesse 1991, 109). "The 'author' in the modern sense ... is the product of the rise in the eighteenth century of a new group of individuals: writers who sought to earn their livelihood from the sale of their writing to a new and rapidly expanding reading public"

(Woodmansee 1984, 426; see also Frank 1986; Trabant 1991). Mark Rose (1993, 56) concludes:

> The emergence of the mass market for books, the valorization of original genius, and the development of the Lockean discourse of possessive individualism . . . occurred in the same period as the long legal and commercial struggle over copyright. Indeed, it was in the course of that struggle under the particular pressures of the requirements of legal argumentation that the blending of Lockean discourse and the aesthetic discourse of originality occurred and the modern conception of the author as proprietor was formed.

The translation of these bourgeois concepts of individualism and property into laws of artistic copyright occurred first in England in 1709 and then in Prussia in 1794 (Hesse 1991, 110; Rose 1993). The legal notion of the author, first recognized in France in 1777, followed a half century of discussion. For example, in *Mémoire sur les propriétés et privilèges exclusifs de la librairie, présenté en 1774,* Linguet asked: "What is a literary privilege? It is a recognition made by public authority of the property of the author or of those to whom he has ceded it. It is the literary equivalent of a notorial act which . . . assures the rights of citizens. . . . The privilege is a seal that guarantees peaceful enjoyment; but it is not the source of that enjoyment. . . . A privilege grants nothing to the author, it only ensures protection" (cited in Hesse 1991, 115). After the Revolution, advocates of copyright laws used patriotic and political arguments in addition to commercial ones. Copyright not only protected publishers from ruinous pirate editions; it also protected the state against sedition and libel by establishing authorial accountability. The new laws made the author legally responsible for the text by defining it as his property (Hesse 1991, 118, 120).

With the debasement of handicraft and artisan labor by capitalism and later, because of industrial production, an analogy emerged between divine and artistic or scientific creation. This new conception went hand in hand with the emergence of patents for scientific invention and of copyrights for literary authorships. Art works and artisan techniques and ideas had always been property—that is, in all societies and times, certain persons and not others had the right to use them. But only in the capitalist era did art become a commodity (Brown 1989). "Before the existence of patents and copyrights, the value of ideas was preserved by the maintenance of secrecy and by strictly private and elitist consumption. But once ideas can be owned, their value lies in disowning them by making them public—not only in the economic sense of the creation of surplus value, but also in the sense that the very meaning of conceptual ownership depends upon the knowledge of others of your ownership, upon their capacity to know your ideas without also being able to extract material profit from them" (McKeon 1987, 123-24). With prose works, for example, writing took priority over speaking because printed works could be more readily copyrighted, reproduced, and marketed than oral presentations. Objectivity came to be associated with print, and it was felt that an idea did not really belong to its author until it had been published.

With the establishment of more universal norms of aesthetic excellence and authorship in the French Academy (and after, in an imitation of science), it became easier to say which practices were proper and, hence, who was or was not an artist. The establishment of canons of proper aesthetic representation provided demarcations for membership and enabled the formation of professional associations that articulated and enforced these definitions of aesthetic propriety. In turn, members of the new professions received new titles that entitled them to greater control over their cultural products. Thus, aesthetic propriety, cultural property, and professional privilege each supported the others.

From the eighteenth century onward, and especially after the decline of monarchies and the rise of capitalist elites, science and efficacy increasingly replaced theology and divine right as the hegemonic social discourse. With this, artists claimed the same privileges as those already acquired by scientists (Clignet 1990; Caillois 1974, 28-29; Warnke 1993). To buttress this claim, artists stressed the similarity of mimesis in both artistic and scientific pursuits. "Art is nothing without Science," said Mignot, the architect who advised the builders of the cathedral of Milan. This attempt to homogenize scientific and artistic practices of representation is also evident in the claim of the seventeenth-century critic Roland Friart de Chambray, who insisted that those who would understand Nicolas Poussin's art must "study and judge matters in the manner of mathematicians" (quoted in Bull 1991, 12). John Constable's comment that "painting is a science of which canvases are experiments," expresses a similar spirit, as does Paul Signac's (1987) description of the neo-impressionists' "methodical and scientific technique," and Georges Braque's search for a "method that would be appropriate for verifying paintings."[3]

All these remarks presumed a parallelism in the character of methods and works in the sciences and arts. In the same way that, in the sciences, laboratory experiments are subordinate to hypotheses, so, in the arts, stonecutting was deemed inferior to sculpture because the cutter was believed to express no guiding theory or conception. Artists adopted the rhetorics of the scientific communities of the period. Since scientists were allowed to define truth, artists felt they should be allowed to define beauty. Artists asserted that aesthetic pursuits were governed by the same rules as scientific projects, such as universalism, objectivity, and disinterestedness. For example, on the eve of the French Revolution, René-Antoine Ferchault de Réaumur suggested that "individuals who strive to improve the sciences *and the arts* should consider themselves as citizens of the world" (Merton 1973, 274, emphasis added).

Similarly, in both the arts and sciences, the validation of claims concerning achievement was supposed to be independent of their authors' personal or social attributes. Thus, it was held that careers should reflect talent and achievement, not caste or connection. Correspondingly, champions of "cosmopolitan" art forms were often hostile toward any mode of expression that could be interpreted as ethnocentric or particular. "Regional" art was categorized as a minor genre, and minority artists were expected to transcend the marginality of their race or gender and to reaffirm the universalistic quality imputed to artistic creativity (Rosenberg 1977; Schowalter 1984).

Artists also were expected to display the same gratuitous passion for knowledge as that attributed to scientists; likewise, artists' activities were expected to be inspired by idle curiosity and fair play. A forerunner of this in the visual arts was Rembrandt, who sought to establish greater autonomy by asserting a distinction between commissioned paintings and those made for unspecified patrons (Baxandall 1986). In the same spirit was the assertion of Salvator Rosa that he painted "for his own satisfaction and pleasure rather than to please his clients" (Haskell 1963, 22-23). These sentiments were elaborated during the nineteenth century in the notion of "art for art's sake." This ideology distinguished the "fine" arts from "applied" activities. The first were held in high esteem as pure expressions of spirit; the second were thought to be debasing, a kind of prostitution. Painters asserted their preeminence over printmakers and, later, over photographers. Later, during the early phases of the cinema, stage actors who had already achieved a solid reputation refused to make movies, much as their successors later refused to do commercials. Such shunting off of dirty or impure work to lesser laborers is a well-known technique for creating and maintaining professional status and privilege.

In sum, the relationship between propriety and property changed with the impact of industrialization on the conception of both realism and the rights of artists. Artists capitalized on the new laws concerning scientific property and on the ensuing distinction between the rights granted to scientists and those claimed by inventors. They emphasized analogies between scientific and artistic realism and creativity in both fields. They also asserted their right to define canons of validity and to evaluate individual works in the name of the community at large. Moreover, artists claimed similarities between their roles and those of inventors, in order to affirm their economic rights over their individual creations after these had entered into the public domain. Thus, the creation of modern forms of "scientific" realism in aesthetic representation was not simply a matter of refining and elaborating the respective modes of mimesis. Such refinement also provided norms of propriety that facilitated the professionalization of producers of culture and, with this, their enhanced privilege and property, at least to the extent that their works became staples in the new markets for culture.

The Novel as a Sourcebook for Textual Realism

The view of realism as a social and historical construction can be further elaborated with reference to the novel. Realism in the novel was produced by the homology between orthodox aesthetic forms and the dominant ontology of artists and their publics: the modern novel projects fictional realities that express and reinforce the modern social realities of psychological individualism and economic capitalism within an atomistic, causal universe.

Like science, the novel expresses the shift from a medieval to a modern conception of realism. From Plato to Aquinas, to Shakespeare and Shaftesbury, reality had been thought to inhere in universal forms that existed independently of instantiations in any particular time, place, or person. Thus, true or correct representations by definition could not be novel. By contrast, though modern realism preserves the medieval respect for universals, these no longer are divine essences revealed by God. Instead, universals for modern persons take the form of natural laws discovered by the individual cogito and confirmed by empirical perception (Hasan 1928, chaps. 1 and 2; Aaron 1952, 18–41; Watt 1957, 9–34). Individual sense perception, like the individual cogito, was elevated to the status of a primary means for knowing the laws of nature, which were seen to inhere in perceptible external experience. Whether in its formulation by Descartes or by Locke, truth was now seen as derived from individual cognition or experience, formulated into mathematical laws of nature, and independent of inherited belief or collective tradition.

The novel also expresses the time sense of modernity, in which *nostrum aevum*, our own age, was renamed *nova aetas*, the new age. For Christians the new world had meant the still-to-come age that would dawn only on the last day. By contrast, the secular concept of modernity welcomes the novelty of the future and the discovery and exploration of new geographic or aesthetic frontiers (Habermas 1987, 4, 6; Koselleck 1985, 241). This can be seen in the famous *querelle des anciens et des modernes*, in which the "moderns" used critical and historical arguments to challenge the established practice of imitating classical models. In opposition to the supposedly timeless norms of beauty and of human nature, the moderns advanced a conception of relative beauty and historically conditioned human nature. The future was now contained in the present and the present at each moment gave birth to the new.

These conceptions accorded with the rise of the individual as a subjective agent, which can be seen in the psychological atomization of Protestantism, in the freedom of wage workers from manse and guild in the emerging market economy, and in the legal individualism of citizens in the new nation-states. Georg W. F. Hegel (1956, 442) noted this principle of individuation at the beginning of the 1800s. With the Reformation, Enlightenment, and French Revolution, he said, "right and morality came to be looked upon as having their foundation in the actually present will of man." As Stephen Heath (1986, 109) notes:

> Realism, in fact, is produced in the novel as a social narration of the individual as problem: what, where, how is the meaning of the individual in this prosaic world, confronted thus by society, by history? The novel ceaselessly makes sense for the individual, brings him or her—hero or heroine but also simultaneously the reader as its addressed agent—into this new field of reality, into recognition, knowledge, meaning. Crucially, its realism is a response to instability: the novel coincides with the development of a new form of social organization, that of capitalism, in which, precisely, society and the individual become the terms of reference, in which the social relations of the individual—'the individual and society,' as we have learnt to say—become a problem as such.

Instead of tales and stories told to a communal audience, the novel wrote about, spoke to, and helped constitute a mass public of discrete individuals. The novel was the literary version of new social practices and epistemological assumptions. Its very name expressed the primacy of newness; its form provided a vehicle for representing unique experiences of unique individuals in unique situations. Novels are composed by a sole author, read in isolation by a single reader, and apprehended by a solitary consciousness. After printing, literacy, and middle-class readers had become widespread, authors could more fully sustain themselves with earnings from the market. Authors thereby could be more individualistic than, for example, architects, whose financial means of production were still controlled by churches, academies, and states.

The novelist, like the scientist, was expected to faithfully represent experience, and this had come to mean for fiction the particular experiences of particular persons in particular times and places. Formerly it was assumed that the repertoire of possible experience was already established, and that art, therefore, was to draw on traditional plots and characters to display reality. Shakespeare, for example, used traditional plots and characters—it mattered little whether they were set in medieval Scotland, Renaissance Verona, or ancient Rome. By contrast, Defoe, Richardson, Balzac, Flaubert, and their heirs created highly individuated characters set in specific places and times. Indeed, much of the textual space of their novels is devoted to providing the local empirical details by which realism has come to be known. Thus, writers of novels are thoroughly grounded in the world of *things* (Bayley 1991, 12). As masters of the mundane, novelists establish their authority and mesmerize the reader with facts, as in Boris Pasternak's depiction of the stationary train and the suicide of Zhivago's father: "There was a faint stench from the lavatories, not quite dispelled by eau de cologne, and a smell of fried chicken, a little high and wrapped in dirty wax paper." Similarly, Henry James wrote of Anthony Trollope, "his great, his inestimable merit was a complete appreciation of the usual." Such a quantity of the quotidian is a main reason why novels are generally much bigger than earlier kinds of fiction: they are packed with spatial and temporal minutia that previously were considered irrelevant. This also partly explains why the novel requires less social and historical commentary than other literary genres: novels supply such details themselves within the initial text.

As René Descartes and John Locke had provided a new subjectivist conception of the person as an identity of consciousness over a duration of time, writers from Laurence Sterne to James Joyce have explored the personality as an interpenetration of past and present self-awareness (Descartes 1954; Locke [1690] 1974, Bk. II, chap. 27, sec. 9, 10; Watt 1957, 21). Moreover, unlike earlier narratives whose action moved forward through accidental encounters, chance events, or mistaken identities, the novel, in its new realism, is emplotted with a more cohesive structure based on the principle of causal connections through time. Heroic novels usually make the protagonist the cause of exterior events; stream-of-consciousness novels usually construe the narrator's interior states as caused by external happenings. In both, however, and in the many writings that could be placed between, there is a clear temporal sequence of causality of individual consciousness and action that forms the modern plot.[4]

The modern habitus also includes a skepticism toward language. Scientists established their power in part by distinguishing their own prose from the eloquence of jurists, humanists, and theologians, and soon novelists followed this lead. Because truth for moderns is of the mind and the world and no longer primarily in God's *word*, language seemed to play no positive role in its representation. Language only got in the way of direct intuitions or perceptions. "Eloquence," said Locke (Bk. III, chap. 10, sec. 33–34), "like the fair sex," involves a pleasurable deceit. Hence, "plain language" came to be preferred to refinements of style. As in science, a flat denotative prose in the novel was seen as the necessary price of fidelity to the object or experiences represented. "The function of language is much more largely referential in the novel than in other literary forms; the genre itself works by exhaustive presentation rather than by elegant concentration" (Watt 1957, 30). This explains why the novel is the most translatable of literary genres, perhaps *the* international literary form, and also why even great novelists, such as Dostoevsky, Dreiser, or Zola, often write with little grace.

With the growth of a middle-class reading public, patronage of writers shifted from the court and church to a mass of individual purchasers of individual books. "The Wealth of the Nation," Jonathan Swift said, "that used to be reckoned by the Value of Land, is now computed by the Rise and Fall of Stocks" (Swift [1710] 1940, 6–7, 119). The shift from landed to commercial wealth also enabled writers like Swift to enjoy prosperity, or suffer penury, as independent creators. Unlike architects or orchestra conductors, their means of production and the unit cost of their products were both relatively cheap. This, combined with the rise of a large and literate middle class, freed writers from both the constraints and privileges of ecclesiastical or aristocratic patronage.

Part of the novel's character as a distinct genre is that it cannibalizes and incorporates canonical genres as well as "nonliterary" writings.

Like modern individuals, the novel thereby composes its own conventionality against the authority of traditional conventions. It defines itself through negation. The novel is thus an inherently self-conscious genre, since it bares its own devices of construction. This, at least, is the ideal of modern literary form as articulated by critics such as Mikhail Bakhtin or Bertholt Brecht. It is also the ideal of the modern, authentic, auto-created self expressed by writers from Jean-Jacques Rousseau to Jean-Paul Sartre. The "estrangement effect" of the novel is the literary counterpart of the social and psychological "alienation" of modern persons, each a precondition of the possibility of self-knowledge and literary truth, and both the counterparts of a reified market-driven social order.

The moral challenge for premodern persons was sincerity—to be what they seemed, a truth to the social role. For moderns, the challenge is authenticity, to be true to one's inner self. Thus, the novel is preoccupied with questions of truth and virtue or, rather, truth to oneself as virtue—not so much its achievement as its definition and even its possibility. In this, the novel expresses social shifts and tensions between older and newer moral codes. This conflation of "truth" and "virtue" in the novel mediated the epistemological and existential concerns of the emerging middle class. The novel was the cultural genre that enabled early modern authors and audiences to address, on the level of narrative form and content, both moral and social crises simultaneously (McKeon 1987, 212–18, 222; Kaplan 1988). As a commentary on human conditions, God's justice in heaven was replaced by "poetic justice" in the novel. Whereas formerly right and morality referred only to God's command, modern authors secularized spiritual norms into aesthetic forms. Religious faith was replaced by "that willing suspension of disbelief for the moment, which constitutes poetic faith" (Coleridge [1817] 1965, II:xiv:169; see also Hegel 1956, 442).

Realism in the Late Capitalist or Postmodern Mode

The late capitalist or postmodern relationship between realism and power in aesthetic representations is marked by a shift of emphasis from production to consumption and, with this, an accentuation of the turnover and the differentiation of artistic commodities available in differing markets. With the invasion of cultural worlds by capitalism, there also has been a systematic celebration of the concept of relativity (Horwitz 1977) and, hence, a devaluation of anything that could be called realistic. Such relativization comes with the proliferation of new art worlds and market sectors and the ensuing profusion of competing avant-gardes, each with a shorter life span than the last (Kostelanetz 1993). For example, abstract expressionism in the forties and minimalism in the early sixties were championed by academic critics and the curators of New York museums. Pop, photorealism of the early seventies, and neo-expressionism of the early eighties were patronized by dealers, investors, and collectors. Figurative and pattern painters (of the early seventies) were supported by regional museums and corporate art acquisition managers (Crane 1987, 41; Bürger 1984).

All this of course has affected the character of art. In the postmodern period, autonomous artists have tended to react against commercialized culture by rejecting codified meanings as corrupt. This exhaustion of meaning is expressed in prose forms by the radical dislocation of the temporality of language. Contemporary narratives tend to subvert their narrativity in favor of a self-referential structure. In the postmodern antinovel, for example, even the author does not know what is going on. "Narration" fragments into a series of perpetual presents, "character" ends with the death of the subject, and "plot" becomes an absurdist montage of temporalities. As Luis Buñuel replied when asked if there were beginnings, middles, and ends in his films, "Yes. But not necessarily in that order."

Similarly, postmodern music abandons the formerly necessary order of classical harmony, rhythm, and melody, as well as the tonality of romantic impressionism. Rather than simply criticize processed media culture from the viewpoint of authentic human experience, postmodern artists collapse image and experience into a play of signifiers. This can be heard in the works of Philip Glass and John Cage. Unlike critics of modern technology such as Louis Mumford, these postmodern musicians see technology as pregnant with the aesthetic values of heterogeneity, randomness, and plenitude. "Since the theory of conventional music is a set of laws exclusively concerned with 'musical' sounds, having nothing to say about noises, it has been clear from the beginning that what was needed was a music based on noise, on noise's lawlessness" (Cage 1981). Cage thereby reappropriates technology into a postmodernist aesthetic. By literalizing the belief that spirit can shape matter, postmodernists reduce meaning and nonmeaning to a relativized sameness. Like the marketplace of the information society, the world in postmodern representation becomes a "network of neutral and purely contingent relationships" (Leed 1980, 35; see also Baudrillard 1980, 141).

This postmodernist spirit also is expressed in pictorial art by such creators as René Magritte ("This is not a pipe"), M. C. Escher (a hand drawing a hand drawing a hand), Claes Oldenberg (a baseball glove as big as a house), or in advertising (This is not an ad). These derealizations also are achieved through formal, technical means, as in Salvador Dali's *Portrait of Gala* (1935) with its distinct and disconnected surfaces (Altieri 1983, 6, 3). Much the same could be said of the patchwork of surface impressions that is the surreality created by TV except that, unlike TV, Dali created his surreality ironically. As Dali profaned modern linear time by melting watches, so Justen Ladda sacralized the profane boxes of Tide and Clorox by making them into a gigantic image of Durer's hands in *Prayer*. Other contemporary artists, such as Marcel Duchamp, argue that in order to resist capitalism it is not sufficient to emphasize the variability of interpretations attached to artifacts; artists also must make sure that the artifacts themselves do not last (Lasch 1978; 1984; Thompson 1979).

A postmodern fragmentation of the real appears in a 1992 exposition of drawings, "Allegories of Modernism," at New York's Museum of Modern Art (MoMA). Instead of the purity and decorum of modernism, this show displayed impure and indecorus fragments that referred only to other fragments. Robert Rauschenberg's work of pastiche and palimpsest illustrates this in its mixing of the verbal and the visual, its international hybridization of styles, and its apparent disregard for all aesthetic categories (Danto 1992). Hal Foster (1987) notes that "purity as an end and decorum as an effect" are privileged by modernism. In the same volume, Claude Owens speaks of "the fragmentary, the imperfect, the incomplete" and of works so characterized as having affinities with "the ruin." Now the title of the MoMA show begins to make sense. Modernism itself lies shattered in fragments, an artistic ruin. But because the works in "Allegories of Modernism" are themselves fragments, they compose allegories of the ruin that modernism has become—"a new vision of the real."

In this context the artist's goal is not to represent Truth or Beauty but to contest multiple aesthetic verisimilitudes, multiple versions of the beautiful and the true. In effect, the task of the contemporary artist is to bring chaos into order. A work must embody multiple masks as it seeks to unmask the regimes of signification that structure experience. In the postmodern, contemporary moment "the real is no longer what it used to be. . . . There is . . . a panic-stricken production of the real and the referential. . . . The very definition of the real becomes: *that of which it is possible to give an equivalent reproduction*" (Baudrillard 1983b, 12-13, 146, emphasis in original). In this situation the only realism that is possible is deconstructive verisimilitude (Denzin in this volume). That is, the artist can only produce a work that reproduces these multiple versions of the real, showing how each version impinges on and shapes the phenomenon being represented. A work's verisimilitude is given in its ability to reproduce and deconstruct the reproductions and simulations.

Such ironies of the dominant system are not a threat to that system. Instead, the established system that commoditizes art preserves itself by turning even protest into an item of consumption. As Andy Warhol said, "Good business is the *best* art" ("Selling" 1988, 60). Thus, the postmodernist protest succeeds by imitation even as it is defeated by co-optation. The very relativity of postmodernism illuminates and justifies artistic creations and evaluations as mere variations of the marketplace, rather than as distorted or accurate reflections of any absolute. Art becomes fashion, and fashion becomes the latest fad of consumer choice.

Such an abandonment of one single, stable paradigm generates in turn an accelerating number of coexisting and reciprocally negating aesthetic proprieties, legal cultural properties, and canons of realism. With the development of a large-scale cultural industry catering to increasingly diversified market sectors, there is a parallel fragmentation of various art worlds. Existing definitions of rules of aesthetic propriety and rights to artistic property die young, while newer ones are born in such a profusion that each subverts the others. This encourages an inflation of the interpretations offered of existing art works even as their respective turnovers and life cycles are accelerated. The blurring of rules also erodes the professional solidarity of artists to one another. In such a context, no authoritative definition of realism can survive.

This "realism" of "anything goes" in the art market is similar to "everything comes and goes" in the stock market. In the absence of reliable aesthetic criteria, it remains possible and useful to assess the value of art works according to the profits they yield. Such realism accommodates all tendencies, just as capitalism accommodates all "needs," providing only that the tendencies are marketable and the needs have purchasing power. Thus, pop artists break with the austere canons of high modernist paintings and embrace the consumer culture as their inspiration. What Madison Avenue was for Andy Warhol, the landscape of Las Vegas was for Venturi (1972) and other postmodern architects who celebrate fantasy and eclecticism against the rectilinear realism of modernism. We learn, in *Learning from Las Vegas,* to glorify the billboard strips, gigantic neon sculptures, schlock spectacles, and pop aesthetics of casino culture.

Realism asserts truth and preserves consciousness from doubt. Almost a century ago in 1905, Paul Cezanne wrote to the painter Émile Bernard, "I owe you the truth in painting and I will tell it to you." Since then, from Manet through synthetic cubism and Matisse, painters have gradually abandoned the task of representing reality just as reality has resisted the power of painting to realistically represent it. The last generation of American artists who could undertake to speak or paint the truth without being self-conscious or ironic about it was probably the avant-garde of the 1940s, many of whom felt that museum shows or commercial success were acts of self-betrayal (e.g., Breslin 1993). Instead, painters are increasingly preoccupied with problems intrinsic to painting itself, including problems of representing the real, being true, and being art (Michael Fried [1965], quoted in Franscina and Harrison 1982, 115; see also Bourdieu 1984, 3). In an age that is quintessentially one of doubt, self-conscious representations of reality can only be ironic, for there are no longer any fixed conventions to which one can judiciously conform or against which one can seriously rebel. Thus, revolts and revolutions against line, language, metaphor, or mode of representation all sound hollow today, since they too have been commoditized, marketed through the dominant institutions, sometimes against the intentions or wishes of their makers, sometimes at the artist's instigation. For example, postwar New York artists embraced abstraction because it seemed to be a way to represent and protest the modern age of alienation and atomic terror. But their "political apoliticism" was soon deployed by various U.S. government agencies as an example of the liberties of the Free World in contrast to Soviet totalitarianism (Guilbaut 1983).

More important than political or commercial co-optation, however, has been the end of the Real. Or, more precisely, late consumer capitalism reverses the statuses of "reality" and "art" in a world that is now experienced as mediated images. Reality becomes a dream world of commodities and signs that aestheticizes everyday life even as it commodifies art (Benjamin 1982, 1236, 1249; see also Buck-Morss 1983; Williams 1992). Then "Art" expires not only because it has lost its ontological priority and sacral aura but also because the quotidian is now thoroughly impregnated with and even visibly constituted of artificial images. With the banalization of culture and the poeticization of the banal, we see in postmodern representations "the liquification of signs and commodities," "the effacement of the boundary between the real and the image," "floating signifiers," and "depthless culture" (Kroker and Cook 1987; Crary 1987; Featherstone 1989).

The postmodern commoditized realism of "anything goes" also involves contradictions in the roles and expectations of artists. With the development of television and recording facilities, the improvement of editing turns performers into athletes who are judged by whether they can reach a "high C" or, conversely, into simulacra of performers who are neither Milli nor Vanilli. Ideologies of art simultaneously stress the depersonalization of the creative process and the glorification of self-images (Gablik 1985, 38–40; Lasch 1978; Lichtman 1982, 225). But these self-images are themselves a creation of the market. Even great conductors such as Sir Colin Davis cannot "record whatever they like. In fact, they have great difficulty, unless they're chosen, groomed, and advertised by their record companies . . . [which] try to market a 'great conductor' " (Davis 1991, 105). In such a context, Roy Lichtenstein's mocking aesthetics of newsprint and comics, Warhol's art of soup cans, or the minimalist and ironic works of playwrights such as Samuel Beckett, antinovelists like Nathalie Sarraute or Alain Robbe-Grillet, or composers such as Cage or Glass, all are reflections both *of* and *on* late capitalist society. This does not mean that the older canons of realism have been supplanted. On the contrary, they remain significant because the vast majority of popular and even many high cultural expressions still conform to realistic codes of representation, however brutal, self-mocking, or phony these may have become. More significantly, these older codes continue to condition the reception of sur-, neo-, hyper-, and antirealist works, as well as postmodern culture in general.

With the loss of shared canons, representation becomes more personal and more depersonalized. Thus, we have an increase in both idiosyncratic freedom and collective alienation. On the one hand, there is the inflationary emotionalism of artists like Burden who "have themselves shot in the arm because one cannot know what it feels like to be shot if one is not shot" or Parr, who uses violence to "get the public implicated" (quoted in Gablik 1985, 49–50). On the other hand, we find manifestos like Mark Rothko's for "a new aesthetics of exclusion, as in his twelve rules for a new academy: no texture, no brushwork or calligraphy, no sketching or drawing, no forms, design, color, light, space, time, movement size or scale; no symbols, images or signs; neither pleasure nor pain" (Clignet 1990, 240). All these interventions erode the orthodox boundaries between simulation and stimulation, creators and publics, presence and representation, and with these, the very understanding of what "realism" could possibly be. Art as a privileged object or experience is now rendered visible as a social construction, and definitions of aesthetic realism are seen to vary culturally and historically, each depending on the reigning code and context.

Coda

Prior to industrialization, academic or individual patrons of art controlled the definitions of both aesthetic propriety and artistic property. Those who owned or commissioned works of art also controlled the definition of realistic representation. During the early phases of industrialization, the growth of private capital stimulated innovations in the economic patronage, aesthetic propriety, and legal property of art. This occurred first in the least expensive and most easily marketable art forms, such as literary books, and later in such media as painting, sculpture, and theater, and finally in architecture and public works. The elites of each period legitimized the emerging practices of new cohorts of artists, just as they used art to legitimize their own political power. Indeed, the shift in rhetoric allowed public authorities to elaborate a legal framework that protected individual creativity. The new ideology allowed artists to ride in the company of scientists and on the coattails of inventors and to claim the right to retain property rights on their artistic works, whose meaning and value were to be determined by the artists' intentions.

The situation is now more complex. Part of this complexity lies in the de-essentialization or de-ontologization of the Real, the True, and the Beautiful. All such ultimates are now radically relativized, and it is no longer possible to establish authoritative and consistent relations between aesthetics, politics, and reality. Moreover, with the increased liquidity of capital, the rise of the mind industry, and the marketing of art by agents, dealers, and museums, art has increasingly turned into a commodity. As the market for art grew and divided, turnover of artists, objects, and codes of aesthetic judgment became more rapid. The result has been the collapse of foundational criteria of aesthetic evaluation. In response or in resistance to market and other forces, artists change the size of their works, their raw materials, production process, or conditions under which these works can be viewed. In so doing, however, artists also challenge any singular reigning definition of aesthetic production and, hence, of artistic property rights.

The main findings of our examples and discussions can now be summarized. "Realism" is a social and stylistic creation. Its principal technique is the thickening of a generic code of representation that is homologous with the dominant ontology of its public. As such, definitions of realism vary culturally and historically from the realism of the Homeric epic for its audiences to the realism of Balzac's novels, each depending on the reigning code and context. In larger societies with a more complex division of social labor, the production of "high" or "national" culture requires significant social investments. That is, to establish and maintain a "regime of signification" involves training and socialization of specialized practitioners, institutions and academies, funding for the support of certified practitioners through retainers and commissions, and the like. Such large-scale investments come not from the artistic or general community, but from the elites who by definition control a disproportionate share of resources for cultural investment. Those artists who become professionalized through academies achieve status, privilege, and prosperity on the condition that they work within artistic paradigms that accord with the ontological and ideological interests of elites. Shifts in class power thus invite shifts in modes of artistic production. This is seen, for example, in the simultaneous rise of importance of the novel and of the middle classes. As the practice of purchasing cultural legitimacy has become more diffuse and fragmented in postmodern society, "realism" has declined along with shared and enforceable standards of what is real, true, beautiful, or art. Artists have a new freedom but also are faced with the penurious struggle for stardom or mere survival in an increasingly commodified market world of art.

Notes

The section on "The Professionalization of Producers of Art" is coauthored with Remí Clignet. Ian Watt's work greatly influences my thinking about the novel. The section on "The French Academy" draws heavily on Vera Zolberg's writings.

1. Alternate accounts of artistic realism are found in MacCabe (1981, 216-35), Abercrombie, Lash, and Longhurst (1981, 115-40), and Bergeson (1984, 187-221). Colin MacCabe identifies realist culture with "closed texts" and nonrealist representations with "open texts," but he tends to ignore the social and historical dimensions of textual production and reception. Nicholas Abercrombie and his colleagues are thoroughly sociological but of somewhat limited historical scope in saying, "To be realist a cultural form must be compatible with an ontology rooted in a secular and scientific cosmology ... that is primarily mechanistic" (1981, 118). Albert Bergesen tries to impose Basil Bernstein's (1984) conception of restricted and elaborated codes respectively onto

"realism" and "abstraction" in styles of New York art from 1940 into the 1980s.

2. One exception was the Imperial Academy founded in Russia in 1757 on the model of the Academy in France. Its graduates faithfully turned out rather stale neoclassical works on mythological and Biblical themes. The Academy exercised paternal supervision over an artist's career even after graduation—down to specifying a painting's subject matter and style. In addition to being the arbiter of lucrative commissions and travel stipends to study the old masters in Europe, the Academy awarded prizes that came with a particular civil service rank and salary (Gambrell 1993, 52). Until 1870, Russian art was almost entirely under the control of the Imperial Academy. Private patronage, greater autonomy of artists, and artistic innovation flourished with the decline of the Russian Empire and its Academy in the late nineteenth century, only to be suppressed in the late 1920s by the Soviet state, which imposed its own academism of socialist realism.

3. For example, "the application of the principles of the exact sciences to the artistic portrayal of facts ... [marked] the victory of the scientific outlook and technological thought over the spirit of idealism and traditionalism" (Hauser 1958, 65). Like the pointilism of Pissarro and Seurat, cubism was announced as a disciplined method for the scientific representation of reality. "But whereas Pissarro and Seurat still sought to represent reality as we see it, Picasso and Braque sought for reality beyond the appearances. Thus they confronted the epistemological problem to which natural scientists had called attention and which had inspired the theories of Karl Marx and Sigmund Freud, namely that the essential structures of reality elude the naked eye and ear. Like science, modernist art represented the desire to cope with the fleeting and contingent world of appearances with a search for the invariant and immutable" (Klamer 1992, 18).

4. The historical emergence of the individual subject is seen in other arts as well. For example, portraits of contemporary individuals were first painted in Renaissance Italy and were a departure from the earlier religious iconographic art. Still, the Renaissance images are of the social personalities of their subjects, expressing their class or rank with a direct gaze at the viewer. In the North and later almost everywhere in Europe, a more interior and psychological representation prevails. See Praz (1974, 164) and Rosenberg (1964, 58, 282).

References Cited

Aaron, Richard Ithamar. 1952. *The Theory of Universals*. Oxford: Oxford University Press.

Abercrombie, Nicholas, Scott Lash, and Brian Longhurst. 1992. "Popular

Representation: Recasting Realism." Pp. 115–40 in *Modernity and Identity*, ed. Scott Lash and Jonathan Friedman. Oxford: Basil Blackwell.

Althusser, Louis. 1970. *For Marx*. Translated by Ben Brewster. New York: Random House.

Altieri, Charles. 1983. "Surrealist 'Materialism.' " Paper presented at the conference "Dali, Surrealism, and the Twentieth-Century Mind," St. Petersburg, Fla.

Appollinaire, Guillaume. 1980. *Calligrammes*. Translated by Anne Hyde. Berkeley: University of California Press.

Barthes, Roland. 1964. "La litterature, aujourd'hui." In *Essais Critiques*. Paris: Editions du Seuil.

Baudrillard, Jean. 1980. "The Implosion of Meaning in the Media and the Implosion of the Social in the Masses." Pp. 137–48 in *The Myths of Information: Technology and Postindustrial Culture*, ed. Kathleen Woodward. Madison, Wisc.: Coda.

———. 1983a. *In the Shadow of Silent Majorities*. New York: Semiotext(e).

———. 1983b. *Simulations*. New York: Semiotext(e).

Baxandall, Michael. 1986. *L'Oeil du Quattrocento*. Paris: Gallimand.

Bayley, John. 1991. "Pasternak's Fairy Tale." *New York Review of Books*, Mar. 7, 12–15.

Bell, Daniel. 1979. "Modernism and Capitalism." Introduction to *Cultural Contradictions of Capitalism*. New York: Basic.

Benjamin, Walter. 1982. *Das Passagen-Werk*. 2 vols. Frankfurt: Suhrkamp.

Bergesen, Albert. 1984. "The Semantic Equation: A Theory of the Social Origin of Art Styles." Pp. 187–221 in *Sociological Theory*, ed. Randall Collins. San Francisco: Jossey-Bass.

Bourdieu, Pierre. 1977. *Outline of a Theory of Practice*. Cambridge: Cambridge University Press.

———. 1984. *Distinction: A Social Critique of the Judgement of Taste*. Translated by Richard Nice. Cambridge, Mass.: Harvard University Press.

Brecht, Bertolt. [1967] 1977. "Against Georg Lukacs." Pp. 68–85 in *Aesthetics and Politics*, by Ernst Bloch, Georg Lukacs, Bertolt Brecht, Walter Benjamin, and Theodor Adorno. London: NLB (first published in *Schriften zur kunst unde Literatur*. Frankfurt: Suhrkamp Verlag).

———. [1954] 1967. "Uber sozialistichen Realismus." *Gersammelte Werke* 19. Frankfurt.

Breslin, James E. B. 1993. *Mark Rothko: A Biography*. Chicago: University of Chicago Press.

Brinkmann, Richard. 1976. *Wirklichkeit und Illusion*. Stuttgart: M. Niemeyer.

Brown, Richard Harvey. 1987. *Society as Text: Essays on Rhetoric, Reason, and Reality*. Chicago: University of Chicago Press.

———. 1989. "Art as a Commodity." Pp. 13–28 in *The Modern Muse: The Support and Condition of Artists*, ed. C. Richard Swaim. New York: American Council for the Arts.

Buck-Morss, Susan. 1983. "Benjamin's Passagen-Werk." *New German Critique* 29:211–40.

Bull, Malcolm. 1991. "How Smart Was Poussin?" *London Review of Books* 4 (April): 12-13.

Bürger, Peter. 1984. *Theory of the Avant Garde.* Manchester, U.K.: Manchester University Press.

Cage, John. 1981. *Empty Words.* Middletown, Conn.: Wesleyan University Press.

Caillois, Roger. 1974. *Approches de l'Imaginaire.* Paris: Gallimard.

Clapp, Jane. 1972. *Art Censorship.* Metuchen, N.J.: Scarecrow Press.

Clastre, Pierre. 1987. *Society Against the State: Essays in Political Anthropology.* New York: Zone.

Clignet, Remi. 1985. *The Structure of Artistic Revolutions.* Philadelphia: University of Pennsylvania Press.

———. 1990. "On Artistic Property and Aesthetic Propriety." *International Journal of Politics, Culture, and Society* 4, no. 2: 229-48.

Coleridge, Samuel Taylor. [1817]. 1965. *Biographic Literaria,* ed. George Watson. London: J. M. Dent.

Corvisier, Andre. 1978. *Arts et Sociétés dans l'Europe du XVIIIe Siècle.* Paris: Presses Universitaires de France.

Crane, Diana. 1987. *The Transformation of the Avant-Garde: The New York Art World.* Chicago: University of Chicago Press.

Crary, J. 1987. "The Eclipse of the Spectacle." In *Art After Modernism,* ed. B. Wallis. New York: Godine.

Danto, Arthur C. 1992. "What Happened to Beauty." *Nation* (March 30): 418-21.

Davis, Sir Colin. 1991. "Some Immortal Peacock." Interview in *Economist* Sept. 28: 105.

Descartes, René. 1954. *Descartes: Philosophical Writings, A Selection,* ed. Elizabeth Anscombe and Peter Geach. Edinburgh: Thomas Nelson.

DiMaggio, Paul J. 1987. "Classification in Art." *American Sociological Review* 52: 440-55.

Dorment, Richard. 1993. "The Genius of Gin Lane." *New York Review of Books,* May 27, 17-20.

Eisenstein, Sergei. [1929] 1963. "The Cinematographic Principle and the Ideogram." *Film Forum.* London.

Elias, Norbert. 1978. *The Civilizing Process.* Translated by Edmund Jephcott. New York: Urizen.

Featherstone, Mike. 1989. "Postmodernism and the Aestheticization of Everyday Life." Pp. 265-90 in *Modernism and Identity,* ed. Scott Lash and Jonathan Friedman. London: Radius Books.

Fisher, Walter. 1987. *Human Communication as Narration: Toward a Philosophy of Reason, Value, and Action.* Columbia: University of South Carolina Press.

Foster, Hal. 1987. *Discussions in Contemporary Culture.* Seattle: Bay Press.

Foucault, Michel. 1980. *Power/Knowledge: Selected Interviews and Other Writings, 1972-1977*, ed. Colin Gordon. New York: Pantheon.

Frank, Manfred. 1986. *Die Unhintegesbarkeit von Individualität*. Frankfurt am Main: Suhrkamp.

Franscina, Francis, and Charles Harrison, eds. 1982. *Modern Art and Modernism*. New York: Harper and Row.

Fried, Michael. 1990. *Courbet's Realism*. Chicago: University of Chicago Press.

Gablik, Suzi. 1985. *Has Modernism Failed?* New York: Thames and Hudson.

Gambrell, Jamey. 1993. "Art and the Great Utopia." *New York Review of Books*, Apr. 22, 53-59.

Guilbaut, Serge. 1983. *How New York Stole the Idea of Modern Art: Abstract Expressionism, Freedom, and the Cold War*. Chicago: University of Chicago Press.

Habermas, Jurgen. 1987. *The Philosophical Discourse of Modernity*. Translated by Frederick Lawrence. Cambridge, Mass.: MIT Press.

Hallyn, Fernand. 1990. *The Poetic Structure of the World: Copernicus and Kepler*. New York: Zone.

Harms, Wolfgang. 1986. "Significant Objects: A Possibility of Realism in Early Narratives." Pp. 12-27 in *Realism in European Literature*, ed. Nicholas Boyle and Martin Swales. Cambridge: Cambridge University Press.

Hasan, Saiyid Zafar. 1928. *Realism*. Cambridge: Cambridge University Press.

Haskell, Francis. 1963. *Patrons and Painters*. New York: Knopf.

Hauser, Arnold. 1958. *The Social History of Art*. Vol. 4. New York: Knopf.

———. 1982. *The Sociology of Art*. Translated by Kenneth J. Northcott. Chicago: University of Chicago Press.

Heath, Stephen. 1986. "Realism, Modernism, and 'Language-Consciousness.'" Pp. 103-22 in *Realism in European Literature*, ed. Nicholas Boyle and Martin Swales. Cambridge: Cambridge University Press.

Hegel, Georg W. F. 1956. *The Philosophy of History*. New York: Dover.

Hesse, Carla. 1991. "Enlightenment Epistemology and the Laws of Authorship in Revolutionary France, 1777-1793." Pp. 109-37 in *Law and the Order of Culture*, ed. Robert Post. Berkeley: University of California Press.

Horwitz, Morton J. 1977. *The Transformation of American Law*. Cambridge, Mass.: Harvard University Press.

Hulse, Clark. 1990. *The Rule of Art: Literature and Painting in the Renaissance*. Chicago: University of Chicago Press.

Hume, David. 1882. "On the Standard of Taste." In *Essays Moral, Political, and Literary*. London: Longmans, Green.

Jakobson, Roman. 1971. "On Realism in Art." Pp. 38-46 in *Readings in*

Russian Poetics: Formalist and Structuralist Views, ed. Ladislaw Matejka and Krystyna Pomorska. Cambridge, Mass.: MIT Press.

Kaplan, Amy. 1988. *The Social Construction of American Realism.* Chicago: University of Chicago Press.

Klamer, Arjo. 1992. "About Modernism, Art, and Economics." Unpublished ms. Department of Economics, George Washington University, Washington, D.C.

Koselleck, Reinhardt. 1985. "Neuzeit." Pp. 231–66 in *Futures Past: On the Semantics of Historical Time.* Cambridge, Mass.: MIT Press.

Kostelanetz, Richard. 1993. *Dictionary of the Avant-Gardes.* Pennington, N.J.: A Cappella Books.

Kramer, Hilton. 1982a. "Editorial." *The New Criterion* 1, no. 1.

———. 1982b. "Postmodern: Art and Culture in the 1980s." *The New Criterion* 1, no. 1: 36–42.

Kroker, A., and D. Cook. 1987. *The Postmodern Science.* New York: St. Martin's Press.

Lasch, Christopher. 1978. *The Culture of Narcissism.* New York: Norton.

Leed, Eric. 1980. " 'Voice' and 'Print': Master Symbols in the History of Communication." Pp. 41–61 in *The Myths of Information: Technology and Cultural in Postindustrial Culture,* ed. Kathleen Woodward. Madison, Wisc.: Coda.

Levine, Joseph M. 1991. *The Battle of the Books: History and Literature in the Augustan Age.* Ithaca, N.Y.: Cornell University Press.

Locke, John. [1690] 1974. *Essay Concerning Human Understanding.* New York: AMS Press.

Lichtman, Richard. 1982. *The Production of Desire.* New York: Free Press.

Luhmann, Niklaus. 1987. "The Representation of Society within Society." *Current Sociology* 35, no. 2: 101–8.

Lyotard, Jean-François. 1985. *The Postmodern Condition: A Report on Knowledge.* Minneapolis: University of Minnesota Press.

MacCabe, Colin. 1981. "Realism and the Cinema: Notes on Some Brechtian Theses." Pp. 216–35 in *Popular Television and Film,* ed. T. Bennett et al. London: British Film Institute/Open University Press.

MacIntyre, Alasdair. 1980. "Epistemological Crises, Dramatic Narrative, and the Philosophy of Science." Pp. 54–74 in *Paradigms and Revolutions: Applications and Appraisals of Thomas Kuhn's Philosophy of Science,* ed. Gary Gutting. Notre Dame, Ind.: University of Notre Dame Press.

Matisse, Henri. [1943] 1972. "Matisse-en-France." Pp. 110–11 in *Dessins: Thèmes et Variations,* by Henri Matisse. Paris: Martin Fabiani. Translated in Louis Aragon, *Henri Matisse: A Novel.* Vol 1. New York: Harcourt Brace Jovanovich.

McKeon, Michael. 1987. *The Origins of the English Novel, 1600–1740.* Baltimore: Johns Hopkins University Press.

Merton, Robert K. 1973. *Sociology of Science.* Chicago: University of Chicago Press.

Mesnard, André-Hubert. 1974. *La Politique culturelle de l'Etat.* Paris: Presses Universitaires de France.

Mousnier, Roland. 1984. *The Institutions of France under the Absolute Monarchy, 1598–1789, Vol. II: The Organs of State and Society.* Translated by Arthur Goldhammer. Chicago: University of Chicago Press.

Ortega y Gasset, José. 1956. *Velázques.* Madrid: Revista del Occidente.

———. 1977. *Idea del Teatro.* Madrid: Revista del Occidente.

Panofsky, Erwin. [1927] 1991. *Perspective as Symbolic Form.* New York: Zone.

Paulson, Ronald. 1991. *Hogarth.* New Brunswick, N.J.: Rutgers University Press.

Praz, Mario. 1974. *Mnemosyne: The Parallel Between Literature and the Visual Arts.* Princeton, N.J.: Princeton University Press.

Riffaterre, Michel. 1984. "Intertextual Representation: On Mimesis as Interpretive Discourse." *Critical Inquiry* 11, no. 1: 141–62.

Rose, Mark. 1993. *Authors and Owners: The Invention of Copyright.* Cambridge, Mass.: Harvard University Press.

Rosenberg, Harold. 1977. "Being Outside." *New Yorker,* Mar. 24: 69–75.

Rosenberg, Jakob. 1964. *Rembrandt, Life and Work.* London: Phaidon.

Schowalter, E. 1984. "Women Who Write Are Women." *New York Times Book Review.* Dec. 16.

"Selling of Andy Warhol, The." 1988. *Newsweek,* Apr. 18, 60–72.

Shapiro, Michael J. 1988. *The Politics of Representation: Writing Practices in Biography, Photography, and Policy Analysis.* Madison: University of Wisconsin Press.

Signac, Paul. 1987. *D'Eugène Delacroix au néo-impressionnisme.* Paris: Hermann.

Stern, J. P. 1973. *On Realism.* London: Routledge and Kegan Paul.

Swift, Jonathan. [1710] 1940. *The Prose Works of Jonathan Swift, vol. III: The Examiner and Other Pieces Written in 1710–11,* ed. Herbert Davis. Oxford: Blackwell.

Thompson, Michael. 1979. *Rubbish Theory: The Creation and Destruction of Value.* Oxford: Oxford University Press.

Todorov, Tzvetzn. 1977. *The Poetics of Prose.* Ithaca, N.Y.: Cornell University Press.

Trabant, Jürgen. 1991. "Le style est l'homme même. Quel homme?" *Comparativo* 2-3:57–72.

Valkenier, Elizabeth Kride. 1990. *Ilya Repin and the World of Russian Art.* New York: Columbia University Press.

Veblen, Thorstein. 1979. *The Theory of the Leisure Class.* New York: Penguin.

Venturi, Robert, Denis Scott-Brown, and Steven Izenour. 1972. *Learning from Las Vegas.* Cambridge, Mass.: MIT Press.

Warnke, Martin. 1993. *The Court Artist: On the Ancestry of the Modern Artist.* Cambridge, Mass.: Cambridge University Press.

Watt, Ian. 1957. *The Rise of the Novel: Studies in Defoe, Richardson, and Fielding.* Berkeley: University of California Press.

White, Harrison C., and Cynthia A. White. 1991. *Canvases and Careers: Institutional Change in the French Painting World.* Chicago: University of Chicago Press.

Williams, Raymond. 1973. "Base and Superstructure in Marxist Cultural Theory." *New Left Review* 82:31–49.

———. 1981. *Sociology of Culture.* New York: Schocken.

Williams, Rosalind H. 1992. *Dream Worlds: Mass Consumption in Late Nineteenth-Century France.* Berkeley: University of California Press.

Woodmansee, Martha. 1984. *The Author, Art, and the Market: Rereading the History of Aesthetics.* New York: Columbia University Press.

Zolberg, Vera. 1989. "Remaking Nations: Public Culture and Postcolonial Discourse." Unpublished ms. Department of Sociology, New School of Social Research, New York.

8 Dangerous Liaisons: The Reproduction of Woman in Roland Barthes and Jacques Derrida

Linda S. Kauffman

A remarkable conjunction of events took place in Paris between 1975 and 1977: Jacques Lacan offered a seminar on the love letter (FS); Roland Barthes conducted a seminar on *The Sorrows of Young Werther*, which was later transformed into *A Lover's Discourse* (ALD), and Jacques Derrida began writing *The Post Card: From Socrates to Freud and Beyond* (PC), which was followed by the publication of Julia Kristeva's *Tales of Love* (1987). Each of these texts engages—directly and indirectly—in dialogue with the others, and each attempts to confront the dilemma that Kristeva (1987) describes: "The delight and anguish of that freedom [to invent love] are intensified today because we lack a code of love; no stable mirrors for the loves of a period, group, or class. The analyst's couch is the only place where the social contract explicitly authorizes a search for love—albeit a private one."[1] The crucial contribution of Barthes in *A Lover's Discourse* and Derrida in *The Post Card* is their attempt to unsettle the dichotomies between public/private, erudition/eros, and male/female and to rewrite the social contract by shifting the exploration of love from the analyst's couch to the social arena.

The French have always been pretty interested in love, but what distinguishes their investigations from those of the Americans is that in contemporary America love is represented as a disease, dysfunction, or addiction for which we can find the cure by reading such books as *Men Who Hate Women and Women Who Love Them; Kiss Sleeping Beauty Goodbye; The Dance-Away Lover, The Peter Pan Principle,*

Co-dependent No More, and Women Who Love Too Much. These books are targeted for an exclusively female audience; they are relentless in their insistence on compulsory heterosexuality; and they reproduce such tired stereotypes as that of Woman as victim, love junkie, and masochist. *These* are the books that are seriously engaged in reproducing femininity for mass consumption. Such books are manifestations in popular psychology of the stranglehold exercised by the American psychoanalytic establishment, which disseminates the ideology of normality, wholeness, uniqueness, coherence, and unity of the individual subject. In so doing, it represses Freud's most radical assertion: that our subjectivity is not our own. This—rather than sexuality—is the scandal of psychoanalysis.

Poststructuralists Who Love Too Much: it does not have quite the same ring to it! The French theorists investigate love's philosophical foundations, its linguistic structure, psychic configurations, ideology, and their effects. Long before Pierre-Ambroise-François Choderlos de Laclos (1741-1803), the French were interested in writing the *social* text of love, in classifying its *representations*. Indeed François de La Rochefoucauld's (1613-1680) famous maxim could serve as the motto of both Barthes and Derrida: "There is only one love and a thousand *copies* of it"—an aphorism that radically undermines the claims of uniqueness and individuality so central to the Americans' conception. In the literary salons of seventeenth-century Paris, Questions of Love were consistently the focal point of philosophical debate. Barthes quotes another of La Rouchefoucald's maxims, one that is particularly relevant to discourse theory: "Some people would never have been in love if they never heard love talked about."

Barthes's and Derrida's deconstructions of love have important implications for contemporary feminism, which is presently at a critical crossroads. I am alluding to the exhortations of some critics, such as Nancy Miller, Elaine Showalter, Nina Baym, Nina Auerbach, Carolyn Heilbrun, Naomi Schor, and Jane Tompkins, to return to personal criticism. Their cautionary tales construct a narrative in which naive feminists play the role of the virtuous Madame de Tourvel in Laclos's *Les Liaisons dangereuses* (1782) and in which theorists like Barthes and Derrida play the role of Valmont, dangerously enticing us with their elegant, seductive poststructuralist rhetoric. Tompkins (1989) defines theory as "male" and warns that "theory is one of the patriarchal gestures women ought to avoid." She argues that "the female subject par excellence which is herself and her experiences, has once more been elided by literary criticism." It is no accident that Tompkins's work valorizes Sentimental Power or that in the same essay ("Me and My Shadow") she exhorts her readers to get in touch with their feelings by reading M. Scott Peck, Leo Busgalia, David Burns, and the other popularizers of feel-good psychology in America (David Burns's book is actually entitled *Feeling Good*).

I call this *strain* (in both senses of the word) in feminist thought the therapeutic school of feminism. I do not believe there are such constructs as either "male theory" or, conversely, "women's ways of knowing." I do not believe in "Sentimental Power." What some seem to have forgotten is that such dichotomies return us to an earlier mode of discourse that celebrated the uniqueness of the female self, an argument based on the philosophy of individualistic subjectivism. Ironically, the argument that women can only write about themselves and their experiences has been the cornerstone of *sexist* criticism of women writers and poets ranging from Sappho to Anne Sexton: the emphasis on form, craft, and artifice is overlooked entirely by critics eager to connect the ink with which one writes to the body that bleeds, lactates, and weeps. Such dichotomies simply lock us back into the very stereotypes (male intellect versus female intuition, the head versus the body, etc.) that we have spent so much time dismantling.

My aim in this essay is not to serve as an apologist for either Barthes or Derrida, for their amorous discourses are neither faultless nor feminist. In some ways they replicate the very tradition of phallic discourse that they claim to be trying to displace. But by shifting the paradigm from individual therapy to conceptual transformation, their texts offer themselves (sometimes consciously, sometimes unconsciously) to feminist intervention. By mining the topos of femininity so systematically, their amorous discourses meticulously show how Woman is "produced."

Roland Barthes and Jacques Derrida show what feminism stands to gain by questioning the connections between gender and identity in the two texts examined here. If Viktor Shklovsky keened the death of story, plot, and character in *Zoo, or Letters Not About Love* (1923), *A Lover's Discourse* and *The Post Card* hammer the nails into the coffin. In multiple senses, *A Lover's Discourse* and *The Post Card* are wakes, simultaneously commemorating and contributing to the deaths of the author, of Literature, and of the unitary subject. Both texts are archeological "desedimentations" of Western mythologies about literature and culture. Their aim is to stretch language to its limits and "beyond"—beyond the pleasure principle, the narratable, the constraints of genre and gender. Most remarkable of all, they try to go beyond totalizing theories—including even poststructuralism, on those occasions when it threatens to become potentially totalizing. Just as Shklovsky goes beyond Russian formalism in *Zoo*, Barthes and Derrida expose the aporias of poststructuralism in their texts. It is as if they unweave by night the theories they weave by day, a metaphor they each consciously invoke. Their projects overlap in numerous ways, but in this chapter I will focus solely on one major switch point (what Derrida calls *coup d'aiguillage*): the ways in which Woman is "produced" in these texts.

The concept of the simulacrum is crucial to the production of Woman, for Barthes and Derrida see Woman as a writing effect rather than an intrinsic essence. Insofar as their discourses attempt to "write from the place of Woman," we may ask, what is that place, and how is Woman conceived? Do they invent a new conceptual space named "Woman," or do they merely reinscribe outworn stereotypes? What are the implications of using Woman as a rhetorical topos and figure?

Before we can assess their representation of the feminine, we have to know what is being represented, which entails a reconsideration of genre. Both authors choose the epistle because from the *Heroides* to Héloise, from *Letters of a Portuguese Nun* (LPN) to *Clarissa,* it has traditionally been considered the feminine mode par excellence. Derrida describes his project as a "fiction," one that consciously parodies "epistolary or detective literature (from the Philosophical Letters to the Portuguese nun, from the *liaisons dangereuses* to Milena)" (PC 179). He mimics the disorder of the Portuguese nun's rhetoric since, in the seventeenth century, to write *à la Portugaise* meant specifically to be carried away by passion, irrationality, and disorder (Kauffman 1986). Just as the nun laments, "I no longer know who I am or what I am doing," Derrida echoes, "I no longer know what I am doing, and how I am 'scratching,' if I am erasing or writing what I am 'saving.' I no longer know which complicity to count on. . . . You have taken back your name. You have taken mine and I no longer know who I am. Your wife, of course, but what does that mean now?" (PC 229). I will return to Derrida's comic disruption of gender categories presently. For the moment, I want to point out similar allusions to the *Portuguese Letters* in Barthes's text. In the nun's last letter, her epiphany comes when she writes, "I discovered that it was not so much you as my own passion to which I was attached; it was remarkable how I suffered while struggling with it even after you had become despicable to me through your wretched behavior." Barthes admits that "it is my desire I desire, and the loved being is no more than its tool. I rejoice at the thought of such a great cause, which leaves far behind it the person whom I have made into its pretext. . . . And if a day comes when I must bring myself to renounce the other, the violent mourning which then grips me is the mourning of the image-repertoire itself: it was a beloved structure, and I weep for the loss of love, not of him or her" (ALD 31). *Letters of a Portuguese Nun* is a crucial antecedent for Barthes and Derrida because of the myriad ways it reproduces the fictiveness of epistolary production. The lover and addressee constitute a double-edged interiority: from the very first paragraph, the nun refers to her grief, "imaginative as it is" (339). Writing fuels imagination which fuels desire; the purpose is to keep the circuit of desire open long after the beloved has ceased to matter.

Derrida similarly exploits the ambiguities of address when he asks, "When I call you my love, my love, is it you I am calling or my love? You, my love, is it you I thereby name, is it to you that I address myself?" (PC 8). This query is both an echo and an analysis of the first words of *Letters of a Portuguese Nun,* for *tutoiement* is self-reflexive as well as being a familiar form of address to the beloved. It signals from the outset the self-divisions of identity and the insistence of the interior voice. The nun's first words exploit this ambiguity: "Consider, my love, how extremely lacking you have been in foresight. You have been betrayed, miserable one, and you have betrayed me with false hopes. A passion on which you have built so many prospects for pleasure can give you now nothing but mortal despair, equalled only by the cruelty of the separation which causes it" (LPN 339). Although the nun seems to be addressing the chevalier who seduced and abandoned her, her primary addressee is interior, for it is she who has lacked foresight; it is she who has been betrayed by false hopes. Blurring of the boundaries between interior/exterior, self/other, and subject/object recurs throughout Barthes's and Derrida's discourses.

The *Letters of a Portuguese Nun* is a crucial antecedent for Barthes and Derrida for other reasons: it has been the focal point in a three-century debate about the relationship of signature to authenticity, of feminine versus masculine writing styles, and of identity's foundation in gender. Many critics (including La Bruyère, Laclos, Stendhal, Sainte-Beuve, and Rilke) insisted that only a woman could have written in a style so passionate, disordered, and vehement. The letters had such a phenomenal impact on both sides of the English Channel that to write à *la Portugaise* became a veritable code for a certain style of writing-to-the-moment, at the height of passion and distress. Barthes and Derrida would also be aware of the researchers' discoveries in the early 1960s that seemed to prove definitively that—far from being the spontaneous overflowing of powerful feelings in a woman's hand—the letters were written by a man. Although the dispute is far from settled, Barthes and Derrida are less interested in its resolution than in its symbolic significance. Thus, to argue that Barthes and Derrida write "from the place of Woman," one must acknowledge that that place is unlocatable, unstable, oscillating. Elsewhere, Derrida defines the place of Woman as a "nonplace"; to write from it or in it is to situate oneself in the realm of the undecidable (Derrida 1979, 111-13, 119-21). Although interpretation, desire, destinations also may be undecidable, they do not have the same equivalence. Woman has a special status; Derrida's deconstructive project of invagination represents Woman as a destabilizing force that makes propriation, property, propriety, and paternity undecidable. This project has an apocalyptic and utopic aspect, as Derrida explains elsewhere. He seems to echo Shklovsky's praise for the painter who was not bad, though saccharine; just as Shklovsky instantly amends the statement by reflecting that the painter was probably a good painter *because* of the saccharine quality, Derrida reflects that Woman, "because she is a good model, she is in fact a bad model. She plays at dissimulation, at ornamentation, deceit, artifice, at an artist's philosophy. Hers is an affirmative power. And if she continues to be condemned, it is only from the man's point of view where she repudiates that affirmative power and, in her specular reflection of that foolish dogmatism that she has provoked, belies her belief in truth" (Derrida 1979, 67-68). The equivocal punning illustrates the intransigence of binary thinking: truth/artifice, man/woman, affirm/deny. Derrida and Barthes consciously strive to denaturalize gender, to defamiliarize metaphor, and to undermine the assumptions of Western metaphysics by exposing its reliance on binary oppositions. By approaching the feminine as a writing effect, the multiplicity of signifiers creates chains of supplements without origin or end.

Barthes also exploits the traditional associations of the feminine with solitary waiting, weaving, and writing. Just as the Portuguese nun transforms the chevalier's absence into "an ordeal of abandonment," Barthes notes: "Historically, the discourse of absence is carried on by the Woman: Woman is sedentary, Man hunts, journeys: Woman is faithful (she waits), man is fickle (he sails away, he cruises). It is woman who gives shape to absence, elaborates its fiction, for she has time to do so; she weaves and she sings; the Spinning Songs express both immobility (by the hum of the Wheel) and absence (far away, rhythms of travel, sea surges, cavalcades)"

(ALD 14). Having defined Woman's mythic place, Barthes proceeds to situate himself in it. He is the One Who Waits: he waits for the telephone to ring; he waits in cafés; he waits in hotels, filled with anxiety. Like the Portuguese nun, he turns his role as lover into a vocation; his behavior and dress become ascetic: "I shall chasten my body: cut my hair very short, conceal my eyes behind dark glasses (a way of taking the veil)" (ALD 33). As victim, as sufferer, he thus assumes the feminine posture: he tries to make his beloved feel guilty by "representing his unhappiness"; he accentuates his pathos. (The code of pathos is perhaps the most gender-inflected of all codes, as Barthes suggests in S/Z when La Zambinella appeals to Sarrasine on "her" knees, arms outstretched [Barthes 1974, 168-69, 195].) Barthes would argue that, rather than seeing men as masculine or women as feminine, gender is situational, structured by differential relations. Even when the lover is male (as in *Werther*), whenever the situation involves passion, especially in its etymological sense of suffering, he is feminized: "In any man who utters the other's absence *something feminine* is declared: this man who waits and who suffers from his waiting is miraculously feminized. A man is not feminized because he is inverted but because he is in love. Myth and utopia: the origins have belonged, the future will belong to the subject in whom there is something feminine" (ALD 14). Barthes traces the topos of femininity from Werther to Marcel Proust to Rohmer; the figures he finds range backward and forward in literary history, and by reenacting the repertoire he takes his place as a fictional character, consciously "novelized" as well as feminized. This is not an act of appropriation, since the feminine, as we have seen, is marked specifically by its disruption of the proper, propriety, and property. Nor is it an act of nostalgia or some weird kind of womb envy. Those clichés reveal how deeply ingrained the habit is of assuming that gender is the foundation of identity.

As the peripatetic professor in *The Post Card*, Derrida seems to fulfill the "masculine" role of being constantly in motion. But he simultaneously assumes the stereotypically passive feminine role. He is simultaneously mobile and immobile, seizing every opportunity on the train to be *en train d'écrire en genoux*; his knees are his laptop desk. *Genoux* in French sounds like *je nous*, as in *Je nous écrit* (one part of "To Speculate" is entitled "I Writes Us" [PC 273]). The purposeful polyphony of *genoux/je nous* exploits the ambiguity of the lover as "several"; he plays different roles, has several functions, and speaks in different voices. *Je nous* also signifies the ways in which the lovers are (or desire to be) united (sexually, emotionally, intel-

lectually): "I" am "myself," but "I" am also in "you" and a part of "us."
The subject/object dichotomy divides each of us from ourselves as
well as from each other; like language itself, each of us is irreparably
self-divided.

Derrida effects a perceptible displacement in the stereotyping that
identifies the male as active and the female as passive. Despite his
travels, his role is feminine: like Barthes, he, too, is the One Who
Waits. Just as Shklovsky writes under an injunction not to speak of
love, Derrida laments numerous interdictions: the Law of the Father,
the entire system by which the "postal principle" interdicts desire,
and the beloved's determination to end the affair: "You terrify me,
you are bad for me, when will I cease to be afraid of you, of the entire
picture that you send back? I don't even know if I desire it. Perhaps I
would no longer love you, and yet I don't love you, not you, to the
extent that I am afraid and to the extent that, as I am doing here, on
the eve of this return from which I fear the worst, I am writing under
your threat" (PC 38). By passively waiting to learn the outcome of his
lover's determination, Derrida "accepts" the feminine role. She acts,
he receives; she decides, he acquiesces. His repeated refrain is *J'accept,*
which parallels what Barthes calls the "non-will-to-possess." Indeed,
one of Barthes's and Derrida's major motives for writing from the place
of the feminine is to subvert the phallic dominance that has ordered
and tyrannized discourse from Socrates forward. This is why Barthes's
discourse has so many allusions to Zen, Tao, and the Nietzschean
notion of the non-will-to-possess: "I let desire circulate within me . . . to
let come (from the other) what comes, to let pass (from the other)
what goes; to possess nothing, to repel nothing: to receive, not to
keep, to produce without appropriating" (ALD 232–34). The feminine
signifies not just the undecidability of ownership but the relinquishment
of all designs of mastery and competition. To ask whether the amorous discourses of Barthes and Derrida succeed or fail is to participate in the very logic they strive to circumvent, the logic that divides
all activity into win/lose, victory/defeat, vanquisher/victimized.
Barthes observes:

> The world subjects every enterprise to an alternative; that of
> success or failure, of victory or defeat. I protest by another logic: I
> am simultaneously and contradictorily happy and wretched; "to
> succeed" or "to fail" have for me only contingent, provisional
> meanings (which doesn't keep my sufferings and my desires from
> being violent); what inspires me, secretly and stubbornly, is not a
> tactic: I accept and I affirm, beyond truth and falsehood, beyond
> success and failure; I have withdrawn from all finality, I live

according to chance (as is evidenced by the fact that the figures in my discourse occur to me like so many dice casts). (ALD 22-23)

Derrida has the same reasons for poking fun at the antics of scholars scurrying to interpret everything in terms of *arrive* or *do.* He, too, emphasizes chance, fortune, and gambling in references ranging from Matthew Paris's fortune-telling book to his own obsession with numerology. *Jacques sept,* for instance, sounds identical to *J'accept;* as with "Giacomo Joyce," Derrida shows how language aurally as well as ontologically enacts its own slippages. Even as he deconstructs origins and apocalypse, he is fascinated with them, along with all first and last things, including the origins and endings of the epistolary genre and of love affairs. He makes much of the fact that his first and last names each have seven letters and relates that to the seventh book of Plato and the number seven in the Book of the Apocalypse. "Sept" also sounds like the "set" of set theory, the paradigm of his entire epistolary project (PC xiv-xv, xxvii). More generally, he examines the implications of accepting the beyond—of destiny, of good and evil, of the pleasure principle. His postscript, "Du Tout," may be Derrida's attempt to take step after step "beyond the abyssal limits of theoretical production where reading and writing, fact and fiction, become undecidable. And this postscript shows either that he could not do it at all, or how those steps relate to the 'all' of psychoanalysis" (Spivak 1984). Just as language is singular in its resistance to singularity, Derrida's and Barthes's achievements resist definition in terms of success or failure. Their aim is precisely to posit a (feminine) alogic, one whose asymmetry renders undecidable the outcome of all competition and rivalry (Socratic, Platonic, Oedipal, Freudian, etc.).

Since gender is commonly perceived as the fundamental attribute of identity, one of the main ways that Barthes and Derrida subvert attempts to read their discourses autobiographically is by undermining gender categories. At some points Barthes refers to his lover as male, but he often resorts to a variety of strategies to avoid identification by gender—a difficult feat, given the structure of the French language. Instead of referring to the addressee as "he" or "she," he frequently refers to "the loved object," in order to remind us repeatedly that the addressee has been objectified in the lover's image-repertoire. He emphasizes the specularity of the lover's imaginary processes for the same reason; what the lover perceives is a projection of internal obsessions, neuroses, and desires. The technique resembles that in *Roland Barthes* (1977) where he sometimes refers to "I" and sometimes to "he"; from the first page, he mandates that what follows "must be considered as if spoken by a character in a novel." In *A Lover's Discourse*, as he explains to Philippe Roger: "I was careful to de-emphasize the sexual difference. Unfortunately, French is not a language that makes this kind of thing very easy. 'The beloved object' has the advantage of being an expression that doesn't take sides on the sex of whom one loves. . . . The beloved is inevitably an object, is not experienced at all as a subject. 'Object' is the right word, because it indicates the depersonalization of the beloved" (Barthes 1985, 293). Derrida frequently exploits the same ambiguity in *The Post Card* by using indirect objects without antecedents, as in his use of the word *lui*, which can refer either to him or her (PC xxiv). At some points, he uses feminine pronouns when referring to the beloved but elsewhere he repudiates the notion that his letters are addressed to a woman: "To reach the conclusion . . . that I am certainly writing to a woman . . . would be as daring, in your case, as using it to infer the color of your hair" (PC 79). *Envois* forces readers to recognize the extent to which they project the binary oppositions writer/reader and man/woman into the reading process:

> *La séance continue,* how do you analyze that? I'm talking grammar, as always, is it a verb or an adjective? These are the right questions. . . . (I am saying this in order to reassure you: they will believe that we are two, that it's you and me, that we are legally and sexually identifiable, unless they wake up one day). . . . Now all possible accidents might happen in the interval that separates the subject (who says I) and his attribute. By saying I only, I do not unveil my sex, I am a subject without a sexual predicate, this is what had to be demonstrated about "S is p," this is the performance. (PC 178-79)

When gender is undecidable, the entire psychoanalytic structure that erects Oedipus as the master trope is displaced. Barthes's and Derrida's discourses demonstrate that whether one invokes the imaginary processes of identification or the symbolic processes of differentiation, one is oedipalized in either case. Whether viewed as a family crisis or as a structure in which mother and father are replaced by institutions functioning as Mother and Father, it is difficult to go beyond the oedipalizing constraints of Western thought.[1] That is why Derrida places so much emphasis in the *au delà*, the "beyond" in his subtitle. Barthes, too, explores the possibility of living beyond the father's law, beyond all law. "The great problem," says Barthes, "is to outplay the signified, to outplay law, to outplay the father, to outplay the repressed—I do not say to explode it, but to outplay it" (Barthes 1982). Paradoxically, psychoanalysis was the first "science" both to explore that possibility and to repress it (Deleuze and Guattari 1983 [hereinafter cited as DG], Chaps. 2 and 4; Rubin 1975; Rose 1986, 80–81, 101–3). As long as sexuality is kept within narcissistic, oedipal, and castrating coordinates, it will always be subject to repression (DG 351); to displace those coordinates, Barthes and Derrida exploit a libidinal economy that oscillates between male and female, hetero-sexuality and homosexuality. Derrida writes: "I owe it to you to have discovered homosexuality, and ours is indestructible. I owe you everything and I owe you nothing at all. We are of the same sex" (PC 53).

Their discourses, however, are not merely celebrations of trans-gression. One cannot simply step outside the entire discursive appa-ratus of lack, castration, law, cure. Nor does transgression become a reality simply by formulating a wish. Instead, they consistently reveal their own entrapment in discursive systems that define by dividing and differentiating. They formulate (directly and indirectly) a dia-logic series of fragmentary philosophical questions, a mode that has its own venerable tradition, dating from the Socratic dialogues to the Questions of Love formulated in the literary salons of seventeenth-century Paris: How might we envision a "beyond" that is social, utopic, post-Freudian, and postrepresentational? What might desire be like if we could separate it from the Oedipus complex? How might we stimulate desiring-production in the unconscious? What role(s) does the feminine play in desiring-production? Their discourses can perhaps best be described as provisionary, speculative responses (rather than answers or solutions) to the questions raised by Gilles Deleuze and Félix Guattari:

> How to produce, how to think about fragments whose sole relation-ship is sheer difference—fragments that are related to one another only in that each of them is different—without having recourse either to any sort of original totality (not even one that has been lost), or to a subsequent totality that may not yet have come about? It is only the category of multiplicity, used as a substantive and going beyond both the One and the many, beyond the predicative relation of the One and the many, that can account for desiring-production: desiring-production is pure multiplicity, that is to say, an affirmation that is irreducible to any sort of unity. (1983, 42)

This passage illuminates Barthes's and Derrida's motives for refus-ing to resolve their discourses into a unified whole, their resistance to all reductive systems, and their valorization of paradox, fragmentation, contradiction, and multiplicity. It also explains their repeated allusions to "desiring-production," by which I mean the activity of the unconscious, which cannot be contained, assimilated, or censored. Derrida describes the unconscious in a continuous process of production: "Trrr goes the machine on which I am preparing in sum the critical apparatus of our love letter in order to take them away in advance from every center of, as they say, genetic criticism. Not a sketch will remain to uncover the traces. Trrr, *je trame*, I weave, *je trie*, I sort, I treat, I traffic, I transfer, I intricate, I control, *je filtre*, I filter" (PC 232).

At many points, it almost seems as if Derrida's text is a duet with *A Lover's Discourse*, for Barthes says, "I spin, unwind, and weave the lover's case, and begin all over again (these are the meanings of the Greek verb *meruomaî*: to spin, to unwind, to weave)" (ALD 160). That they both figure the unconscious as feminine is hardly a new idea when we consider the etymology of "hysteria." They evoke Penelope at her loom, unweaving by night what she weaves by day, as well as Arachne the spider, weaving her intricate web. Derrida's allusion to "transfer" refers to psychoanalytic transference; "traffic" similarly suggests Freud's discussion of " 'associative traffic' apropros of hysteria and hypnosis" (ALD 90), an allusion repeated by Barthes. Thus, for both theorists, the production of Woman is intricately interwoven with the production of psychoanalysis. Their amorous discourses are experiments in delirious writing, in writing hysteria, discourses of the other.

Lacan, whose seminar on the love letter (hereinafter cited as FS) preceded the publication of Barthes's and Derrida's texts, haunts both and is evoked directly and indirectly in numerous allusions. In this seminar, Lacan elaborates his theory that, to man, woman is a symptom. He defines "symptom" as "that something which dallies with the unconscious" (FS). To constitute a symptom, the patient must believe in it:

> In the life of a man, a woman is something he believes in. . . . Anyone who comes to us with a symptom, believes in it.
>
> If he asks for our assistance or help, it is because he believes that the symptom is capable of saying something, and that it only needs deciphering. The same goes for a woman, except that it can happen that one believes her effectively to be saying something. That's when things get stopped up—to believe in, one believes her. It's what's called love. . . . Hence the common saying that love is madness. (FS 168-70)

Both Derrida and Barthes use their discourses to reflect on the processes of the mirror stage, that stage of development when, according to Lacan, the infant first perceives the subject/object dichotomy and establishes a specular image of ideality, unity, and harmony from which she or he feels alienated. Lacan maintains that life becomes an endless quest for supplementary signifiers to fill a lack that by definition cannot be filled. Like Shklovsky, Barthes and Derrida echo the Freudian theory that all our cultural products are constructed on the way to love. All three would further agree that love is a destination at which we never arrive, no matter how many letters we send in advance. The love letter is thus a metonym of the fort-da game: just as Ernst acts out (if not masters) his anxiety over his mother's departure by miming it (gone/here), the love letters of Barthes and Derrida reproduce that oscillation of presence/absence, mastery/powerlessness; they both consciously mime Ernst's motives and desires.

The extent to which Derrida and Barthes identify with Ernst and his game is startling, for each situates himself as the infant. *Infans* means the one who lacks speech; the infant is trapped between the needs of the body and the demands of speech. He needs because he is in the body; he demands when he enters speech, the realm of the symbolic. Desire is the lack, the gap that lies between need and demand. Barthes reflects,

> Absence is the figure of privation; simultaneously, I desire and I need. Desire is squashed against need: that is the obsessive phenomenon of all amorous sentiment. ("Desire is present, ardent, eternal: but God is higher still, and the raised arms of Desire never attain to the adored plenitude." The discourse of Absence is a text with two ideograms: there are *the raised arms of Desire,* and there are *the wide-open arms of Need.* I oscillate, I vacillate between the phallic image of the raised arms, and the babyish image of the wide-open arms.) . . . I invoke the other's protection, the other's return: let the other appear, take me away, like a mother who comes looking for her child. (ALD 16-17)

In stressing oscillation, Barthes evokes Lacan's description of the "fluttering" motion of the infant: one cannot fix on any one motion or response and define it as paradigmatic of the mirror stage in its entirety. It is a destabilized point and perception that comes and goes in fits and starts. Desire is "squashed of all need"; since one is no longer a child, one is able to fulfill one's physical needs oneself. In amorous discourses, however, lovers nevertheless revert to infantile demands, irrational needs. Thus, Werther is as jealous as a two-year-old when Lotte divides a cake and, later, an orange—not because he is starving but because he does not want Lotte's attention distracted, nor does he want to share her with others (ALD 111, 145).

Barthes's fascination with eating in *Werther* is uncanny, for in the epistolary tradition male lovers invariably have voracious appetites, ranging from Lovelace (in contrast to Clarissa, who ceases to eat) to Humbert. Werther longs to devour Lotte; Humbert yearns to swallow Lolita's kidneys, lungs, liver. Barthes and Derrida allude repeatedly to the same voracity. Barthes compares the tantrums staged by the lover to "the Roman style of vomiting: I tickle my uvula . . . I vomit (a flood of wounding arguments), and then, quite calmly, I begin eating again" (ALD 207). Derrida not only illuminates the psychoanalytic implications of this desire but links it to epistolary production: "The letter 'interiorized' in whatever mode (sucked, drunk, swallowed, bitten, digested, breathed, inhaled, sniffed, seen, heard, idealized, taken by heart and recalled to whoever, or on the way to being so, *en voie de l'étre*) . . . the letter that you address yourself . . . then cannot arrive at its destination. . . . This is the tragedy of myself, of the ego, in 'introjection': one must love oneself in order to love oneself, or finally, if you prefer, my love, in order to love" (PC 195). Derrida puns here on *envois, en voie,* and *en voix.* In loving, one wants to introject the other; introjection is the process in analysis by which the patient transposes objects and their inherent qualities from "outside" to "inside" himself. It is concretely expressed in the oral mode: "expressed in the language of the oldest—the oral—instinctual impulses, the judgment is: 'I should like to eat this,' or 'I should like to spit it out'; it is in contrast to 'incorporation,' which applies to what one takes into the body; 'introjection' refers to what one takes into the psyche" (Laplanche and Pontalis 1974, 229-30).

Another key process and motive in these texts involves identification, which is related to introjection. Derrida "identifies" with Matthew Paris's postcard of Socrates and Plato; elsewhere he identifies with Socrates and compares his beloved to Plato, finger raised, tyrannically dictating to him (PC 38). He also identifies with the Wolfman. When the Wolfman dies on May 7, 1979, Derrida writes: "A little bit of me is gone. Had I told you that I am also Ernst, Heinele, Sigmund, Sophie, and HAlberstAdt. . . . This is the story that I write myself, *fort:da* . . . question concerning the Wolfman: does an 'incorporated' letter arrive at its destination? And can one give to someone other than oneself, if to give, *the* giving must also be introjected? Have we ever given ourselves to each other?" (PC 194-95). That question, which haunts all lovers, brings us back to the obsession with possession and with the contradictions inherent in *je nous*. What one desires from the beloved is total incorporation and introjection, but if one's desires were granted, what would one be receiving that was authentic or unique? Or that differentiated the lover from oneself? Barthes shares this obsession with the vagaries and paradoxes of positioning in the amorous structure; he, too, demonstrates how the personality is constituted and specified by a series of identifications, some of which come from life, some from literature. Literature works by the same transferential system as psychoanalysis:

> Werther identifies himself with the madman. . . . As a reader, I can identify myself with Werther. Historically, thousands of subjects have done so, suffering, killing themselves, dressing, perfuming themselves, writing as if they were Werther (songs, poems, candy boxes, belt buckles, fans, colognes à la Werther). A long chain of equivalences links all the lovers in the world. In the theory of literature, "projection" (of the reader into the character) no longer has any currency: yet it is scarcely adequate to say I project myself; I cling to the image of the lover, shut up with this image in the very enclosure of the book. (ALD 131)

Humbert Humbert's identification with Werther is also relevant here. Just as Werther identifies with Heinrich, the madman within the novel, Goethe's contemporaries identify with Werther, Barthes identifies with Werther and Heinrich, and readers identify with Barthes, who addresses his book to "the United Readers and Lovers." He mocks commodity culture, which manufactures candy, buckles, fans, colognes in imitation of Werther (and eventually turns *A Lover's Discourse* into a bestseller). Commodity culture is a desiring-machine; it simultaneously tantalizes, manufactures, and withholds what is desired. ("Mass culture is a machine for showing desire: here is what must interest you, it says, as if it guessed that men are incapable of finding what to desire by themselves" [ALD 136–37].) One cannot get "beyond" the mirroring; one cannot keep from being "reduced to a certain personality" (ALD 130). Like Derrida's postal system, with its circuits of delivery and return, "the structure has nothing to do with persons; hence (like a bureaucracy) it is terrible. It cannot be implored—I cannot say to it: 'Look how much better I am than H.' Inexorable, the structure replies: 'You are in the same place, hence you are H. No one can *plead* against the structure' " (ALD 130).

By stressing psychoanalysis, I may seem to have digressed from discussing the production of Woman, but the psychoanalytic process of identification provides a clue to the fascination with the topos of femininity. One way to account for Barthes's and Derrida's shared interest in producing Woman is to argue that their shared emphasis on identification enables them to work through the paradoxes of structure and system. They write as Héloise and Mariane (the Portuguese nun) because the feminine is the already written. The already written has been installed in the same place in which they find themselves.

With that insight in mind, we can see the motif of "catching up" and the repetitive miming of the *fort-da* game as an aspect of the production of a subject. One loves one's own ego identification (Heath 1983, 101). It is one's own ego that one loves when one is "in love," one's own ego realized in the imaginary. The subject is a production— multiple, unfinished, in process. Paradoxically, while the subject is produced in language, language ceaselessly divides it. The Symbolic is the term for the constitutive division; the Imaginary is the term for these effects of subject identity, for the very props of subjectivity in which the individual "I" seeks reflection as a totality, and coherence. Love, Barthes suggests, is the catching up of the Symbolic in the Imaginary (Heath 1983, 102). This helps to explain why, in the absence of the beloved, the lover plays with language: "Absence persists—I must endure it. Hence I will *manipulate* it: transform the distortion of time into oscillation, produce rhythm, make an entrance onto the stage of language (language is born of absence: the child has made himself a doll out of a spool, throws it away and picks it up again, miming the mother's departure and return: a paradigm is created). Absence becomes an active practice, a *business* (which keeps me from doing anything else); there is a creation of a fiction which has many roles (doubts, reproaches, desires, melancholies). This staging of language postpones the other's death" (ALD 16). Barthes and Derrida both record their desire not just for the lost mother but for preoedipal verbal states, which are figured as maternal in the imaginary. Derrida alternately fantasizes about suckling the breast and having the capacity to breast-feed. At times he associates the mother with language itself; he is the devouring, vengeful son of a phallic mother: "Our mother language sucks everything, the dirty vampire, I'll get her back for it" (PC 228). Elsewhere, he sexualizes the operation he performs in and on language, referring to it as "this whore of a language" (PC 158) and throwing himself "onto language like a feverish virgin ('wait till you see what I'll do to her') who still believes that the tongue can be taken on, that things can be done to her, that she can be made to cry out or can be put into pieces, penetrated, that one can inscribe one's claws in her as quickly as possible before the premature ejaculation" (PC 184). The last two words signal a comic diminishment of the grandiose fantasies in the rest of the passage. They also circle back to the repetition compulsion. Any "ejaculation" of victory over language is always premature because it has already been anticipated, written, and thus defeated in advance. Conversely, laments about language's intractability, its ineffability, are also repetitions. Language is both a *fort-da* game and a self-reflexive comment on *fort-da*. It is an "old lady," whom Derrida sees as "impenetrable, virgin, impassive, somewhat amused, all-powerful. . . . One day I heard her . . . mock their infantile compulsion: to believe that they violated everything by breaking the two in order to throw the pieces far away, and then to yell loud [*fort*], very loud" (PC 184). Derrida's identifications extend from Earwicker's desire for Issy in *Finnegans Wake* to Freud's desire for the mother/daughter Sophie. Desire underwrites narrative: Plato projects his desire to have his will written in Socrates's dead hand, just as Freud engages transferentially with his patients' desires. Writing prolongs and extends transferential relations: the introjection and projection of needs, demands, and desires results in a "reconstituted nearness." Just as Barthes comments on "the pleasure of the text" when we are enclosed in it, Derrida lays bare his strategy in writing *The Post Card* when he says,

> ([I] enclose myself in a book project, to deploy all possible ruses, and a maximum of consciousness, intelligence, vigilance, etc., while remaining, in order to remain (as you said to me one day) enclosed in this puerile (and masculine) enclosure of naiveté, like a little boy in his playpen, with his construction toys. That I spend the clearest part of my time taking them to pieces and throwing them overboard changes nothing essential in the matter. I would still like to be admired and loved, to be sent back a good image of my facility for destruction and for throwing far away from me these rattles and pieces of tinkertoy), finally you will tell me why I still want this, and in a certain way for you, in order to prepare in your absence what I will give you on your return, at the end of time. (PC 51)

Barthes's and Derrida's production of the feminine is sometimes associated with what is "puerile (and masculine)"; both participate in a larger strategy of "desiring-production." They want to reproduce the vicissitudes of psychic life, the process by which the unconscious is continually producing desires, fantasies, identifications that transgress all boundaries. Rather than channeling their desires into prescribed modes of oedipalization, they want to simulate and stimulate the free play of genres and genders.

Feminist Critiques of Barthes and Derrida

Some critics have misunderstood what desiring-production is and how it functions in the realms of fantasy where all imaginings are permissible. Perhaps because at many points Derrida specifically refers to the addressee by using feminine pronouns, some feminists have blithely assumed that in the text there is a real woman whose identity is suppressed. They have thus indicted him for silencing her. As Shari Benstock comments, "He stole her voice, consumed it in his own desire. . . . She is robbed of name, signature, personality, gender, body, voice" (1984, 182–83). Alicia Borinsky similarly protests, "The woman who has generated the conflict and received the letters is obliterated" (1989). Such responses wrongly assume that *The Post Card* has a single addressee and that she is an identifiable woman. Through such responses, these critics sentimentalize victimized Womanhood. Focusing single-mindedly on gender, they overlook the implications of genre, for amorous discourse is *always* an effort to bury the beloved (male or female) with/in language: its sheer volubility smothers the beloved object—whether the object is male or female. Rosa Coldfield in William Faulkner's *Absalom, Absalom!* is a good example of the feminine enactment of this impulse: she buries Sutpen (or, more accurately, reburies him, since he is already dead) beneath an avalanche of voluble grievances over ancient wounds. Rosa's discourse represents a specific type of complaint, which Barthes defines as the Loquela: "the flux of language through which the subject tirelessly rehashes the effects of a wound or the consequences of an action: an emphatic form of the lover's discourse" (ALD 160; see also Kauffman 1986, chap. 7). Barthes emphasizes that the beloved, objectified by the lover's fixation on his own discourse, inevitably seems to disappear: "If you were only the dedicatee of this book, you would not escape your harsh condition as (loved) *object*—as god; but your presence within the text, whereby you are unrecognizable there, is not that of an analogical figure, of a fetish, but that of a force which is not, thereby, absolutely reliable. Hence it doesn't matter that you feel continuously reduced to silence, that your own discourse seems to you smothered beneath the monstrous discourse of the amorous subject" (ALD 79). Just as the author is a fiction, Woman, like the simulacrum, is a concept that disproves its own validity and defies the boundaries of model and image. The letter is a metonym for the beloved's body; letter writing simulates the lover's voice (*en voix*) speaking to the beloved. As Barthes notes:

> Language is a skin: I rub my language against the other. It is as if I had words instead of fingers, or fingers at the tip of my words. My language trembles with desire. The emotion derives from a double contact: on the one hand, a whole activity of discourse discreetly, indirectly focuses upon a single signified, which is "I desire you," and releases, nourishes, ramifies it to the point of explosion (language experiences orgasm upon touching itself); on the other hand, I enwrap the other in my words, I caress, brush against, talk up this contact, I extend myself to make the commentary to which I submit the relation endure. (ALD 73)

Derrida similarly describes amorous discourse as a site of sensuous production, comparing the texture of language to the sensuousness of flesh, corps to corpus. Evoking Barthes's "the figure is the lover at work" (ALD 4), Derrida echoes: "This is my body, at work, love me, analyze the corpus that I tender to you, that I extend here on this bed of paper, sort out the quotation marks from the hairs, from head to toe" (PC 99).

These two passages reveal the extent to which Derrida's and Barthes's discourses are dedicated to desiring-production as an activity in and of the unconscious. They also serve to reveal inescapable contradictions in the theoretical foundations of poststructuralism, contradictions Derrida and Barthes consciously accentuate. For example, Derrida's entire deconstructive project seeks to displace the hierarchies that idealize speaking over writing and presence over absence; if the beloved were present, the lover would not need to write. The *je crois te parler* motif, then, reinscribes the very dichotomies Derrida theoretically seeks to displace. He dramatizes these contradictions when he confesses, "You are the only one to understand why it really was necessary that I write exactly the opposite, as concerns axiomatics, of what I desire, what I know my desire to be, in other words you: living speech, presence itself, proximity, the proper, the guard, etc. I have necessarily written upside down—and in order to surrender to Necessity" (PC 194).

Although such confessions seem to go against the grain of deconstruction, Derrida reminds us that the "confession" may be spurious; it may merely be one of the things, along with dates, signatures, titles, and references that he "abuses." The confession recalls the paradoxes of set theory; like Epimenides's Cretan lie, Derrida's confession relies on an irreducible doubleness; it is that which disproves its own validity and thus cannot be relied upon as a model of sincerity, authenticity, or even of deconstructive strategy. The recording of that which resists one's theories, contradicts one's axioms, turns all the tranquil categories of genre and gender upside down is precisely the activity of desiring-production. Deleuze and Guattari's description of the subject in the process of desiring-production is an apt corollary to Barthes's and Derrida's project:

[He] has his own system of co-ordinates for situating himself at his disposal, because, first of all, he has at his disposal his very own recording code, which does not coincide with the social code, or coincides with it only in order to parody it. The code of delirium or of desire proves to have an extraordinary fluidity. It might be said that the schizophrenic passes from one code to the other, that he deliberately *scrambles all the codes,* by quickly shifting from one to another, according to the questions asked him, never giving the same explanation from one day to the next, never invoking the same genealogy, never recording the same event in the same way. (DG 15)

Throughout their discourses, Barthes and Derrida demonstrate the extraordinary fluidity of the codes of delirium and desire. They are "feminized" through rhetoric that reproduces the disorder and delirium of the epistolary heroine. Hysteria is a writing effect in a double sense: one writes to record one's hysteria, and writing augments it at every turn. Delirium permits the unspeakable to be spoken: irrationality, paranoia, vengeance, and obsession are all made legible. The amorous discourses of Barthes and Derrida are "dialogic" in that their interior voices resist all systems and logic and substitute another value—insistent, infantile, and preternaturally self-reflexive. Barthes reflects: "I am mad to be in love, I am not mad to be able to say so, I double my image: insane in my own eyes (I know my delirium), simply unreasonable in the eyes of someone else, to whom I quite sanely describe my madness: conscious of this madness, sustaining a discourse upon it" (ALD 120). Another paradox: if one is "mad" or "possessed," can one simultaneously be self-possessed? Can one "know" one's delirium? These lovers are possessed by love, by knowledge, by acute self-consciousness, despite their lack of belief in a "self." Derrida confesses that he writes to "get rid of delirious images. You know them better than I, which is what always will prevent me from being delivered of them, you were there before me. . . . And then I am not writing falsely knowledgeable letters in order to keep me from the delirium which possesses me, I am writing delirious letters, knowledge walls them up in their crypt and one must know crypts, delirious letters on the knowing letters that I make into cards. I summon them to appear, that's all" (PC 96). Derrida compares the cryptic messages on postcards to crypts, which contain remains, just as he reminds us at the outset that what we are reading may be the remainder of a correspondence. He describes crypts as being both inside and outside nature: they highlight the significance of death while disguising its content.[2] The postcard performs a similar function: it signifies desire while disguising its content.

Like Barthes waiting in the hotel, Derrida suffers numerous apprehensions: he fears that the affair will end badly; he worries about numerous miscommunications, flaws in the postal system, and misinterpretations. "It's not that you are absent or present when I write to you but that I am not there myself when you are reading," as if his presence and the immediacy of speech could ward off misunderstandings. Even while invalidating the illusion of full presence, he inscribes a certain nostalgia for it. (Whether he really feels this nostalgia or is simply memorializing its traces remains undecidable.) Like Barthes, he wants to defamiliarize these illusions in order to expose their force and signification.

Derrida's fears are fulfilled when the letter he sends *poste restante* goes astray; as in Poe's "Purloined Letter," the fate, contents, and significance of the lost letter become one of the major switch points in the text as well as the source of numerous quarrels with his lover. His motive for highlighting this interpolated tale (whether he invented it or whether it really happened cannot be determined) is to demonstrate that the letter can always *fail to* reach its destination. The vicissitudes of the unconscious are less traceable and tractable than (in his view) Lacanian psychoanalysis will admit. To Derrida, there are more pathways, prevarications, and detours than are dreamed of in Lacan's philosophy. Barthes does not share Derrida's view of Lacan nor is he interested in using *A Lover's Discourse* to prove Lacan wrong. Nevertheless, he comments on the tendency of dominant discourses (including psychoanalysis) to turn into authoritative prescriptions:

> The several systems which surround the contemporary lover offer him no room (except for an extremely devaluated place): turn as he will toward one or another of the received languages, none answers him, except in order to turn him away from what he loves. Christian discourse, if it still exists, exhorts him to repress and to sublimate. Psychoanalytic discourse (which, at least, describes his state) commits him to give up his Image-repertoire as lost. As for Marxist discourse, it has nothing to say. If it should occur to me to knock at these doors in order to gain recognition *somewhere....* for my

"madness" (my "truth"), these doors close one after the other; and when they are all shut, there rises around me a wall of language which oppresses and repulses me—unless I *repent* and agree to "get rid of X." (ALD 211)

Like Héloise and the Portuguese nun, Barthes refuses to "repent," to let himself be recuperated by any of the socially sanctioned systems that might "cure" him of his "addiction." He is nonetheless aware that he cannot replace those sanctioned systems with any positivistic belief, which is why "truth," even if it *feels* like his own, must be defamiliarized with quotation marks. Contemporary society's rhetoric of normative health, its positivistic faith in determining whether one loves "too much", its guarantees of "cures" for "addictive" "dysfunctions" is the new mythology, the new religion—one that belies the regimented, behavioristic bent in society's approach to subjects, all of which Derrida and Barthes resist.

Since no discursive system sanctions the lover's discourse, Barthes and Derrida produce an endless chain of supplements. It is precisely because the language of love is impossible that Derrida and Barthes have chosen it: not to co-opt it or make it conform to societal norms but to perform it—with all the irresolvable contradictions that entails. Derrida's allusion to Necessity echoes Barthes's explanation of what makes his book a necessity: the lack of models, the lack of a language of and for love in the modern world.

Although some feminists have misunderstood the role and function of Barthes's and Derrida's amorous discourses, I am not implying that their discourses are faultless or intrinsically feminist. Feminist appropriations of deconstruction do not require a wholesale endorsement. Instead, they imply a reciprocal critique—what I call a strategy of infidelity—for, as with Shklovsky and Nabokov, in the process of producing Woman, Barthes and Derrida frequently reinscribe traditional stereotypes of femininity. For instance, associating Woman with the relinquishment of mastery (as in Barthes's "non-will-to-possess") is an idealization. Ironically, the traditional love letter negates such idealizations. Instead of victimized or wisely passive heroines, we find remarkably cunning assertions of mastery: Héloise's unrepentant desire is accompanied by a virtuoso display of her erudition in philosophy and theology. Richardson's Clarissa refuses to be a passive victim; instead, she refutes her persecutors point by point and exercises her will, particularly in her last will and testament. In *The Turn of the Screw*, the governess masterfully attempts to usurp the master's authority and to fix the one "true" meaning of her tale, exonerating herself from murder in the process (Kauffman 1986, chaps. 2, 4, and 6).

Absence of mastery (over meaning, language, interpretation) does not mean that the effects of power are absent or invisible. Barthes and Derrida sometimes overlook the irreducible difference that gender makes economically, sexually, and politically. The celebration of multiplicity has its dangers. Myra Jehlen (1987) warns that the celebration of plural sexualities may result in women disappearing altogether: "The claim of difference criticizes the content of the male universal norm. But beyond this, it represents a new understanding that if the other is to live, it will have to live as other, lest the achievement of integration be crowned with the fatal irony of disappearance through absorption."

Despite certain limitations, A Lover's Discourse and The Post Card are particularly notable for the ways in which they try to come to terms with otherness without merely absorbing it. Disappearance need not be indissolubly associated with deconstruction, for in these texts numerous strategies are presented to preserve alterity, to make legible that which is threatened by erasure in the dominant discursive structures. To wrest identity away from its grounding in gender, Barthes and Derrida exploit the paradoxes of set theory: gender roles entail "a sort of participation without belonging—a taking part in without being part of, without having membership in a set" (Derrida 1980a, 206). The same strategy can be exploited to prevent women from being assimilated into the category Woman. As Lacan observes, that is the whole point of set theory: "The woman can perfectly well be delineated, since it is all women, as you might say. But if women are 'not all'? Then if we say that the woman is all women, it is an empty set. The advantage of set theory, surely, is that it introduced a measure of seriousness into the use of the term 'all'" (FS 168). Despite his manifold differences from Lacan, Derrida is striving for that same measure of seriousness in his use of "all" throughout The Post Card, perhaps most notably in "Du Tout." Derrida and Barthes open a space that feminists should be urged to keep from closing again, for if feminism and theory have taught us anything, they teach us how seamless the act of recuperation can become.

Ironically, some strategies for dealing with these dilemmas in feminist criticism can be found in Derrida's own work, for he struggles with the same issues when he confronts the scene of writing in the wake of Barthes's death. In "Les morts de Roland Barthes," he uses musical analogies to illustrate the dilemma; the relationship between one's own voice and the voice of the other (Barthes) is comparable to that of a pianist accompanying a soloist:

Two infidelities, one impossible choice: on the one hand saying nothing that one must attribute to oneself alone, to one's own voice; to remain silent or at least have oneself accompanied or preceded by the voice of the friend, in counterpoint. In consequence, to content oneself to cite, in fervent friendship or homage—also by approbation—to accompany that which returns, more or less directly, to the other; to give him the word, to efface oneself before it, and in front of him. But this excess of fidelity would finish by saying nothing, and by exchanging nothing. It turns back to death. It returns there; it restores death unto death.

On the other hand, in avoiding all citation, all identification, even all *rapproachement*—so that he who addresses himself to Roland Barthes or speaks of him may truly come from the other, from the living friend—one again risks making him disappear, as if one could add death to death, and so indecently pluralize it. What remains is simultaneously to make and not make the two [impossible] choices—to correct one infidelity by the other. From one death another: is that where the trouble lies which compelled me to begin with a plural? (Derrida 276-277)

Derrida is faced with the impossible choice of, on the one hand, attributing nothing to Barthes's voice, of limiting himself to citing Barthes's texts. By so doing, he would be faithful to poststructuralist theories of decentering and relativizing the relation of author, reader, and critic. But such fidelity is excessive; not only would it say nothing, it would exchange nothing. This emphasis on the importance of a transformative economy is vital to both the Derridean and the Barthesian projects. The opposite choice is to avoid all citation of and identification with Barthes, to avoid all allusion to the friend still very much alive in Derrida's memory, but that would have the effect of making Barthes disappear, thus adding yet another death to the "deaths" of Roland Barthes.

The use of plural "deaths" reveals Derrida's anxiety at being confronted with such questions; one sign of his attempt to work through that anxiety lies in the revelation of the *cheminement*—the tracing of the working-through process. I've taken that as my model in this study, trying to work through the conflicts and contradictions between feminism and deconstruction without foreclosing either one. One strategy entails resistance to genre itself: confronted with an occasion in which the genre of eulogy insistently asserts itself, Derrida refuses to eulogize Barthes; he refuses to reduce him to the conventional. Death in the plural marks the metonymic chain of signifiers that multiply ceaselessly: the deaths of author, of the mother, of literature itself. That multiplicity does not detract from or mitigate the literal death of Roland Barthes. Multiplicity, in fact, signals the extent to which death defies representation. The advent of modernity, Derrida observes, commences with finding literature impossible (Derrida 276). Barthes echoes this view when he observes (in an analogy full of significance for feminist criticism) that modern litera- ture has been playing a "dangerous game with its own death." Mod- ern writing "is like that Racinean heroine who dies upon learning who she is, but lives by seeking her identity." Not only is that another way of figuring the feminine but it has important implications for feminist investigation: rather than imposing consensus, feminist criti- cism is poised to forestall the death that comes with positiveness. (Dostoyevsky said, "Positiveness is the beginning of death.") Feminist criticism lives by continuing to seek its identity, by seeing identity as a process—that, indeed, has long been one of its strengths. By exposing the intractability of language, one prevents language from closing itself off, embalming itself.

Feminist criticism faces the same challenge today. Indeed, Derrida's multiple dilemmas in confronting Barthes's death are a parable of the dilemmas confronted by feminist criticism in the last decade: How can we engage poststructuralist theory without losing sight of the material body? What does it mean to be constituted as a subject in and of language? In and by institutions? Which texts (and ideologies) survive and why? What material and economic conditions contribute to their survival or demise? If "positiveness is the beginning of death," how is feminist criticism going to avoid becoming either a passing fashion or worse—the new orthodoxy? A feminist appropria- tion of the infidelity Derrida proposes may provide a possible strategy: we can be unfaithful to formulations that we may subsequently find inadequate. In *Discourses of Desire*, for example, I remark, "I have tried to expose the devaluation of the sentimental as another form of repression, with ramifications as serious at the end of the twentieth century as sexual repression was at the end of the nineteenth" (Kauffman 1986, 316). I now see that the valorization of the sentimen- tal has led in directions I could not have predicted—although per- haps I should have been able to predict them. Specifically, I do not believe in "women's ways of knowing" (Belenky, Clinchy, Goldberger, and Tarule 1986) or "Sentimental Power" (Tompkins 1985), yet I unwittingly became a party to such idealizations in the passage above. A conscious strategy of rejecting one's own postulations if they are subsequently found wanting is one way for feminist criticism to keep from embalming itself. Far from striving for consensus, we learn most from the ruptures, limitations, and contradictions in our own thought. We can also consciously highlight the ways in which our desires may be in conflict with the theoretical stances we endorse, as Derrida does when he confesses that the very act of writing *envois* defies all the axiomatics of deconstruction.

Derrida's dilemma is that he wants to remember Barthes without merely eulogizing him; he wants to pay homage and acknowledge his debt while simultaneously marking his difference. Since feminists' debt to Barthes and Derrida has been incalculable, we, too, can acknowledge it without losing sight of the grounds of difference. The new conceptual space Derrida and Barthes have opened has utopic possibilities, as Gayatri Spivak explains, for it "is concerned with forging a practice that recognizes its condition of possibility in the impossibility of theoretical rigor, and that must remain apocalyptic in scope and tone, 'render delirious the interior voice which is the voice of the other in us' " (1984, 25). This passage, quoting from Derrida's "Of an Apocalyptic Tone Recently Adopted in Philosophy," further illuminates "Les morts de Roland Barthes": the voice of Barthes is the voice of the other in Derrida, *in all its alterity*. Spivak's statement does not repudiate the value of theoretical rigor, nor does it relegate theory to some realm of so-called masculine discourse. Instead, it emphasizes the partiality and provisionality of one's theoretical constructs. It further suggests how to retain a sense of "living as other," of sustaining a sense of alterity that resists absorption.

Feminism and deconstruction are mutually indebted and benefit from a mutual reciprocity, despite the insistence of some feminist critics on sustaining the (false) dichotomy between "male" theory and feminist criticism (e.g., Showalter 1983; Tompkins 1989). Some male critics have enforced the same dichotomy, as Spivak observes:

> It is surely significant that, even today, the men who take to him take everything from him but his project of re-naming the operation of philosophy with the "name" of woman. Although sexual relations of reproduction are still crucial in every arena of politics and economics—and the tradition of love letters has been the most powerful ideological dissimulation of those relations, such letters continue to be considered merely frivolous in a world of bullets and starvation. Although Derrida is using them as texts for interpretation and suggesting their complicity with the objective tradition of intellectual discourse, they can still be dismissed as a mark of bourgeois individualism. . . . If, however, we academic women of the First World observe Derrida's minuet with the epistles of love, we might learn that sexuality, "the woman's role," is not in simple opposition to "real politics," and that a vision that dismisses a

man's conduct in love as immaterial to his "practical" stands would not be able to see the generally warping legacy of masculinism. . . . This, I think, is why Derrida reads great men's letters and writes about them as he writes about their "serious" work. (1984, 35)

By defamiliarizing the arbitrary oppositions between "serious" scholarship and love letters, between theory and practice, Barthes and Derrida reframe the questions. One need not choose—indeed, it is not even a question of choosing—between language and experience, deconstruction and psychoanalysis, poststructuralism and institutions. We are simultaneously in language and the body, the "disreal"[3] and the material. Feminist criticism can mark the vicissitudes of psychic life without ignoring the material conditions of real women around the globe. One can deconstruct the ruses of identity and desire while simultaneously analyzing their impact on material bodies and material conditions.

Notes

I thank the University of Chicago Press for permission to adapt this essay from their publication of my *Special Delivery: Epistolary Modes in Modern Fiction* (1992).

1. See Gilles Deleuze and Félix Guattari (1983, 82), hereinafter cited in the text as DG. Barthes alludes specifically to his reading of *anti-Oedipe* (1977, 100).
2. What Derrida says in *The Post Card* about crypts is exhaustively elaborated in "Fors," his preface to *Le Verbier de l'homme aux loups,* by N. Abraham and M. Torok (Paris: Frammarion, 1977).
3. Barthes defines "disreality" (*déréalité*) as the "sentiment of absence and withdrawal of reality experienced by the amorous subject, confronting the world" (ALD, 87).

References Cited

Barthes, Roland. 1974. *S/Z: An Essay.* Translated by Richard Miller. New York: Hill and Wang.

———. 1977. *Roland Barthes by Roland Barthes.* Translated by Richard Howard. New York: Hill and Wang.

———. 1978. *A Lover's Discourse: Fragments.* Translated by Richard Howard. New York: Hill and Wang.

——. 1980. *New Critical Essays*. Translated by Richard Howard. New York: Hill and Wang.

——. 1982. *A Barthes Reader*, ed. Susan Sontag. New York: Hill and Wang.

——. 1985. *The Grain of the Voice: Interviews, 1962–1980*. Translated by Linda Coverdale. New York: Hill and Wang.

Belencky, Mary Field, Blythe McVicker Clinchy, Nancy Rule Goldberger, and Jill Mattuck Tarule. 1986. *Women's Ways of Knowing: The Development of Self, Voice, and Mind*. New York: Basic Books.

Benstock, Shari. 1984. "The Letter of the Law: *La carte postale* in *Finnegans Wake*." *Philological Quarterly* 63:163–86.

Borinsky, Alicia. 1989. "No Body There: On the Politics of Interlocution." Pp. 245–56 in *Writing the Female Voice: Essays on Epistolary Literature*, ed. Elizabeth C. Goldsmith. Boston: Northeastern University Press.

Deleuze, Gilles, and Félix Guattari. 1983. *Anti-Oedipus: Capitalism and Schizophrenia*. Translated by Robert Hurley, Mark Seem, and Helen R. Lane. Minneapolis: University of Minnesota Press.

Derrida, Jacques. 1979. *Spurs: Nietzsche's Styles*. Translated by Barbara Harlow. Chicago: University of Chicago Press.

——. 1980a. "La loi du genre" (The law of genre). Translated by Avital Ronell. *Glyph* 7 (Spring): 177–232.

——. 1980b. *The Post Card: From Socrates to Freud and Beyond*. Translated by Alan Bass. Chicago: University of Chicago Press.

——. 1981. "Plato's Pharmacy." In *Disseminations*. Translated by Barbara Johnson. Chicago: University of Chicago Press.

——. 1984. *Signéponge/Signsponge*. Translated by Richard Rand. New York: Columbia University Press.

Heath, Stephen. 1983. "Barthes on Love." *Sub-stance* 37–38:100–106.

Jehlen, Myra. 1987. "Against Human Wholeness: A Suggestion for a Feminist Epistemology." Paper presented to the Columbia University Seminar on Women and Society (cited in Naomi Schor, "Dreaming Dissymmetry: Barthes, Foucault, and Sexual Difference." In *Men in Feminism*, ed. Alice Jardine and Paul Smith. New York: Methuen).

Kauffman, Linda. 1986. *Discourses of Desire: Gender, Genre, and Epistolary Fictions*. Ithaca, N.Y. Cornell University Press.

Kristeva, Julia. 1987. *Tales of Love*. Translated by Leon S. Roudiez. New York: Columbia University Press.

Lacan, Jacques. 1982. "Seminar of 21 January 1975." In *Feminine Sexuality: Jacques Lacan and the École Freudienne*, ed. Juliet Mitchell and Jacqueline Rose. New York: W. W. Norton.

Laplanche, J., and J. B. Pontalis. 1974. *The Language of Psychoanalysis*. Translated by Donald Nicholson-Smith. New York: W. W. Norton.

Rose, Jacqueline. 1986. *Sexuality in the Field of Vision*. London: Verso.

Rubin, Gayle. 1975. "The Traffic in Women." Pp. 157–210 in *Toward an*

Anthropology of Women, ed. Rayna Reiter. New York: Monthly Review Press.

Showalter, Elaine. 1983. "Critical Cross-Dressing: Male Feminists and the Woman of the Year." *Raritan* 3 (Fall): 130–49.

Spivak, Gayatri. 1984. "Love Me, Love my Ombre, Elle." *Diacritics* 14 (Winter): 19-36.

Tompkins, Jane. 1985. "Sentimental Power: *Uncle Tom's Cabin* and the Politics of Literary History." In *Sensational Designs: The Cultural Work of American Fiction, 1790-1860*. Oxford: Oxford University Press.

———. 1989. "Me and My Shadow." Pp. 121–39 in *Gender and Theory*, ed. Linda Kauffman. Oxford: Blackwell.

9 Somewhere over the Rainbow Dorothy Got Totaled: Postmodernity and Modern Film

Paul Shapiro

Until recently, the traditional Hollywood film ending was characterized by an obligatory happy ending. Such an ending could be interpreted by the audience as life affirmative and by the critic as culturally affirmative. The general aura conveyed by such endings rendered all into optimists, like Browning's Pippa: "God's in his heaven, all's right with the world." Like Pippa, Hollywood has always—until recently—done its utmost to ensure the general audience that "all's right with the world." All clouds were to have silver linings and tragedy was generally banished, even to the point of incongruity. The absurdities of such incongruity are evident in adaptations of literary classics. Gratuity rather than proportion or consistency reigned supreme. Let us recall some acts of excess regarding the film adaptation of literary classics. Such reversals of classic tragedies include Ahab killing the whale and getting the girl, Anna Karenina living in bliss with Vronsky, Dr. Jekyll awakening from a dream, and even Chance Wayne getting only a busted nose, and so on.

This zealous commitment to elysium has been vanquished. Indeed, a new manner of film ending, in which the hero can be thwarted or even killed, has been emerging. Moreover, films may have no conclusive ending or resolution of the plot. Worse yet, evil can be smashingly and leeringly triumphant. If the older style of happy endings represents early modern, the new style of film endings is perhaps indicative of postmodern culture.

This essay will explore this change in film construction. My primary theoretical focus will be a dialogue between postmodern culture theory and classic modernist social theory. The major commitment will be to the viability of classic theory—Max Weber and Georg Simmel—as providing a span to form a bridge for understanding present culture, a span rendered incomplete by postmodern theory. These themes (rather than fashionable film theory) will be the vista for exploring modern and postmodern film—particularly film noir.

This new film type and its ending seems to represent a transformation of late film modernity most strongly visible in film noir. First, the features of the noir universe will be elaborated. Next, the postmodern thriller will be presented as rooted within features of this noir world. A comparison between the moral thematics that delimit action within the modern and postmodern domains follows. Finally, I will discuss how these differing ethical parameters affect the role of the persona/subject and alter his/her capacity for agency.

The general discussion of modernity and postmodernity, which grounds this analysis, will be placed within ongoing current debates between classical modernity theory and recent culture theory. Modernity will be envisioned through Simmel and Weber's images of life as tragic existence. Further, these images seem to point to moral themes that stress that the subject also exists as tragic. Indeed, this tragedy focuses on the unavoidable centrality of persona and agency. As a culture product, film noir belongs within the ethical domain of this modernity, yet it also offers interstices that point toward postmodernity. Modernity stresses the centrality of persona and agent; postmodernity, in contrast, focuses on the axial and moral decentration of subject, milieu, and representation. The ethical problem of modernity then becomes the preservation of the moral unity of the subject within the experience of cultural fragmentation.

Postmodernity actually obliterates the problem of persona and agency via the notion of the death of the subject. In this manner, postmodern film resolves the matter by allowing the actual moral and physical death of the subject. How are such radical endings postmodern? Such films and endings seem to reside within the parameters of postmodernity presented by Frederic Jameson (1983): (1) the death of the subject, (2) the transformation of reality into images, and (3) the fragmentation of time into a series of perpetual presents. These parameters offer a further dimension that affects the representation and legitimacy of the subject—the collapsing of milieu. Modernity can be characterized by the boundaries of milieu, as represented by front and backstage (Goffman 1959).

Postmodernity provides a new turn for the authenticity of milieu. Thus, the boundaries of stages collapse. Indeed, this collapse of front/backstage further undermines the legitimacy of subject and agency, a legitimacy (as with front- and backstage) essential to the noir world. The role of the noir hero in setting the moral and authentic boundaries of these arenas is altered, as is the villain's rendering these domains as realms of concealment. The postmodern milieu, by decentering milieu itself, may further accelerate the decentration, death, or loss of significance of the agent.

What is the significance of this new postmodern realm? The modern/noir tension of fragmentation versus unity, the delineation of front and backstage, is rendered morally superfluous. The total universe exists as morally decentered. What is then the political import of this postmodern universe? A Brechtian alienation effect is hardly likely. Instead, it is more likely that such a film universe and its new manner of ending may lie more comfortably within the areas of cultural affirmation and uncritical acceptance. Such aspects fall within the culture industry's agenda of mass pacification (Horkheimer and Adorno 1972). Thus, we may propose that noir and postnoir have a political as well as cultural edge. Like Marx regarding history, we can observe the transformation of the tragedy of modernity into the postmodern farce. Film noir and its travails (even new travesties) become the signpost of this transformation.

The Tragedy of Modern Culture

Georg Simmel (1971) portrayed modernity as being characterized by a *tragedy of culture,* which occurs in the following manner. Man seeks emancipation from existing forms. Such forms act to constrain the full thrust of his creative desires. The new, emancipatory creative product will itself ironically act as a new form that constrains new creative desire. These new forms then must be transcended by new creative effects that in turn will also emerge as new constraining forms, and so on.

Max Weber (1958) also proposed a parallel tragic situation. He envisioned modern man as existing within an overwhelming surplus and array of cultural objects and possibilities. The overabundance of both objects and possibilities ironically acts to confuse and frustrate the prospects of choice. Paralysis of choice results. This ensuing dilemma renders life empty and meaningless rather than fulfilled. (Quite possibly Weber adumbrated Baudrillard's notions of overstimulation and the obscene.)

Weber also offered a secondary tragedy within modernity by expanding his notion of cultural paralysis to include implications from Friedrich Nietzsche's notion of a transvaluation of values. Nietzsche (1966) noted that there are no certain criteria of values in modernity. Thus, values have no grounding in truth; humans can create and choose value schemas that express their aesthetic and emancipatory needs. Nietzsche celebrated this value flux as a new dawn. Weber instead saw this phenomenon as a further tragedy of modernity. Weber noted a polytheism of values wherein the most sacred values have no grounding of certainty and worth. All that remains is a heroic and uncertain act of existential choice. The persona must choose to ground its own authenticity in an act of will, without certain or provable moorings. The self must act alone to prevent its own obliteration and trivialization.

The Postmodern Farce (Anything Goes)

This new transvalued universe that humbled Weber and elated Nietzsche is now the realm of the postmodern farce. In this domain, bildung and heroism, key aspects of tragic high modernity are being rendered obsolete. The paralysis of culture and form that Weber and Simmel predicted exists now as suspension of the realizability of desire. Experience is no longer unique to the privacy of the persona. Instead, it has been transformed into collective dippings that exist now as manufactured and discardable units of spectacle and amusement.

Modern culture theorists, both optimists and pessimists, are divided over the implications of this postmodern condition. The optimists carry on the Nietzschean celebration of the new dawn. They look upon the paralysis not as tragedy but as the break to a new emancipation. Jean-François Lyotard (1984) has outlined their position. All previous narratives based on certainty are dethroned. Instead mininarratives shall exist in a nonhierarchical pluralism of appreciation and celebration. The subject will be recognized not as the persona of yore but as a bundle of energy units of desire to be constantly projected, regrouped, and rearranged. Previous distinctions of high and low culture and deep and shallow discourse will also collapse. Recombinations and infinities of language gamings will replace the broodings of forensics and existential choice.

The pessimists view postmodernity as a prelude to or even a realization of cultural barbarism. In the ethical plane, postmodernity serves to generate moral paralysis as celebration and provides legitimation for indiscriminate indulgences of desire—a surrender to hedonism. In the cultural plane, it serves to place high culture under siege, corruption, and trivialization by collapsing and obliterating the high/low distinction. Mass culture is fused with high culture and aesthetic fulfillment gives way to narcosis. The fix of postmodernity follows Jameson's model: (1) the death of the subject, (2) the rejection of time sequence in favor of the present as continuum, and (3) the triumph of image over substance. This model carries us beyond Erving Goffman's modernity. Front stage and backstage collapse, as do subject and agency, marking the transformations of both noir and postmodernity.

Fearing Fear Itself: The World of Noir

Film noir and horror noir (1940s and 1950s) provide a grim cinema—a cinema of devastation. Film noir illustrates the tragedies of modernity and its moral topography. What is the moral mapping of this cinema of devastation? It resembles features of the pre-Christian universe of fate and revenge that underlie, for example, *King Lear*. Equilibrium rather than justice is restored, and death and retribution are not proportionate. The violence requited goes far beyond the actual wrongfulness of the deed to be avenged. Thus, morally excessive destruction results, over abuse of the innocent, hapless, and guiltless. The key point of noir is that an imperfect morality exists. It acts to restore moral viability to the fragmented persona of the hero as well as some semblance of moral equilibrium to the universe. (We may note that the destruction embodied in film noir as highly personalized and intimate in impact becomes wanton mass destruction of image and spectacle in postmodernity, with no centering ethical core.) In film noir then, the traditional, obligatory, generally joyous happy ending is discarded. The rule here follows *King Lear*—"as flies to wanton school boys are we to the gods, they kill us for sport."

How do human flies get swatted: let me count the ways? Heroes can die arbitrarily. They exist as unwitting and unwilling agents of revenge and moral restoration. In *DOA* (1949, directed by Rudolph Mate), the poisoned accountant is an innocent pawn in a plot of which he is initially unaware. Yet he becomes the instrument of moral equilibrium, resolving the crime and avenging his own impending death. The hero also becomes an unwitting and unwilling bearer of knowledge and truth. In this manner the hero acts as agent to clarify and restore the proper boundaries of front and backstage. These stage domains are both the moral and spatial boundaries of the noir universe.

Film noir also has a burden of undeserved, excessive brutality and destruction placed on the innocent and weak. The merest indication of possible suspicion or complicity serves as a warrant for condemnation. The loyal and devoted become victims. Their only reward is posthumous revenge served by the hero. Such is the fate of the heroine in *Manhunt* (1941) and the lonely, friendless little girl in *Confidential Agent* (1945). A variation involves the vulnerable protagonist who shows deep moral weakness among other character flaws. Such a figure should merit charitable mercy but in the noir world is discarded violently as a disposable annoyance.

This character is well delineated in the Val Lewton horror noirs, as tragic victims marked by cursed heritages or strategic character flaws. In *The Seventh Victim*, the female protagonist is mentally ill and morally weak. She betrays a cult of devil worshippers. This act exposes the concealment of front and backstage. The cult hounds her to suicide. Indeed, the cult remains thriving, upper bourgeois and, worst of all, unpunished. This ending looks forward to both postmodernity and to a cinema of atheism. Why? It has no conclusive ending. The final scene of suicide has deep shock impact. It is abrupt, unexpected, unprepared. There are no further scenes of aftermath and resolution. This dispensing of a moral or even a resolution looks forward to a postmodern sense of ending. This Lewton oddity provides the hint that God is asunder or unable to curb evil (i.e., God is dead). Thus, the subheroes offer ineffectual admonitions to the cult as disregarded pleas for Christian charity. Their appeals, of course, are unheeded.

Two other noir films that share aspects of a Lear world and latent postmodernity are Fritz Lang's interrelated films *Scarlet Street* (1945) and *Woman in the Window* (1944). Both films share the same director, basic cast, and similar plot themes. They deal with the naive male innocent as hapless victim—a middle-aged, unhappy, sexually innocent, milquetoast played by Edward G. Robinson. His front stage is the shabby, unfulfilling rut of lower middle-class respectability. Fate presents itself as agent of entry into the backstage of the demimonde in the form of the femme fatale. She acts to propel our hero out of his staid middle-class protective cage into her exciting and always destructive backstage of the noir world—evil, danger, and seduction. The price of his new knowledge and adventure is to exchange his grubby Eden for death and despair. The hero makes the shift from Chekovian sadness to the lower depths, an arena that would outdo Gorky's worst visions of degradation, madness, and poverty. The main narrative of *Scarlet Street* falls within tragedies shared by noir and modernity. The hero experiences both fragmentation and entrapment between front and backstage. Yet the ending is inverted, and modernity points toward postmodernity.

By contrast, the earlier *Woman in the Window* did not attempt such a reversal; it had a contrived happy ending. The noir world becomes a dream sequence, as though the dire thrust of the narrative would have left even a noir audience aghast. But in *Scarlet Street*, Lang went for broke. The film ends with the collapse of front stage into backstage. Robinson's character is now insane and degraded. He attends an exhibition of his own art that is now credited to the femme fatale he murdered. His wife is happily reunited with her "long dead" husband. A voice-over is heard of the evil pimp and femme fatale united in a tender *noir-liebestod* that belies the viciousness, sado-masochism, and levels of treachery of their earthly existence. Hero figures are thus thwarted, and moral equilibration is burst; front and backstage are thereby collapsed into each other. In these two films, Lang presents the Robinson characters as children in men's bodies. Like children, they are naive, impressionable, and easily tricked. They are also childlike in their capacity to be bullied and in their response of uncontrolled rage and revenge.

Whereas Lang explores the imagery of the man-child, the actual world of childhood and adolescence in the noir world was treated by Alfred Hitchcock in *Shadow of a Doubt* (1943), which deconstructs the aura of *Our Town* and was scripted by its author, Thornton Wilder. This film follows the pattern of a fairy tale. The heroine cries wolf legitimately and properly but the adults are oblivious to her warnings. Like the pattern of Victorian thrillers, evil takes the form of a regarded, seemingly benign, avuncular uncle (parallel to Le Fanu's *Uncle Silas*). By her own grit the heroine must then make it through the evil mansion and/or dark haunted forest. The child adolescent must save not only herself but the adults as well. The emergence of the heroine as noir agent serves also as her rite of passage into the adult world, a world that is oblivious to the evil that is so obvious and present to the child. This occurs due to the atavisms of childhood surviving in various levels of the adult world. In this regard, Hitchcock's work parallels Lang's thrillers. The actual levels of atavism are the small town, the small-town family, and the villain who also bears the same name as the heroine—a moral doppelgänger effect. The small town and small-town family are clichéd images of American normalcy that exist as stages of childhood fixation. The small-town mentality, like a child, is generally innocent in itself and unknowing of its own impressionability, trustingness, and dazzlement. They are dazzled by sophisticated, courtly, suave Uncle Charlie. Uncle Charlie also represents the big city as Satan entering into Eden. Uncle Charlie, a homicidal sexual misogynist, is himself a childhood atavism. His sexual maladjustment and pathology occur as a fixation manifested by childlike maliciousness and destructiveness. Uncle Charlie is a lost emotional orphan when in the city, and becomes a vicious prodigal son when reunited with his family.

Niece Charlie acts as agent of noir modernity. She exposes and restores front and backstage. She learns of Uncle Charlie's murderous backstage and must morally equilibrate the universe by vanquishing his evil. This is also the fairy-tale motif of the rite of passage via the exposure and death of the monster. A postmodern moment emerges, however: Uncle Charlie dies while trying to kill niece Charlie. Niece Charlie, for the sake of family and town, conceals Uncle Charlie's background. The price of maintaining the childlike naïveté of family and town is the concealment of truth, which confers moral entry into adulthood. Uncle Charlie is revered and buried as a hero. Thus, front and backstage are collapsed; the moral telos of noir is reversed. Uncle Charlie dazzles the town and family in death as well as life. He exists solely as sheer imagery, a decentered subject. His capacity to dazzle both alive and posthumously renders him not a persona but rather a presence as a moment of spectacle. The magnification and expansion of spectacle is a major aspect of postmodernity. Niece Charlie is now placed into an anomic moment that reverses noir resolution. Front stage and backstage are simultaneously delineated and collapsed. The heroine is agent and anti-agent. She preserves the modernist integrity of her moral persona but fragments her own moral cognition. Her truth remains private. The authenticity of her public personality tends toward postmodern decentration because of its immersion in lies and spectacle. In this regard, *Shadow of a Doubt* has modern elements with postmodern omens that presage the noir pastiche of *Blue Velvet*.

The Noir Persona as Subject and Agent

We can turn now to aspects of agency and subject that fall within the noir domain through a theoretical frame that incorporates insights of several thinkers: Max Weber on fraternization, Stanford Lyman on anhedonia and civilization, Erving Goffman on front/back stage, and Robert Merton on deviance and anomie. I will contextualize this framework with specific noir examples. Max Weber (1958b) discussed the notion of the fraternization process. This process seems to be implicitly presented as a major civilizing force. Weber argued that salvation religions demand the member to practice an ethic of fraternization. The member is enjoined to extend the loyalty and love due to natural family members to the stranger as a fellow brother. Weber further observed the dilemmas of this process. It may come into conflict with the requirements of other life areas, such as family, economy, politics, aesthetics, or eroticism. Religion must either remain in a state of conflict with these areas or compromise the rigor of this ethical imperative.

Lyman (1986) gives an unusual twist to Weber's argument. Lyman treats male bonding as being a special form of fraternization whose consequences are hedonistic and anticivilizational. He proceeds to offer a counterprinciple of an ascetic feminine ethos. This is the Ariadne principle, which uses eroticism as a civilizing force. Why is male bonding an anticivilizational force while the Ariadne motif acts as a civilizational force? Lyman's discussion of this issue serves also to raise further issues regarding the capacities of subject and agency within the noir universe.

Male bonding is characterized as a sphere of irresponsibility, adventure, and exhilaration that exists out of civilization's reach. The male motif is unravelled by two erotically rooted feminine motifs— Ariadne and Jezebel. Ariadne serves to tame and convert the male into an agent of civilization; Jezebel acts to entangle the male within her web of ambition and death. The cinema of front stage, bourgeois respectability uses the Ariadne principle as its means of agency to integrate the male away from male bonding (fraternization) into domesticity (feminization). Though the Ariadne motif is erotic in appeal, it is ascetic/anhedonic in its consequence. The female imperative urges the male to forego palship, escape, and adventure to win love's reward. This renunciation places the male under the guidance of the female at the service of the higher fraternization—community and civilization. Male bonding as fraternity is replaced by conjugal bonding. In Freudian imagery, Ariadne becomes the agent of the superego that tames the male id into the Freudian criteria of normalcy—work and love. The irony here is that sexuality, the weapon of Ariadne, serves to act as an agent of inner worldly asceticism that seduces the male into renunciation.

Lyman provides film examples of Ariadne's workings. He focuses on World War II dramas where the male under feminine urging enters into military obligation and under feminine nurturance is integrated back into peacetime family and civilization. This theme represents the triumph of Penelope over Ulysses. Lyman discusses films such as *Since You Went Away, Mr. Lucky,* and *The Best Years of Our Lives.* More recent postwar films show Ariadne in various life spheres—politics, art, the corporate world, science—acting to tame men into these life areas.

What is the future of fraternization qua feminization? Lyman suggests that male bonding and male heroes have become feminized. They act now as agents of nurturance, sentiment, and sensitivity (e.g., *Kramer vs. Kramer* and *Tootsie*). Man can no longer exist even as *Annie Hall*. Lyman suggests that Ariadne and Pygmalion have been defeated and are yet to be transformed.

In the noir world Ariadne the Good is transformed into Jezebel the wicked femme fatale. Jezebel as persona provides new vistas to enact intentional dramas of subject and agency. Ariadne acts to render the world into a prim middle-class front stage. Jezebel instead operates within the backstage of the demimonde. Her goal is to infect and infiltrate the front stage as shill to her backstage world. She generates a Marxian frame between the underworld as primary base for the middle-class superstructure. The male hero as moral agent acts to restore a proper separation of front and backstage, whereas Jezebel attempts to maintain her illicit linkage. Both generate storms of bloodlust against each other that draw in the innocent for destruction. The male can also be Jezebel's agent as erotic slave. If Ariadne attempts to maintain the ethicality of civilization through erotic agency, Jezebel instead uses her eroticism to ensure her sheer survival.

This pending aura of anomie and transvaluation, which envelopes noir modernity, becomes the dominant aura of postmodernity. Thus, Lyman writes: "Two noir films 'Kiss Me Deadly' and 'Vertigo' adumbrate the theme that a world without community and norms governing love and death is irretrievably meaningless—a limbo land of absurdity from which there can be no escape except into madness and death. . . . Death and deviltry are also distributed to the innocent and to the good" (1986, 30). In postmodernity, the madness and paranoia that characterize Jezebel's attempt at amoral reordering of the universe will comprise everyday life. The amoral distribution that Lyman fears in noir modernity will become the postmodern felicific calculus, as in Woody Allen's *Crimes and Misdemeanors*. The exploration and exploitation of anomie as a device for social mobility here becomes the innovation practiced by Jezebel in the noir world. Front and backstage become for her guideposts to be moved rather than boundaries to be feared and honored. Her use of deviance as a tool for social mobility and social change is consistent with Robert Merton's (1957) analysis of deviant behavior, anomie, and social innovation.

How then does anomic innovation perform as agency to alter front and backstage in noir world? In film noir, there are two dimensions of front/back stage: (1) the separate gnostic worlds of bourgeois civility (front stage and light) versus the demimonde (backstage—corruption and darkness), and (2) the seeping linkages of these two worlds as backstage base to front stage superstructure. The respectable middle-class world is always at risk of losing its delineation and of being infected by the noir backstage. The noir domain of shade underlies the front stage of bourgeois gentility. This facade launders the subterranean mix of violence, corruption, and dishonor that form the noir world.

The male noir hero acts to restore ideality over illusion and equilibrium over disorder. He is both restorer and disrupter who combines Merton's types of ritualist (rule fetishist) and rebel (rejecter of means and goal). The hero acts as Weber's ghost that haunts modernity—the last inner worldly ascetic (i.e., the last Calvinist and exposer of idols). The overthrown idols are Jezebel's false seductive gods. The idols he dethrones are the false respectabilities of subverted front stage, fake idols of gentility deeply infected by noir iniquity. The proper boundaries of front and backstage are restored by establishing the proper categories of stigma—primitive classification appropriate to modernity—discreditable or discredited personas. The hero must exist between categories of stigma. His role of disruptive agency places him in eternal marginality. His self is always in risk of permanent decentration as the price of its authenticity; he may extricate himself from being discredited but never entirely without falsehood.

If the hero acts as Weber's instrumental Calvinist, then Jezebel enchants as the Circe of the anomic; she seduces the hero to ensure her manipulations of front stage. Jezebel is Ariadne transformed from front stage ritualist to the manipulator and mistress of the noir world. As Ariadne she existed within a fatalistic situation. She, the civilizer of men, became their prey and debris. Jezebel is the means of escape. Lyman (1986, 30) writes of Jezebel the innovator within anomie as, "... released from the sacred bonds of community and the individual released from their restraints. Crime becomes a deviant route to restoring his lost faith in the future. Crime seems to promise the way to realizing the shiboleths of the American Dream—great wealth and a gorgeous wife." The femme fatale in her prior role of Ariadne was precluded from personal success because her central ethicality excluded usage of deviance. Jezebel must not only transform herself out of Ariadne; she must also transform the male from conformist or ritualist into deviant (a dual use of her agency of innovation). The male thus becomes an ego tool to fulfill Jezebel's id. The Ariadne pattern is thereby inverted between them. Front and backstage become linked as base and superstructure. The new goal is to conceal the risk of discredibility and its tensions and strains. Stigma as well as backstage now become the domains that Jezebel as agent must conceal and dissimulate.

Even male villains in the noir world become Jezebel impersonators. This may be the noir origin of male feminization that Lyman attributes to postmodernity. The noir male villain is dapper, suave, and sadistic. He exists as discreditable rather than discredited. The hero must discredit the villain's aristocratic front stage. This sneering, chortler of *bon mots* and good taste (Clifton Webb or Sidney Greenstreet) must be exposed as an androgynous, misogynistic, pseudo-dapper, effete male bitch. The male bitch image alludes to the hint of overt homosexuality, which could not be fully presented within the codes of the time. Closely related in image to the male bitch is the dapper, suave stranger/interloper whose backstage is homicidal psychosis (e.g., Claude Rains, Franchot Tone, or Joseph Cotton). If the overt homosexual villain must be presented in a veiled fashion, the stranger/ interloper then represents a closet image of a latent homosexual. His hidden backstage of sexual disposition is dissimulated as misogynistic murderous rage. Such uncertain masculinity in either guise is filtered as the archness of front stage, as in Cotton's Uncle Charlie in *Shadow of a Doubt*.

American Postmodern versus American Gothic: Mighty Casey Strikes Out and Out to the Last Syllable of Recorded Time

Some key features of the postmodern thriller are related to film noir and its transformations. These key elements include the antievanescence of evil and the omnipresence of the spectacle. These two general key elements affect two more specific key elements—death (displacement) of the persona and the frustration (neutralization) of agency.

How does postmodern film relate to and contrast with film noir? A comment by Alfred Hitchcock gives us an indication. In an interview Hitchcock described suspense as an intentional transformation of the following situation. A bomb exploding in a room without prior notice to either the characters or audience would not provide suspense and would be a wasted attempt at providing a thrill. Suspense would occur in the following revision of the situation. The characters in the room are not aware of the presence of the bomb and routinely go about their business. The audience is, however, aware of the bomb and fearfully focuses on its moment of imminent detonation. The audience experiences the sensation of suspense; they must hope and wait to see if the characters leave. Hitchcock placed a proviso here. The bomb must not actually go off; this would be too disturbing to the audience. Thus, even in Hitchcock's noir universe, the Hollywood ending thwarts unrelenting devastation. In the postmodern thriller, however, the bomb can and must go off. This becomes the desired and savored expectation of the audience.

Why this transition and transposition of possibility, fate, and destruction? Why the amoral rendering of moral tone? In postmodernity, that exploding bomb falls within the realm of the spectacle. In the spectacle, all that matters is imagery and bedazzlement. The subject does not exist as a unique persona for empathy and concern, as in noir. It exists as an isolated facet submerged into an overwhelming visage of the spectacle. Thus, the subject and his capacity for agency is decentered and relegated to inertial beings who go beyond Marx's peasants as sacks of potatoes or inertial voyeurs as monad units of couch potatoes. This decentration will transform the symbolic worth of the noir hero, whose eventual and final frustration is converted into uselessness, thus confirming a triumph of the spectacle.

The postmodern and its theme of the spectacle therefore serve to unwrap plot and narrative—the scaffold underlying noir. The description given by a scriptwriter of recent film captures this new sense of time and linearity as being disposable—"things don't end anymore, they just stop." Thus, the capacity for an ending to serve as a clear and ultimate moral guidepost becomes decentered. This now acceptable lack of a centered ending opens an arena where the spectacle is triumphant. The flow and resolution of narrative is inconsequential. Postmodern film thus informs the audience to wait for the moments of spectacle. Narrative now exists as mere artifice and diversion from the Great Diversion. The moral advice to everyman goes beyond the maxim—if it isn't broke, don't fix it. If it is broken (backstage) but appears fixed (front stage), let someone else worry about the actual reality of breakage and repair. It is better they should get killed than you! Thus, the moral dimension of front and backstage are trivialized and rendered a concern for suckers and fools.

Who is this sucker who never learns the finality of the spectacle and remains obsessed with an anachronistic concern about making things be what they seem? He is the hero—that noir moral center who is now relegated as victim of the spectacle. Postmodern heroes may be killed or ultimately thwarted. Evil can triumph and be realized as a prime agency of the spectacle. At best, evil can become temporarily containable but never fully eradicated. Thus, it can be revived to engender itself anew for more spectacle. It can be the center of imagery but be ironically decentered as the center of moral concern. This is done by rendering evil as clinical in impact (e.g., a plague that spreads and infects impersonal others). Evil thus becomes amorphous, lacking in tangibility and focus. Once evil is transformed into spectacle, it packs an overwhelming impact. The impact is such that the curbing of evil provides only temporary respite without redemption or reward for the hero. The hero must engage in over-sacrifice as the price of this mere curbing. This sacrifice levels the hero. His excessive effort negates consideration regarding the worth and realization of everyman's own redemptive heroic fantasies. The notion and worth of heroism becomes morally vacant and trivialized. Evil, the agency of spectacle, gains new focus for and attraction to the observer. Heroism is reduced to a cynical utilitarian equation for everyman's knowing rejection. How does evil manifest itself? Two modes of appearance are central: (1) extremely exotic, weird, or distant locales—fought by superhero elites whose aspect is equally exotic and beyond experience, and (2) evil as latent base that is interlinked to the superstructure of everyday life. Front and back-stage thus tend toward fusion and collapse, a reversal of both moral noir ethos and heroism. Thus, any disruption of the understructure of evil destroys its propping of the mundane. Such disruption destroys the normal and releases more evil. The noir ethic is reversed, as evil seeks its own equilibrium. The hero violates laissez-faire. Evil in this guise polices itself. Everyman should be neither perturbed nor concerned—"they only kill each other."

By subverting heroism and collapsing front and backstage, post-modernity becomes antirepresentational. Why? Heroism and evil require recognizable moral and visual representation, that is white and black hats. Evil is now given recognition as spectacle, not mor(t)al enemy. Heroism is now rendered ineffectual and thus unreliable. The observer now lacks any criterion of moral judgment to evaluate the imagery, which exists as its own representation without criteria or need for further consideration. Imagery becomes all. Ethical argumentation is thereby rendered superfluous. Because ethical argumentation is characterized by causal and historical referents, such discourse violates the postmodern obliteration of time and narrative. Postmodern chronology then turns reality into image and spectacle. There is no longer room or need at the Postmodern Inn for notions of ethicality. The moral of postmodernity then becomes: "the world can't spiritually elevate us in an authentic manner. Let then its appearance as perpetual presents at least enthrall us as spectacle."

The new postmodern omnipresence of the spectacle and decentration of the subject can be seen in an emerging film type that stresses the triumph of evil, the normalcy of paranoia, and betrayal as a mundane and acceptable ethic. These films may be called political noir. They maintain the noir focus on front stage and backstage; they also focus on the hero as agent of equilibration. They differ from standard noir by allowing for the eventual collapse of front and backstage and the subverting of effective heroism. The moral core intrinsic to noir becomes deconstructed. These films either overwhelm the viewer by showing the triumph of rampant amorality or themselves advocate such amorality in a bemused manner. They represent two eras—high Watergate and the greedy eighties. High Watergate examples include *Chinatown* (1974), *The Parallax View* (1974), and *Twilight's Last Gleaming* (1977). These films are ambivalent in their message. Some are Brechtian in tone and generate a sense of unease and nausea, with front and backstage serving as base and superstructure of corruption. The validity of paranoia is confirmed. Trusted figures are actually evil. They exist as both conspirators of evil and a false front stage. Legitimation provides the imagery for this spectacle. The price here is that the hero is killed or thwarted to make the world safe for the maintenance of legitimacy and the continuance of conspiracy. These films suggest two possible impacts. The most positive impact is Brechtian: the informing and unsettling of a politically quiescent audience. The other possibility is cultural affirmation of the postmodern narcosis and its continuing celebration.

In another variation of political noir, evil is rendered as exotic and omnipotent. It then becomes distant, trivial to everyman, an amusing and diverting spectacle. An example of this version is *Madame Sin* (1971), in which Bette Davis and sidekick Denholm Eliot are the ultimate political conspirators within travesty. They are portrayed as deliriously, campily wicked; delightfully daffy Robert Wagner, an elite agent, thwarts their schemes. He is finally killed by one of Madame Sin's luscious agents during lovemaking. The two villains are soon again at work in a fadeout of them conspiring, chortling and unscathed. Evil is here triumphant as agency and eccentrically appealing as image's spectacle. The veneer of exoticism is distanced from everyday life. The tone conveyed is culturally affirmative. The elite hero is distanced from conveying meaningful ethical identity and is ultimately impotent (except sexually) and uninfluential. Everyman is best advised to pursue mere everyday life and not bother with the realities of higher politics (real front and backstage), which is simultaneously dangerous and trite. Such a film falls clearly within the parameters of the culture industry, providing both entertainment and enlightenment in the guise of cynical inside information.

Conclusion

If the noir hero is rendered as an ineffectual shard in postmodernity and evil exists as both prime entertainment spectacle and victorious vanquisher of the moral, what subject or persona shall represent us all and provide grace and succor for everyman? Everyman is in need of salvation, even in the ethical free fall of postmodernity. Salvation from what? Salvation from the boredom engendered by the spectacle—gluttonies of sensate overload. Jean Baudrillard (1983) refers to this experience as obscenity: cycles of overwhelming desire, attempted satiation, frustration, and finally, paralyzing boredom. Who then within the spectacle can save us from the spectacle? The noir world is based on human agency as redemptive. Postmodernity, instead, subverts the worth of such agency and undermines the legitimacy of the hero. The postnoir hero will be either superhuman or nonhuman—a self-contained purveyor of spectacle. Some examples are Batman, Mad Max, Starman, the Jedi knights, E.T., and Robocop. We will even have spectacle antichrists to replace our noir world array of dapper villains and their psycho henchmen. Our spectacle villians shall be undying, sadistic signifiers—Freddy, Jason, recycled comic book villains Luthor, Joker, Penguin, Hannibal Lector, and so on. They enact the defilement and destruction of the body as their contribution to spectacle. Our heads will be bloody but we hope not bored.

Postscript: Porno as Anti-Noir

This essay has focused on the noir and postmodern worlds as contrasting moral universes. Among the key inversions that occur in postmodernity are the eviscerations of heroism and moral agency as well as front and backstage. Indeed, the backstage of noir world is the demimonde—the arena that noir heroism must prevent from infecting the front stage. Part of the moral equilibration achieved in the noir world was to expose the seemingly hedonistic front stage of the demimonde as being actually the backstage domain marked by misery and anhedonia. Pornography, however, provides a counterworld to the noir world, by celebrating and exalting the hedonistic front stage image of the demimonde. In porno-world, front and backstages become superfluous. The body becomes its own sole spectacle, replacing all other appearances and domains.

The body as actor without subject is so ultimately explicit that front and backstage become meaningless as dichotomies. The subject becomes irrelevant and decentered, as the body becomes all. Narrative and subject exist as trite devices, rendering any moral dimension equally meaningless. The viewer, however, is not yet free. He or she experiences Baudrillard's notion of "obscenity" but within film obscenity. Hedonism is turned to frustration. The surfeit of the object(s) of desire only serves to overwhelm desire. Desire is forced always to assert and benumb itself.

A Dantesque tour of such a demimonde underworld emerges from the underground to mark the pornographic film *The Devil in Miss Jones*. This final image will be taken from that classic tour de force of avant-garde pornography. *Devil* explicitly offers an image of a postmodern hell in which the main torment is the infinite immersion into Baudrillard's experience of the obscene.

The heroine, Miss Jones, commits suicide due to virginal frustration. She sells her soul to the devil for a week of pure and ultimate sensual pleasure. The pupil is an apt and creative learner. She becomes enthralled and immersed into the ideal of pornography as spectacle and fulfillment. The final image is of a post-Christian anhedonia worthy of Dante's tormented souls (that is, if a tenth ring can emerge for the spirit of Times Square sleeze). The image that follows debases the heroine within the spectacle as well as the spectator.

Hell's terrain, in this image, pays homage to high modernity. It is a Beckett-like, desolate, desert landscape. The sexually awakened and now voracious heroine seeks to couple with the only male—a depraved cretinous imbecile. The imbecile ignores her. He instead deeply observes a fly—the symbol of Satan. Thus, neither backstage nor front stage are discernible. The initial phase of hell is that this dichotomy exists solely in the separate desires of the damned. Thus, Miss Jones's hell is in not being able to lure the idiot away from his private self-enclosed theater of front stage. She tries to attract him through an eternally continuous act of joyless masturbation. The heroine thus experiences anhedonia. The act of pleasure serves only to distance her further from the object of pleasure, while not yielding her any pleasure. Desire is thus thwarted by its own act (agency) of pleasure and exhibitionism. The heroine has come full circle. Frustration first began with no available sexual agency. Frustration concludes with her inability to enlist an ever present but unavailable agent/object of desire. To paraphrase Jean-Paul Sartre, hell is being unable to amuse oneself or other people. Her lack of pleasure, however, can provide pleasure to the male viewer. The voyeur isn't experiencing sensuality but sadism derived from another's humiliation. One wonders if the exploitation and humiliation involved is reciprocal— an exchange of debasement within shared dimensions of spectacle, a spectacle that must implode to achieve a further transformation into newer spectacle.

Thus, in the postmodern hell, the subject becomes decentered and anhedonic. The secular spectacle of the fulfillment of the flesh reverts to a quasi-Christian mortification of the flesh. The body becomes the spectacle whose denial of itself provides a new spectacle based on damnation and retribution. Lust transvalues itself into images by Hieronymus Bosch but not for detached amusement. Things thus fall apart; the postmodern cannot hold. All worlds become transvalued. The Hollywood ending (cinema as Herbert Spencer) yields to the evanescence of goodness. Noir world is vanquished into the postmodern spectacle.

The once morally equilibrated noir world is now turned amoral. The noir world has been transformed into the postmodern. This postmodern world is post-Calvinist and antiheroic. In postmodernity then, God pines, as enfeebled and decentered evil is now triumphant. Moral icons are transformed into secular nonhuman super redeemers. Human heroes, who previously enforced the noir primacy of the great chain of being, are now destroyed for interfering with the great chain of signifiers. Even Porno-X is not immune; it turns Calvinist in tone. The only shards of noir heroism linger in desperate struggles for mere survival, as in Robocop. Heroes who survive earn only consolation prizes for their deeds: existence without redemption, disillusionment without further understanding, and ultimately, not laurels, but crowns of thorns. We can only hope to survive as Mad Max, neurotic superhero detectives, or Batman.

After the spectacle there comes only the sequel.

References Cited

Baudrillard, Jean. 1983. *Simulations.* New York: Semoitext(e).

Benjamin, Walter. 1969. *Illuminations.* New York: Schocken.

Brecht, Bertold. 1964. *Brecht on Theatre,* ed. John Willet. New York: Hill and Wang.

Debord, Guy. 1987. *Society of the Spectacle.* London: Rebel Press.

Freud, Sigmund. 1962. *Group Psychology and the Analysis of the Ego.* New York: Bantam Books.

Goffman, Erving. 1959. *The Presentation of the Self in Everday Life.* New York: Anchor.

——. 1961. *Asylums.* New York: Anchor Books.

——. 1963. *Stigma.* Englewood Cliffs, N.J.: Prentice-Hall.

——. 1967a. *Interaction R.* New York: Bantam Books.

——. 1967b. *Strategic Interaction.* New York: Ballantine Books.

Horkheimer, Max, and Theodor Adorno. 1972. *Dialectic of Enlightenment.* New York: Herder and Herder.

Jameson, Frederic. 1983. "Postmodernism and Consumer Society." Pp. 111–25 in *The Anti-Aesthetic,* ed. Hal Foster. Port Townsend, Wash.: Bay Press.

Lacan, Jacques. 1977. *Écrits.* New York: Norton.

Lyman, Stanford. 1986. "Anhedonia and Modern Film." Unpublished ms.

Lyotard, Jean-François. 1984. *The Postmodern Condition.* Minneapolis: University of Minnesota Press.

Merton, Robert. 1957. *Social Theory and Social Structure.* Chicago: Free Press of Glencoe.

Nietzsche, Friedrich. 1966. *Beyond Good and Evil.* New York: Vintage Books.

Simmel, Georg. 1971. "The Tragedy of Modern Culture." Pp. 375-93 in *Georg Simmel: On Individuality and Social Forms,* ed. Donald Levine. Chicago: University of Chicago Press.

Weber, Max. 1958a. *The Protestant Ethic and the Spirit of Capitalism.* New York: Scribner.

——. 1958b. "Religious Rejections of the World and Their Directions." Pp. 323-59 in *From Max Weber,* ed. Hans Gerth and C. Wright Mills. New York: Oxford University Press.

——. 1958c. "Science as a Vocation." Pp. 129-56 in *From Max Weber,* ed. Hans Gerth and C. Wright Mills. New York: Oxford University Press.

10 Rhetoric, Ethics, and Telespectacles in the Post-everything Age

Bruce E. Gronbeck

Among the many sociopolitical, technological, and economic changes that have altered American politics in the last third of the twentieth century, two have been especially disruptive to traditional democratic thought. First has been the rise of "New Politics." While New Politics has been defined in various ways, most agree that the consensus model of American governance was dealt a fatal blow in the 1960s and 1970s. The melting pot politics so characteristic of nineteenth-century tribalism and clientelism (Piven and Cloward 1989) gave way to power politics.

Traditional melting-potism is nowhere better illustrated than in the Statue of Liberty, a gift to the United States from the French government in the age of immigration. Positioned in the New York harbor, looking toward Ellis Island and the sea, the statue was immortalized two years before its arrival in Emma Lazarus's poem, "The New Colossus." Inscribed on the pedestal of the statue were these lines:

> Give me your tired, your poor,
> Your huddled masses yearning to breathe free,
> The wretched refuse of your teeming shore,
> Send these, the homeless, tempest-tost to me,
> I lift my lamp beside the golden door! (Lazarus [1883] 1989)

Together with Israel Zangwill's 1908 play, *The Melting Pot*, and the construction of American identity on its coins (*e pluribus unum*, "Out of many, one"), our nineteenth-century political ideology turned around a fund of common values to which we always could appeal in times of political acculturation or controversy. A primary tenet of political argument, ever rational, was that we can dispute about means, not ends, and those ends were, in Richard Weaver's language (1953), uncontested terms. Daniel Webster could appeal to "Union and Liberty" in 1850, the U.S. Immigration and Naturalization Service could term potential citizens "huddled masses yearning to breathe free" even while remaking their histories and futures ideologically, and Albert Beveridge could end the nineteenth century reciting America's shared political virtues in his imperialistic "March of the Flag" speech. Political dialogue was envisioned in melting-potism as consensus-building, with various parties arranging themselves around communal valuative property.

Traditional American democratic thought thus assumed we could engineer binding agreements through group representatives who, especially if they were of the gentry class, would speak for—even instead of—their constituencies with disinterestedness yet vision and, along with their peers, come to political decisions constructed around doxastic (generally agreed upon) beliefs, attitudes, and values.

The New Politics destroyed that consensus model. Daniel Bell's *The End of Ideology* ([1960] 1962) was a herald for what was to come in the decade of revolution. Bell charted the demise of nineteenth-century universalistic, holistic, intellectual ideologies, particularly Marxism and the mass society tenets of the West, in a world that featured economically (not politically) motivated wars as well as ethnic-racial uprisings in Africa and the Middle East. Classical ideologies to Bell had to die in the face of nationalism: anticolonialism, modernization, industrialization, and Pan-Arabism marked the new world.

The fact that Bell critiqued the left rather than the right narrowed his influence in later years but certainly not in the early 1960s. His program of anti-institutionalism and localism fit that decade well. Anti-institutionalism represented the attempt to erode the influence of bureaucracies and marked the Berkeley Free Speech Movement and its attack upon the "multiversity." Such attacks powered the civil rights and women's rights movements and, of course, Vietnam protests. The second force, localism, led to much talk about grassroots movements: the localist philosophy of the seemingly radical Port Huron Statement of 1962 reverberated through environmentalism, Common Cause, other citizens' lobbies, and neighborhood reclamation projects. Bottom-up social change preached the gospel of working on your own turf, improving your community first before assaulting larger units of society. Citizen action committees were built more around issues and demographic characteristics than abstract ideologies (Barbrook and Bolt 1980).

We thus came to understand that competing groups with incommensurate values align and realign themselves issue by issue, situation by situation, bringing only temporary closure to political conflicts we are bound to relive every time circumstances change. The classic philosophy of "out of many, one" was rewritten as "out of many, many more" (Connolly 1987; Gronbeck 1990; Lee 1994). The New Politics is person-centered, power-based, and always, always, circumstantial in its force. New Politics discourse reminds us often of marketing talk, where audiences are segmented and then targeted with specific messages tailored to their particular needs and lifestyles.

Equally disruptive of the classic models (especially of political campaigning) has been the rise of electronic media. Radio's broad reach of voice and ideas moved American thought toward a kind of plebiscitism (Lowi 1985) that led the independent candidate H. Ross Perot in 1992 to think he could conduct actual electronic town meetings as president. The coming of film, notably in the 1924 campaign biography of Calvin Coolidge (Morreale 1994), illustrated the political power of visual discourses—the ocularcentrism so disturbing to Jacques Ellul (1985). Television's instantaneous transmission of sight and sound made possible a level of standardization of ideas that inspired Alvin Toffler's (1971) thesis of massification. Toffler argued that television's dual power was to massify people and to convince them to accept depersonalized treatment. And fourth, of course, the computerization of politics has fostered both the compilation and simplification of ideas in modern theories of political informatics (Armstrong 1988; Gronbeck 1990). Informatics becomes the study of the simultaneous amassing and reduction of data, a hallmark of the age that explains why Americans decry their level of political knowledge even while they are drowning in political information. The communication technologies have created connections between and among political institutions and constituencies never dreamed of even in the homogeneous city-state democracies of ancient Greece.

Following the rise of both New Politics and the electronic media, the political world of the United States has been radically altered. In this essay I wish to pursue those changes: first, I will discuss briefly the chief characteristics of the new political discourse and its audiences. That will allow me to examine assaults upon the morality of such a new modelled politics; "teledemocracy" has been attacked for various reasons and with different challenges. Examining those attacks will provide me with lines of argument for a rhetorical view of political morality. I will outline that ethic and suggest its implications as I conclude this essay.

Characteristics of Contemporary American Political Discourse

Political discourse and its audiences have been remade, I would argue, around five propositions. *First, political messages are complex composites of multiple discourses created in verbal, visual, and acoustic languages.* In the age of secondary orality (Ong 1982), political meaning-making occurs at the intersection of ocularcentric, phonocentric, and logocentric discourses. Our political messages depend for their force upon words' interpretations of pictures, pictures' illustration of words, and sounds' emotional shadings of both (Gronbeck 1993).

Second, paradoxically, even as the amount of political information increases in the United States, political messages are shortened and focused. Even as the amount of sheer information increases, voters sense that they lack the requisite political knowledge to make good electoral decisions. Today we are awash in ten-, thirty-, and sixty-second polispots and five-second sound bites on the news but to little avail. Citizens regularly complain about politicians talking about the wrong issues or about the "right" issues in incomprehensible language—sometimes called "professional speak" (*Citizens* 1991, 14). The ad or clip may provide an emotional lift but is of little cognitive comfort.

Third, controversial, partisan propositions (political debates) are giving way to emotion-laden, narrative depictions (storytelling) as the center of political talk. Since Aristotle, reasoned argument has been idealized as the essence of political process. Today, however, much political discourse is narrativized. In a scientized, complicated, distant, enormous society of over 260 million people with a four-trillion dollar debt, an anecdote about an African American man in Tupelo, Mississippi, or a little old lady in Dubuque, Iowa, is reassuring. Through such stories we learn that individuals count, that the abstract can be concretized, that complicated political situations can be reduced to simple morality plays (Fisher 1987; Jamieson 1988).

Fourth, constituencies in the contemporary world are fractured, then added together, not homogenized, in political spectacle. The ideas of segmentation and targeting suggest that coalition-building is even more central to today's politics than it was in the era of melting-potism. Thus, at the 1988 Democratic National Convention, Jesse Jackson sought to build his Rainbow Coalition out of fragments of the American public. He called each segment a patch, identifying farmers, laborers, women, mothers, students, blacks and Hispanics, gays and lesbians, and conservatives and progressives as constituents to be sewn together: "Pool the patches and the pieces together, bound by a common thread. When we form a great quilt of unity and common ground we'll have the power to bring about health care and housing and jobs and education and hope to our nation. We the people can win" (Jackson 1988).

Quilts of unity are visual objects, and contemporary politics runs on the telespectacle. Human action draws its significance from its context; acts derive power from scenes, as Kenneth Burke (1945) said, the thing-contained from the container. The telespectacle is the enactment of political processes upon scenes that direct interpretive and evaluative reactions in particular ways. The granite and oak that comprise the courtroom suggest enlargement of scope, solidity, and permanence. The party national convention is dominated by hordes of party faithful, signs, colorful costumes, balloons, bunting, joyous song, and inspirational speech; the collectivity materializes the chant of ideology and hope, while the rest of the scene adds overtones of excitement, power, confidence, commitment, and indefatigable optimism. Television gives the viewing public a chance to oversee the spectacle, to participate from a point of view controlled by the camera lens. That participation is the source of power in today's politics, for the symbolic dimensions of politics are both origin and outcome of acts of power (Bourdieu [1971] 1977).

Fifth, political parties play reduced roles when the executive elite can build constituencies electronically. One of the unintended consequences of the electronic revolution in politics has been the death of party so far as presidential politics is concerned (Gronbeck 1990; see also Polsby 1983; Wattenberg 1990; Bennett 1992). Candidates and their oligarchical election committees appeal directly to the voter via mass- (television) and mini- (zip-code sorted, computerized mail) media. Candidates and their committees raise the great bulk of their money directly from political action committees (PACs) and private givers, with political parties important only when it is time to mount a convention or reach for a few more votes.

While the idea of candidates in direct contact with their constituencies sounds like participatory democracy at its best, in fact it makes those candidates and their election committees absolutely free; they are accountable to no person or institution for what they say or do. They live out the New Politics vision of anti-institutionalism but without a concern for local politics or for any other part of the political system. In drawing power directly from voters, the president lives a fascist political life where the ability to rule depends upon personal authority—and on high voter-approval ratings in the Gallup poll on presidential leadership and achievement.

The Assault on Teledemocracy

The fragmentation of the electorate in the era of New Politics in combination with the coming of the new technologies have rebuilt American electoral politics in fundamental ways. The new electoral machinery has not been received with universal praise. While it is possible to critique the machine for its cumbersomeness—fifty-three caucus and primary contests before the general election, frustrating bookkeeping thanks to campaign finance reporting rules, a two- to four-year preparation period before announcement speeches—most attacks upon teledemocracy have a strong moral tone. The American way of electing presidents has been assaulted both for what has been lost, its absences, as well as for what has been added, its presences.

The Lost Virtues of the Old Ways

Those most explicit about what has been lost in the electronic age are the French postmodernist social critics, especially Jean Baudrillard. His 1987 essay, "Seduction, or the Superficial Abyss" (1988), focuses specifically on the question of absence. He sees postmodernist politics as seduction and hence the absence of anything real or powerful: "Surface and appearance, that is the space of seduction. Seduction as a mastering of the reign of appearances opposes power as a mastering of the universe of meaning" (1983, 62). Such seduction is possible to Baudrillard because populations have been massified: "The masses scandalously resist . . . rational communication. They are given meaning: they want spectacle. No effort has been able to convert them to the seriousness of content, nor even to the serious- ness of the code. Messages are given to them, they only want some sign, they idolise the play of signs and stereotypes, they idolise any content so long as it resolves itself into a spectacular discourse" (1983, 10).

Public policy in such a situation is dependent upon "resonance," "an illusionary mass outlook" (1983, 24). Elections in this analysis are games, entertainments, at best theatrical performances (1983, 37). Thus, all of politics is seduction—a gesture without love, a move without social consequences, a sham, a simulacra.

Writing with more bite about politics as mere spectacle is Guy Debord, whose *Society of the Spectacle* ([1967] 1983) is a foundational postmodernist document. Beginning with the presupposition that "spectacle is not a collection of images, but a social relation among people, mediated by images" (para. 4), Debord spins out a theory wherein the social is constructed and maintained via mass-mediated spectacle or appearances. In a time of the loss of unity (community), the "alienation of the spectator" (para. 30), and power constituted via appearances rather than material relationships, (political) spectacle affirms our relationships with each other, but only symbolically, in representations of ourselves. Tragically, it ultimately moves us "from partial knowledge into totalitarian falsehood" (ideology), using and destroying rationality simultaneously (para. 108). We thus live in the era of the "illusionary social fact," "the illusion of encounter" (para. 217): "The spectacle obliterates the boundaries between self and world by crushing the self besieged by the presence-absence of the world and it obliterates the boundaries between true and false by driving all lived truth below the real presence of fraud ensured by the organization of appearance" (para. 219).

With boundaries between the false and the true gone, with community obliterated, and with material relationships absent from the exercise of power, Debord argues that spectacle is all that is left—and that is not good.

Quite similar, oddly enough, is the liberal critique offered by Wilson Carey McWilliams (1989) in reaction to the 1988 presidential campaign. He believes the American electoral system is in trouble because of the decline in voting, the manipulative use of media by all parties, and the resulting loss of community and liberal values. He, too, worries about the spectacle we experience with television: "television is a visual medium, confined to what can be seen and hence to externalities. Sight is our quickest sense, but it is also superficial, and the media's discontinuity of image and affect encourages emotional detachment, adaptation rather than commitment" (182). The result is death of community: "Communitarianism sees political society as a moral order, and the laws of such a regime, designed to strengthen what is admirable and right, entail penalties for the wicked as well as rewards for the virtuous" (197). Unless we return to communitarianism, to "a new civility" seen in "the kind of word and deed necessary to affirm, for the coming century, the dignity of self-government" (200), we will not endure.

The Acquired Vices of the New Ways

Perhaps even more critiques of teledemocracy worry about what has been added to or emphasized in the era of New Politics and the new technologies. Robert Denton, Jr. (1991), for example, lays out four characteristics of democracy—accountability, free flow of information, systemically free marketplace of ideas, and collective deliberation —and then uses them to measure the operating efficiencies of teledemocracy. It does not measure up, for our "primetime presidency" has worked to conform messages to the demands of media and not the other way around, to lead to the collusion of the presidency and the press at the expense of the people, and to create a cult of individualism via a rhetoric of personalism. Thus, the power and even the presence of the collective all but disappears. Ronald Reagan's presidency exemplified to Denton all of these characteristics:

> The personalizing medium of television allows the actor in the proper setting to engage us and become part of us in defining the world. Ronald Reagan the "great communicator" was really Ronald Reagan the "great television communicator." His persona, messages, and behavior fitted the medium's requirements in terms of form, content, and industry demands. Reagan, especially in the first term, surrounded himself with professionals of the modern communications technology. (107)

Here, "the central task is how to continue to cultivate an active, democratic citizenry in light of the heavy dependence upon television, an undemocratic medium" (111).

A variant analysis flows from media scholar Neil Postman. After arguing that social knowledge (epistemology) is rooted in modes of discourse and that "typographic America" in the nineteenth century led to "liberal, rational and articulate" discourse (1985, 57), he moves on to assault the "peek-a-boo" politics of the contemporary era, with its stress on show business, brevity, noncontextuality, false narrativation, musical background, and hypervisuality. The problem is that television is a "style of learning," even a "curriculum" (144, 145), and hence the telespectacle shortchanges us by providing truncated, presentist, useless political information. Television fosters a burlesque culture (155).

The Marxist John Welsh ([1985] 1990) launches his assault on teledemocracy from the vantage of the people, the proletariat. To Welsh, the central operating tenet of teledemocracy is mystification. Political power is converted into political rule through "the dramatization of authority," which in turn relies upon "processes of mystifying the social relations" (399). Mystification occurs through the recitation of a pseudo-democratic ideology, pseudo-political debates, the creation of a corrupt cult of personality to run the country, the false politics of bureaucratic self-criticism, and, whenever rulers are in trouble, the diversionary appeals to patriotism. We are submerged in and by the "dramaturgical technology of the American state" (408).

The message of both the critics of absence and the critics of presence is clear: the contemporary electoral system in the United States is seriously flawed, and those flaws constitute grounds for political despair. Concern for both what has been lost and what has been found is articulated by Lance Bennett (1992, 14):

> We have entered a political era in which electoral choices are of little consequence because an electoral system in disarray can generate neither the party unity nor the levels of public agreement necessary to forge a winning and effective political coalition. The underlying explanation is that the political and economic forces driving our national politics have created a system in which the worst tendencies of the political culture—the hype, hoopla, and negativity—have been elevated to the norm in elections, gaining a systematic dominance in campaign content as never before.

In a realist political world, dominated by multilanguaged political discourse that has sacrificed size for frequency and stories for arguments, and in a political world fractured, segmented, and then targeted by spectacle of an anti-institutional, fascist sort, it is easy to note what has been lost or found and to conclude that political morality is no more.

A Rhetorical Ethics for Teledemocracy

I would suggest that such attempts to write off contemporary political morality are too precious; they smell of the lamp and seem oddly out of rhythm with the 1992 elections they attempted to predict. They are also time-bound, governed less by any lengthy examination of American political history than by a concern to sell ideas to today's understandably frustrated public. I would suggest a longer look at the matter of ethics in American democracy. I would argue that public moral judgments have always been constructed rhetorically, argued into existence in times of theoretical and circumstantial crisis. Political ethics do not exist in a philosophical time capsule or in decontextualized sets of actions. They are not tied permanently to a credo or means of communication. Rather, public morality must constantly be reconstructed every time democracy faces a point of decision.

The failure of the Articles of Confederation in the 1780s led to discussions about the American community as constructed locally (within states) and nationally (within a federation); the nullification debates of the 1830s rehearsed the same themes. The operations of the federal government were viewed as antidemocratic (or not) by the reformers of the civil service system in the late nineteenth century. Relationships between democracy and power were featured in debates over limitations of presidential terms following Franklin Roosevelt's twenty-two-year reign. Periodically, America has had to reconstitute its political community in light of circumstantial or structural alterations in its political system. We can think of the coming of New Politics and the new technologies in the same way.

To make theoretical sense of these events and to integrate the themes of this chapter, let me consider the matter of rhetoric, ethics, and teledemocracy in three movements, first discussing my understanding of "community," then offering a definition of political communication that I think rationalizes current practice, and finally dealing with the difficult matter of how we are to understand the rhetorical crafting of political morality.

"Community" as a Boundary Construct

Loose talk about the loss of community abounds as the world hurtles toward the end of the millennium. We should expect no less, for the millennium is a symbolically rich temporal boundary that draws attention, no doubt, to equally intriguing spatial and social boundaries. People define themselves in time and space, as Edward Hall (1959) noted when calling systems of time and space orientation systems. Such orienting systems are central to defining one's sense of sociality; who we are as a collectivity is based on the perception of having a place in time and space.[1] Such perceptions, likewise, are discursively constructed and become "power inscriptions" (Shapiro 1992, 88).

"Community," viewed here as a configuration of social relations understood and constructed symbolically, is almost never lost, strictly speaking. Rather, varied definitions of social relations dominate thought from time to time, situation to situation. As Anthony Cohen (1985, 98) argues, "culture—the community as experienced by its members—does not consist in social structure or in 'the doing' of social behaviour. It inheres, rather, in 'the thinking' about it." And we can think about it in different situations in manifold ways. Our sense of community—our collective identity—is rhetorically constructed. We set our social boundaries or definitions of "we" and "they" via discourses of community.

Temporally, we draw our diachronous boundaries through the rehearsal of traditions, myths, and significant events, which we in

turn use to describe ourselves today. Thus, Americans strongly emphasize 1620 and the Pilgrims coming to uncharted lands when we wish
to don the mantle of God's new Israelites, the chosen people of the
New Canaan, and give ourselves an aura of divinity and roots that
run down the center of Judeo-Christian history. Americans fall back
to 1776, in contrast, when they prefer not to be reincarnations but a
genuinely new people, separated from the Old World and its corrup-
tions; with 1776 as a starting point, we become Yankees, a people
with new forms of government, new models for economic arrangements,
new values—especially for the rights and prerogatives of the individual.
Such moves to temporalize community draw strongly on history and
tradition and hence usually carry with them a kind of sacralization of
the group (Shapiro 1992, 91–95).

Similarly, spatially we create boundaries around ourselves as
"community" by the ways we arrange synchronous associations with
other collectivities. And, again, we are dealing here with a rhetorical
process, one which Kenneth Burke (1950) called "identification,"
understood as a discursively defined, horizontal set of cooperative
and conflictive relationships between groups of people. We are dealing with what Michel Foucault (1986, 23) called "the forms of relations among sites."

To map community spatially is to redefine geographical relationships as geopolitical and geosocial constructs. Calling me an "Iowan"
geographically places me between real, materially identifiable seg-
ments of the Missouri and Mississippi Rivers. Calling me an "Iowan"
geopolitically conjures up images of populism, the ideological programs of the Grange and the National Farmers Organization and
political mood swings of great volatility. Calling me an "Iowan"
geosocially evokes the heartland values of hard work, honest pay for
honest effort, and individualism clearly embedded in a brother's
keeper ethic—self-sufficiency encased in social responsibility. Calling me an "Iowan" separates me from the "coastals" who talk about
New York and Los Angeles, who practice a complex urban politics I
do not understand, and who live out power- and money-driven (i.e.,
pragmatic) values that I find alien to my way of life.

"Community," therefore, is not strictly speaking a commodity,
though it can be commodified as it is every time a baseball team wins
the World Series or a traveler comes home with a British suit or
Nigerian jewelry. Most of the time "community" is a set of social
relations that someone brings to consciousness so as to make claims
upon the beliefs, attitudes, values, and actions of someone else.
Rhetorical evocations of community are efforts to fit audiences with

orientational glasses, which we assume will cause them to see the world in particular ways and then to act in a manner appropriate to what they are seeing.

Constructions of community, thus, are sources of consensus, not in the nineteenth-century sense of systemic or decontextualized ends or purposes but as valuative complexes that audiences in particular settings can be persuaded to accept as grounds for judgment and action. When accepted, they can be evoked in support of specific beliefs, attitudes, values, or actions.

Mass-mediated Discursive Worlds

Let us now consider the vehicles of such rhetorical evocations: most importantly, television, the mass medium of choice among American politicians. Regarding this communication medium, we must remember three things. First, no matter how much emphasis we put on television as the great medium of political communication, it is only one among many. Even if we believe Americans get most of their political information from television, they do not get it all there, and, further, they acquire it from multiple televisual forms—news programs, ads, talk shows. Television should be given neither all of the credit nor all of the blame for what is interesting or banal about American electoral politics. Second, because televisual discourse works across three languages—sight, sound, and words—its messages can be and often are highly complex. Even the thirty-second political ad can both present and evoke a staggering amount of political information. Third, television as a medium is inherently neither good nor bad; rather, it is the culturally conditioned uses of a medium that we must assess when examining it. Iranian television is used for long sermons and lessons, not quick-hitting ads and public service announcements; television in most parts of the world is not so strictly governed by time as it is in the United States; few countries' networks fill the day with game shows, sensationalist talk shows, and cartoons. The uses to which television is put are reflections of the sociopolitical system within which it operates and of that system's modes of institutionalization and habituation. How, then, is television used politically in the United States? Consider the following propositions:

Television commodifies politicians, especially in the electoral process. American television is a regulated, commercial medium of communication; it delivers viewers to advertisers via its programming and hence pays for itself through the buying and selling of commodities (Parenti 1993). During the 1988 general election, the Dukakis-Bentsen campaign spent $22.3 million and the Bush-Quayle campaign spent $30.2 million on television ads and presentations (Alexander and Bauer 1991). The making of the ads is overseen by advertising executives, not politicians, and their products are slipped into the evening viewing schedule between ads for cars and hamburgers.

As commodities, campaigners become both communicators and satisfiers. Sut Jhally (1990) argues that any advertised good is both a communicator of social ideas and power relations and a satisfier of human needs. In his analysis, the discourse surrounding advertised goods seeks to raise and satisfy needs and, in the process, totemizes the object of the discourse—here, the candidate. As totems, campaigners have attached to them a great variety of changing, abstract qualities: personal (yet collectively sanctioned) virtues, powers to solve the unsolvable problems of society, charismatic forces to rejuvenate a declining society, the vision to rule wisely and prudently. Political acts and actors are imbued with totemic virtues and powers through sophisticated manipulations of verbal, visual, and aural sign systems.

Television commentators help form and interpret campaigners by providing us with ways of viewing these commodities. As Joshua Meyrowitz (1985) argues, Americans live their presidential campaigns not on front stage, as mere spectators of political events, nor backstage, as members of the political elites, but at side stage, both watching political events and receiving commentary on those happenings. We also are presented almost nightly with the daily poll results of who is ahead and behind; polls are reified, self-reflexive views of how we collectively are thinking at any given moment. So, we are fed a diet of video clips surrounded with professional ("expert") interpretations and resonant polls that place those clips against an evaluative charting of our own reactions.

Through all of this, we are taught to see by television news and commentary programs. Television anchors, reporters, and commentators become our political worldmakers, using all five of the worldmaking tools that Nelson Goodman (1978) identified.[2] The effects of such processes are a formalization by television of relationships between events or between events and people as well as an interpretation—a way of understanding—what is posed as the heart of the campaign.

I wish to argue, in sum, that candidate-controlled and media-controlled messages are contraposed, each vying with the other for rule over popular perceptions and evaluations of the political environment. Candidate aides and network staffs alike seek to construct a sociopolitical reality capable of forming a backdrop for specific actions, proposals, and, ultimately, electoral judgments. The struggle to control public perceptions is most easily seen in the primary period, when the horse race aspect of a campaign (who's ahead? who's doing better or worse than expected? who can survive the most hits?) dominates candidates' and media's messages. The sheer volume of tracking polls during the general election period also puts the worldmaking efforts of candidates and the media into conflict. One of the most telling ads George Bush ran in 1992 was composed of clips of "citizens" saying confidently that he had "won" the third presidential debate, in obvious reaction to the networks' judgments about a draw.

The Rhetorical Construction of Political Morality

With these introductions to matters of community and mass-mediated political discourse, we can plunge into the primary argument: political ethics has neither disappeared nor been perverted. Rather, political ethics is now, as it has always been, a matter of rhetorical construction. Moral visions must be painted discursively and then argued into judgments about individuals, their acts and their motives.

In an earlier essay (Gronbeck 1991), I argued that there are a dozen ethical positions from which to assess presidential campaigns. In the American political ethos, we have available three ethical pivots: candidates' actions and the *motives* they offer in justification of those actions, candidates' *characters* as revealed in talk and action, and candidates' discussions of issues and the extent to which they illustrate their *competence* as governors. In addition, I suggested that the ethical pivots of motives, character, and competence can be assessed from four different moral vantages or perspectives: from the viewpoint of the *message maker* (who can be held responsible for his or her actions), the *message consumers* (who can be told to test claims in relation to their own experiences), the *messages themselves* (which ought to contain true claims and sufficient evidence for those claims), or the *situation* (which seemingly evokes "rules" for how candidates ought to conduct themselves in various contexts).

Multiplying three ethical pivots by four possible moral vantages produces twelve possible ethical questions that could be asked of any campaign. The point is not whether twelve is the right number but, rather, to suggest that just as we can have many possible political worlds constructed by parties interested in electoral outcomes, so are there numerous moral nodes to which political ethicists may appeal.

This last point finally gets to the center of the question I am posing: how are we to conceive of political morality in an era of telespectacle? My answer is rhetorically, or, better, dialogically. My thinking is very much influenced by Celeste Condit's "Crafting Virtue: The Rhetorical Construction of Public Morality" (1987). Condit opens with sharp attacks on the privatization of morality. She argues that moralists such as Walter Fisher (1984) are so pessimistic about the possibility of making ethical judgments in public that they retreat to private worlds of controlled, rational moral judgments. Or they follow Alasdair MacIntyre (1981) in urging a conversational approach to moral assessment reminiscent of Callicles's and Socrates's dialogue on the morality of rhetoric in the *Gorgias*. The problem with privatization and conversationality is that they avoid matters of public concern; such matters often are reduced to discussions of how individuals ought to live their lives rather than about "how a collectivity comes to 'act morally' " (Condit 1987, 80).

Condit urges us to examine public morality anew, by recognizing that the language of morality is a collective not a personal language, a language of shared meanings with moral import. Ethical judgments always are contextually situated, depend inductively on judgments we have made before, and hence are grounded in objectivated aspects of human behavior. "Ethical principles" are articulated by collectivities in bounded contexts and in the face of objectifiable, practical, that is, political circumstances. They come into play whenever a collectivity is attempting to make "good" or "right" decisions and hence have an optimistic side to them.

Condit then moves into an extended case study of how Americans have defined "justice" for African Americans across time, showing us a moving scene of moral argumentation. In reviewing the narratives and propositional disputes from various epochs, she discusses what she calls the crafting of public morality: the construction of symbolic perspectives on the world and their application in particular circumstances. To think of rhetorical constructions of public morality as a craft is to recognize the hard work that underlies it as well as its reach for goodness, creativity, and perfection (Condit 1987, 94).

I am taken with Condit's arguments on the crafting of public morality because the power train of American politics is fully exposed during presidential campaigning. The machine is open for inspection; and, given that politics treats of the valuation and distribution of shared resources, we cannot help but see materialized the moral engines of our political institutions and the moral commitments of those who drive those institutions. More specifically, I would argue that the following propositions characterize the ethics of political (especially presidential) campaigning in late twentieth-century America.

First, the prototype of American campaign communication is dialogical engagement. This is not to say that campaign communication is explicitly argumentative in a propositional sense, where a candidate provides a "t'aint" for every one of his or her opponent's "tis's." Rather, voter-citizens are always in search of points of comparison, of electoral pivots useful in making voting decisions. Even candidates who assiduously avoid mention of opponents cannot escape dialogical engagement, for it is fostered by both the press (ever on the lookout for the sort of conflict that sells newspapers and earns viewership points) and by the independent voters who dominate American politics. Even when candidates present only telespectacular stories in their ads and films, audiences set the narratives of the different candidates side by side, testing them against each other for narrative fidelity and probability (Fisher 1984).

Second, among the many issues framed in dialogical engagement during campaigns are significant moral issues. Even the most left-brained technocrat running for the presidency cannot escape moral matters. Policies have consequences; someone is always profiting even as someone else is paying for those profits. While politics is not really a zero-sum game, it has enough characteristics of one to guarantee that public policies on everything from the pledge of allegiance to medical reform have differentiated consequences. Those differentiations are not only econo-political but also socio-ethical.

Third, ideologies, policy positions, and candidates themselves all have moral dimensions that are central to campaigns. If the notion that candidates themselves become commodified and even totemized over the course of a campaign makes sense, then they cannot help but signify moral choices, even if such choices are not articulated (but they usually are). Suppose a candidate decries the loss of family values, particularly those associated with the traditional nuclear family, and stands on and for policies that reward family-centered vis-à-vis institution-centered solutions to personal problems, that identify single-parent or nonheterosexual families as flawed, and that blame forces presumably outside of one's personal influence (television, rock music, or social welfare programs) for the degeneration of family values. A morality is thus commodified in a specific context and even can be totemized by the candidate who participates in family values spectacles for primetime television and journalists.

In this sort of situation, an appeal to "family values" is morally charged, for it has been attached to a conservative ideology, stitched into policy positions, and then worn as political raiment by a candidate for office, as part of that candidate's definition of "character."

While commentators ridiculed Dan Quayle in the spring of 1992 for attacking Candace Bergen's defense of single-parenthood on the TV sitcom *Murphy Brown*, Quayle in fact got the last laugh. He managed to articulate an ideology roundly applauded in his circles, seize the center of a family values social policy, and become identified—as could be seen during the 1992 GOP convention—as the family man politician. Silly or not, Quayle acquired a moral profile and even moral force that spring.

Fourth, during political (especially presidential) campaigns, the moral dimensions of ideologies and public policies take center stage and are attached to candidates who perform in moral sociodramas and who likely are assessed by voters on moral terms. To be sure, the morality of ideologies and public policies can be spelled out discursively (linguistically) in speeches, computerized mail, position papers, campaign biographies, and Internet bulletin boards. But, more important in the electronic age, moral positions are visually constructed and performed in ads, press conferences and other newsworthy candidate events, candidate forums, talk shows, candidate films, road shows, party conventions, and infomercials.

The key notion here is *act*, as Kenneth Burke stressed (1945; 1950). Both the (discursive) saying and the (symbolically meaningful) act of saying engage voter-citizens. So, in 1976 Jimmy Carter promised America a government as good as its people and *acted* as a man of the people, being photographed washing out his own socks in his hotel room and carrying his own luggage, as well as making a campaign poster out of a picture of himself in a denim jacket leaning against a ranch fence post. More subtly, George Bush's *act* of broadcasting negative ads in June and July 1988 said as much about his moral character as did the contents of the ads themselves; "going negative" so early in the season was considered at worst a ploy of a desperate man and at best a big political risk—which, of course, paid off (Gronbeck 1992). Thus, the moral dimensions of political campaigning are made salient in coding systems that extend beyond the verbal to the visual, even to all of the public acts a candidate commits. In contexts that shape their interpretations, voters use all of the cues—the fragments of political life—to make political meanings, to construct what Samuel Becker (1983) calls mosaics, which in turn become the ways they view the political world and through which they craft their political decisions.

Fifth, overall in their sayings, showings, and actions, political campaigners craft symbolic worlds framed in moral matters that center both their sociopolitical character and their vision of what politics ought to be like under their rule. Of course, not all political promises are kept but that does not diminish their importance, because it is out of those promises that the citizenry crafts a political morality (1) against which to measure the acts of politicians in the future and (2) with which to examine themselves and their life-world—their self-images and their images of society (Miller and Gronbeck 1994). Not all politicians execute their political jobs in ways that are absolutely consonant with the sociopolitical and moral values they articulated and performed while campaigning. Yet voter-citizens (not to mention the loyal opposition and the press) can use those values as measuring rods in periodic assessment—the monthly Gallup poll on presidential performance, the press evaluations of political activities, the news releases from lobbies and citizen watchdog groups, and even future votes understood as delayed assessments.

As much as anything else, George Bush fell victim to negative moral assessment in 1992. He came into office riding a social ethic built out of patriotism, sympathy ("a kinder, gentler" tone), and change ("the new breeze is blowing" theme of his 1989 inaugural). He left office with his patriotism challenged as hollow, his sympathy seemingly transformed into domestic antipathy, and far too little changed to convince voters he deserved four more years. His moral bankruptcy did him in; he could not credibly perform his own ethic.

Overall, then, given the multiple political players, stables of expert journalists, and innumerable shows viewers can watch, manifold political moralities are engaged dialogically in any given election, with the field of ethical options slowly narrowing as the first Tuesday of November approaches. The choice between candidates—as totemized by themselves and by journalists—becomes, finally, a choice between moral visions where character (linguistically and behaviorally constructed) is the ultimate rhetorical issue.

In this view, the postmodernist impulse of Baudrillard and Debord must be rejected because it ignores political outcomes. Whether or not we are seduced, the fact remains that political institutions fight wars, finance clinics, regulate coal mining, and prohibit incest; in addition, for better or worse, the winners exude a political ethos that pervades political thought and decisions. Baudrillard is shackled to the Word as the only sign system worth treating, unable or unwilling to pursue meaning in oral and visual signs. The same can be said about Postman, who is tied to a conception of discursivity bracketed by literate sign systems. The rhetorical-constructivist view cuts through the smoke and mirrors so fascinating to the French to the power of multiple discursivities that makes very real differences in our lives.

The democratic-liberal view of Denton and McWilliams is likewise turned back not because of its motives—for they are sterling—but because it stresses purity of motive or ideal outcome (primitive communitarianism) without telling us *how* to direct motives practically or reach those outcomes processually. The ideological democrat is chained to ossified propositions that cannot be remolded as socio-cultural circumstances change. The democratic-liberal attack on telespectacles thus ignores the dynamic, pragmatic side of politics that requires attention to its rhetorical foundations. Finally, Welsh's views depend upon a passive, impotent audience without any sources of power; his position is extremely difficult to sustain in light of the ballot box and the importance of television ratings (viewership) to any mass-mediated discourse in the United States.

When Aristotle defined the arts of rhetoric as lying at the boundary between ethics and politics (McKeon 1941, 1356a), he was framing practical discourse as a means of negotiating between public morality and public action. That is as important in the age of the orthicon tube as it was to the small, walled city-state.

A Final Plea for Engagement with the Telespectacle

In conclusion, I would observe that the academy abrogates its duties to the civic world when it ignores the political telespectacles of our time. The concept of "political power" has terribly negative associations for many of my colleagues: endless debates over political correctness, cultural diversity, hate speech on campus, coded discussions of gender, race, and class, and all of the other hot buttons that start wars between colleagues or between school and state.

Even if those issues disappeared, many in the professoriat would continue to resist discussions of the politics of knowledge. These colleagues would not understand the sentiment of Isocrates, who said in his own defense that a teacher "reaps his finest and his largest reward when his pupils prove to be honourable and intelligent and highly esteemed by their fellow-citizens, since pupils of that sort inspire many with the desire to enjoy his teaching" (*Antidosis* 220). Just as the ancients celebrated *phronesis* or practical wisdom, so should we.

The world of the telespectacle is here to stay and whether the Don Quixotes among us tilt with windmills matters not: the windmills are still there, powering the politics of the country. Our scorn affects television ratings and political conventions not one whit. Cursing the darkness only leaves us hoarse. Turning our back on peek-a-boo politics means that someone is going to kick us in the seat of the pants.

The telespectacle can be base or magnificent, dramaturgically moving or maudlin, poetic or prosaic. The telespectacle, for better or worse, is the center of public politics, of the public sphere. Melting pot consensus is gone forever, the assimilationist philosophy of Ellis Island and "The New Colossus" is anachronistic; the literate discursivity of older ages cannot be recovered on a large scale. This is not to say that we should not seek systemic reforms of the type Bennett (1992) urges. But we must recognize that the conversation of the culture is centered not in the *New York Review of Books* but in the television experience. To ignore the conversation—to fail to arm students with the means of verbally and visually decoding it—is folly. Furthermore, that conversation is embued with moral positions that must not be left to do their work in unexamined ways. When the Revolving Door or the Willie Horton ad goes unchallenged, its poison takes a civic toll (Jamieson 1992).

Public education occurs in service to the state, even to the citizenry. Teaching students ways to assess the dynamics of politics, even electronically amplified politics, is entailed in our service contract with that state and citizenry.

Notes

1. The loss of our sense of space brought about primarily by television, J. Meyrowitz (1985) argues, is both liberating and disorienting.

2. Goodman argues that we make our worlds through composition and decomposition (reassembly of aspects of our environment), weighting (identifying key or dominant issues), ordering (sequencing issues), deletion and supplementation (subtracting troublesome or adding needed information), and deformation (simplifying matters).

References Cited

Alexander, H. E., and M. Bauer. 1991. *Financing the 1988 Election.* Boulder, Colo.: Westview Press.

Antidosis. [1929] 1962. *Isocrates.* Vol. 2. Translated by G. Norlin. Cambridge, Mass.: Harvard University Press.

Armstrong, R. 1988. *The Next Hurrah: The Communications Revolution in American Politics.* New York: Beech Tree Books.

Barbrook, A., and C. Bolt. 1980. *Power and Protest in American Life.* Oxford: Martin Robertson.

Baudrillard, J. 1983. *In the Shadow of the Silent Majorities.* Translated by P. Foss, J. Johnston, and P. Patton. New York: Semiotext(e).

———. 1988. *The Ecstasy of Communication.* Translated by B. Schutze and C. Schutze. Edited by S. Lotringer. New York: Semiotext(e).

Becker, S. L. 1983. *Discovering Mass Communication.* Glenview, Ill.: Scott, Foresman.

Bell, D. [1960] 1962. *The End of Ideology: On the Exhaustion of Political Ideas in the Fifties.* New York: Free Press.

Bennett, W. L. 1992. *The Governing Crisis: Media, Money, and Marketing in American Elections.* New York: St. Martin's.

Bourdieu, P. [1971] 1977. "Two Bourdieu Texts [Symbolic Power, Qualifications, and Jobs]." Stencilled occasional paper no. 46. Birmingham, England: Center for Contemporary Cultural Studies.

Burke, K. 1945. *The Grammar of Motives.* Englewood Cliffs, N.J.: Prentice-Hall.

———. 1950. *The Rhetoric of Motives.* Englewood Cliffs, N.J.: Prentice-Hall.

Citizens and Politics: A View from Main Street America. 1991. Dayton, Ohio: Kettering Foundation.

Cohen, A. P. 1985. *The Symbolic Construction of Community.* New York: Tavistock.

Condit, C. M. 1987. "Crafting Virtue: The Rhetorical Construction of Public Morality." *Quarterly Journal of Speech* 73:79-97.

Connolly, W. E. 1987. *Politics and Ambiguity.* Madison: University of Wisconsin Press.

Debord, G. [1967] 1983. *Society of the Spectacle.* Detroit: Black and Red.

Denton, R. E., Jr. 1991. "Primetime Politics: The Ethics of Teledemocracy." Pp. 91-114 in *Ethical Dimensions of Political Communication,* ed. R. E. Denton, Jr. New York: Praeger.

Ellul, J. 1985. *The Humiliation of the Word.* Grand Rapids, Mich.: Wm. B. Eerdmans.

Fisher, W. R. 1984. "Narration as a Human Communication Paradigm: The Case of Public Moral Argument." *Communication Monographs* 51:1-22.

———. 1987. *Human Communication as Narration: Toward a Philosophy of Reason, Value, and Action.* Columbia: University of South Carolina Press.

Foucault, M. 1986. "Of Other Spaces." Translated by J. Miscowiec. *Diacritics* 16:22-27.

Goodman, N. 1978. *Ways of Worldmaking.* Indianapolis: Hackett Publishing.

Gronbeck, B. E. 1990. "Electric Rhetoric: The Changing Forms of American Political Discourse." Pp. 141-61 in *Vichiana,* 3d series, vol. 1. Napoli: Loffredo Editore.

———. 1991. "Ethical Pivots and Moral Vantages in American Presidential

Campaign Dramas." Pp. 49-68 in *Ethical Dimensions of Political Communication*, ed. R. E. Denton, Jr. New York: Praeger.

———. 1992. "Negative Narratives in 1988 Presidential Campaign Ads." *Quarterly Journal of Speech* 78:333-46.

———. 1993. "The Spoken and the Seen: Phonocentric and Ocularcentric Dimensions of Rhetorical Discourse." Pp. 139-55 in *Rhetorical Memory and Delivery: Classical Concepts for Contemporary Composition and Communication*, ed. J. F. Reynolds. Hillsdale, N.J.: Lawrence Erlbaum Associates.

Hall, E. T. 1959. *The Silent Language*. New York: Doubleday.

Jackson, J. 1988. "Common Ground and Common Sense." *Vital Speeches of the Day* 54:649-53.

Jamieson, K. H. 1988. *Eloquence in an Electronic Age: The Transformation of Political Speechmaking*. New York: Oxford University Press.

———. 1992. *Dirty Politics*. New York: Oxford University Press.

Jhally, S. 1990. *The Codes of Advertising: Fetishism and the Political Economy of Meaning in the Consumer Society*. New York: Routledge.

Lazarus, E. [1883] 1989. "The New Colossus." Pp. 289-90 in *Soul of America: Documenting Our Past, 1492-1972*, ed. R. C. Baron. Golden, Colo.: Fulcrum.

Lee, R. E. 1994. "Images of Civic Virtue in the New Political Rhetoric." Pp. 40-59 in *Presidential Campaigns and American Self Images*, ed. A. H. Miller and B. E. Gronbeck. Boulder, Colo.: Westview Press.

Lowi, T. 1985. *The Personal President*. Ithaca, N.Y.: Cornell University Press.

MacIntyre, A. 1981. *After Virtue: A Study in Moral Theory*. Notre Dame, Ind.: University of Notre Dame Press.

McKeon, R., ed. 1941. *The Basic Works of Aristotle*. New York: Random House.

McWilliams, W. C. 1989. "The Meaning of the Election." Pp. 177-213 in *The Election of 1988: Reports and Interpretations*, ed. G. M. Pomper et al. Chatham, N.J.: Chatham House.

Meyrowitz, J. 1985. *No Sense of Place: The Impact of Electronic Media on Social Behavior*. New York: Oxford University Press.

Miller, A. H., and B. E. Gronbeck, eds. 1994. *Presidential Campaigns and American Self Images*. Boulder, CO: Westview.

Morreale, J. 1994. "American Self Images and the Presidential Campaign Film, 1964-1988." In *Presidential Campaigns and American Self Images*, ed. A. H. Miller and B. E. Gronbeck. Boulder, Colo.: Westview Press.

Ong, W. J. 1982. *Orality and Literacy: The Technologizing of the Word*. New York: Methuen.

Parenti, M. 1993. *Inventing Reality: The Politics of the Mass Media*. 2d ed. New York: St. Martin's.

Piven, F. F., and R. A. Cloward. 1988. *Why Americans Don't Vote*. New York: Pantheon Books.

Polsby, N. 1983. *Consequences of Party Reform.* New York: Oxford University Press.

Postman, N. 1985. *Amusing Ourselves to Death: Public Discourse in the Age of Show Business.* New York: Viking Penguin.

Shapiro, M. J. 1992. *Reading the Postmodern Polity: Political Theory as Textual Practice.* Minneapolis: University of Minnesota Press.

Toffler, A. 1971. *Future Shock.* New York: Random House.

Wattenberg, M. P. 1990. *The Decline of American Political Parties, 1952-1988.* Foreword by W. D. Burnham. Cambridge, Mass.: Harvard University Press.

Weaver, R. 1953. *The Ethics of Rhetoric.* Chicago: Regnery.

Welsh, J. F. [1985] 1990. "Dramaturgy and Political Mystification: Political Life in the United States." Pp. 399–410 in *Life as Theatre: A Dramaturgical Source Book,* ed. D. Brissett and C. Edgley. 2d ed. New York: Aldine de Gruyter.

Contributors

JON W. ANDERSON is an anthropologist at the Catholic University of America in Washington, D.C. He has done ethnographic fieldwork in Afghanistan and Pakistan and has published widely in several disciplines on issues of tribal, ethnic, and gender identities and on the tribal and religious culture of Afghans.

RICHARD HARVEY BROWN is a professor of sociology and affiliate professor of comparative literature at the University of Maryland, College Park. His central interest is how social science can serve as a humanizing discourse for modernizing, modern, and postmodern societies. He has edited ten volumes on this and related themes. His most recent authored works include *Society as Text, Social Science as Civic Discourse,* and *Science as Narration.*

THOMAS CUSHMAN teaches sociology at Wellesley College and is a fellow at the Harvard Russian Research Center. He is the author of *Notes from Underground: Rock Music Counterculture in St. Petersburg, Russia* and is currently at work on a comparative-historical study of the discourse of intellectual reputation in academic honorary societies in the United States, Great Britain, France, and Spain.

NORMAN K. DENZIN is professor of sociology, communications, and humanities at the University of Illinois, Urbana-Champaign. He is the author of numerous books, including *The Research Act, Interpretive Interactionism, Images of Postmodern Society, The Recovering Alcoholic,* and *The Alcoholic Self,* which won the Cooley Award in 1988 from the Society for the Study of Symbolic Interaction. He is editor of *Studies in Symbolic Interaction: A Research Annual* and *The Sociological Quarterly.*

RICCA EDMONDSON was born in South Africa and has lived in England, Germany, and Ireland, where she now teaches at University College,

Galway. She was educated at the Universities of Lancaster, Oxford, and Berlin and has worked on subjects including the philosophy of the social sciences, the rhetoric of argument, and the sociology of aging and of the environment. She is a community activist and writes literary and philosophical essays on Irish themes.

BRUCE E. GRONBECK is a professor of communication studies at the University of Iowa, specializing in political rhetoric and mass-mediated culture. A former president of the Central States Speech Association and the Speech Communication Association, he has authored four textbooks, two dozen book chapters, and three dozen articles, and has edited *Spheres of Argument, Communication, Consciousness, and Culture,* and *Presidential Campaigning and American Self-Images.*

LINDA S. KAUFFMAN, professor of English at the University of Maryland, College Park, has published extensively on postmodern literature and critical theory. She is the author of *Discourses of Desire: Gender, Genre, and Epistolary Fictions* and *Special Delivery: Epistolary Modes in Modern Fiction.* She also has written on pornography, *Bad Girls and Sick Boys: Fantasies in Contemporary Culture,* and has edited several collections of essays on feminist theory.

PAUL SHAPIRO is a graduate of the New School Graduate Faculty and teaches sociology at the Fashion Institute of Technology (SUNY) in New York City. His interests center on sociological theory and sociology of the arts and popular culture. He has published several articles and given many conference presentations.

JOHN VAN MAANEN is professor of organization studies in the Sloan School of Management at MIT. He is the author of *Tales of the Field* and editor of *Representation in Ethnography.* He has conducted fieldwork in police agencies in the United States and Great Britain and is currently writing on Disneyland.

Index